COMING OF AGE
IN AMERICA

COMING OF AGE
IN AMERICA

Growth and Acquiescence

Edgar Z. Friedenberg

Vintage Books

A Division of Random House

New York

The author is grateful to the Payne Educational Society Foundation, Inc., for permission to reprint material from the *Journal of Educational Sociology;* to the University of Chicago Press for permission to reprint material from the *American Journal of Sociology;* to Bourne Co. Music Publishers for the poem on pages 119 and 291, "No Man Is an Island," by Joan Whitney and Alex Kramer. © Copyright 1950 by Bourne, Inc.

Manufactured in the United States of America

VINTAGE BOOKS
are published by
ALFRED A. KNOPF, INC. and RANDOM HOUSE

FOR

MICHAEL

AND

DIANE

PREFACE

—◡—

During the two-year period that I have been writing this book, I have also been carrying on a research study of a particular aspect of the influence of a mass society on adolescence. The book and the study are quite separate undertakings. The study is, of course, limited in scope to certain manifestations of the social processes with which the book is concerned. But the observations, formal and informal, that I have had to make in the course of the research have been essential to the book, both as data to be reported and, equally, as a realistic discipline to my conceptions of just how these processes take place in the social institution—the secondary school—to which nearly all adolescents in our society are consigned.

The experience of protracted school attendance cannot be grasped by an abstract approach. By projecting and extrapolating the demographic trends and social and economic developments that affect the school, one can, to be sure, quite accurately predict and precisely dissect the major problems that confront both youth and the educational system. But the results are likely to be bloodless and, for that reason, unduly optimistic. Experience is never categorical; what matters about it is always detailed and personal. Centuries of accumulated data attesting to the ineffectiveness of capital punishment in lowering the murder rate will never move anyone who is capable of supposing that hydrogen cyanide smells like peach blossoms to the condemned.

My metaphor may lead the reader to wonder whether the account to follow will be free from personal bias. I wish to allay such doubts from the outset. It is not. Even if I had begun my investigation without bias—and this is an unlikely event, for unless one is working purely for the record one must have some reason for thinking that what one is studying is important—I should be ashamed to have completed it without bias. The subjects of my study are adolescents, and I brought to the study my feelings about them and my prior judgments as to how they should be treated. These will be apparent to the reader: perhaps more apparent than they are to me.

The technics of scientific investigation are useful in preventing the observer from perceiving phenomena that are not really there even though he wishes they were; and in keeping him from exaggerating the significance of chance events by mistaking them for evidence of a prior relationship. But they do not obligate him to be neutral or dispassionate in assessing the significance of his findings; and they do not exhaust the possibilities of truth.

"Scientific truth," Ortega writes in the opening passage of "The Sportive Origins of the State,"[1]

> is characterized by its exactness, and the certainty of its predictions. But these admirable qualities are contrived by science at the cost of remaining on a plane of secondary problems, leaving intact the ultimate and decisive questions. Of this renunciation it makes its essential virtue, and for it, if for naught else, it deserves praise. Yet science is but a small part of the human mind and organism. Where it stops, man does not stop.

Certainly, in writing this book, I did not. But the relationship between the book and the research study is close. The most important effect of life in a mass society is on the values of the people who share it. Our study is a study of student values as these affect, and are expressed in, the

[1] José Ortega y Gasset, *Toward a Philosophy of History* (New York: W. W. Norton & Company, 1941.)

choices they make about school situations and their attitudes toward school and the possibilities it affords. My colleagues and I were especially interested in how students would face the choice between support for excellence or distinction and a more general extension of opportunity to less well qualified but needier candidates; between well-roundedness and devotion to special talents and immediate personal commitments; between privacy and inwardness and effective socialization in the interests of the welfare of the group.

This book is not, and is not meant to be, a full or formal report of our findings. Our study was conceived quite independently of this book and had technical and specific purposes that lie, in part, beyond its scope. But it provided an incomparable opportunity, and an obligation, for me to immerse myself in the actual day-to-day activities of secondary schools, in a context that kept my mind on the issues we have been discussing. As the research proceeded, I found that what I was learning both supported and required me to modify the positions I had been planning to discuss in this book.

I have now finished a year spent full time in interviewing twenty-five students in each of our nine schools, each of whom I saw three times for as long—with the exception of a few interviews that were truncated by scheduling difficulties—as the student felt our procedure required. The students were selected simply by taking every fourth name from a list of 100 tenth, eleventh, and twelfth graders who had previously rated the social climate and mode of operation of the school on a paper and pencil instrument. The group of 100 were also an unselected, alphabetical list, from which ninth graders were excluded only because we thought they would not have been in the school long enough to have formed a stable opinion of it. In most schools, I also added a few students who had given the school extreme ratings on this instrument or who had been recommended to me as especially interesting by the administration; these additions, of course, impair the randomness of the interview sample, but not of the rating-sample of 100 from which these—including the extras—were drawn. My observations about the students' interview responses will not, in any case, be quantitative. I was the only interviewer in the study and, though the interviews were taped and transcribed, my comments on what the students said and the reasons they gave for saying it are interpretations, subject to personal bias.

All but one of the schools—a private day school for boys in New York City—were co-educational, and located in small towns or small cities. Only one was strictly suburban, but only one was located more than 100 miles from a large city. Two were Southern. Two were of special interest because they were adjacent to centers of missilecraft and intelligence agencies that lie so close to the heart of our national purpose: one school enrolled mostly the children of technicians, while the other included sons and daughters of many high-ranking policy-level officials, military and civil. One school had an enrollment about 70 percent Negro; the small, rather attractive, mostly working-class community in which it was located was separated from its neighbors by the most nearly impenetrable woodland that survived in the region. Local real estate developers had carefully left it intact; had the climate been suitable, they would probably have stocked it with tigers. Another school served a fashionable exurb, while yet another served a consolidated district of small, unprosperous agricultural villages. We selected for the study schools that varied among themselves in the clientele they served as widely as possible.

The central procedure of the study, on which the interviews focused and which provided us with an elaborate but useful statistical basis for comparison among our participants, will be described in Chapter 3, where it is first applied; it is too complicated to explain in advance and, out of context, boring. Before turning to this operation, I wish to explore, in the opening chapter, the moral dimensions of the topic with which the book is concerned and, in the second, to present my detailed personal observations of life in two schools in our sample. The practices that held my attention in these schools are common, with certain variations in degree, to all the schools in our sample. They must, over a period of years, rather strongly influence any adolescent's conception of dignity, of freedom, and of himself.

Besides myself, the professional staff of the study consisted of my co-investigator Carl Nordstrom, Associate Professor of Economics at Brooklyn College; and Hilary Gold, Assistant Professor of Education at Brooklyn. Professor Nordstrom's contribution to the research is at least as great as my own. Each of us wrote three of the six episodes whose use and function as semiprojective tests is discussed in Chapter 3, and which form the heart of our procedure. He devised all the ways in which the data have been analyzed quantitatively, and carried the analysis through, supervised the transcription of all interviews and, with a patience unrivaled since the death of Booker T. Washington, listened to them all, both to check the accuracy of the transcription and to get a feel for what had been said on which to base his own interpretations.

Professor Gold joined us after the study had been set up, at the beginning of our fieldwork. He preceded me at each school by several days, administering the paper-and-pencil test given to the hundred students at each school from whom our twenty-five interview subjects were later drawn. Professor Gold also contributed items to this instrument, of a different kind from those Nordstrom and I contributed or from those that were drawn from the Stern *High School Characteristics Index*. But his most important function was as liaison with the schools. After we had selected them, Hilary Gold was entirely in charge of the arrangements and negotiations that were necessary to establish the study in operation. Of the three of us, Hilary is by far the least rebarbative: he is young, affable, attractive, and since he is, or was, British, school personnel tend to underestimate his intelligence. At the time we began, I should also have described Hilary as unusually sensitive; but I must in all candor admit that he completed his work on the study with his sanity quite unimpaired. Neither Nordstrom nor I would, I think, be inclined to make such a statement about the other.

The research was supported by the Co-Operative Research Division of the United States Office of Education, under Public Law 531 and a contract between the two sovereignties: Brooklyn College and the United States of America. I should also like to acknowledge most gratefully supplementary support provided by the College Entrance Examination Board to cover an essential expenditure—direct payment to the participating schools for administrative services, space, and goodwill. All the schools provided the first without stint, and as much of the others as could really have been expected under the circumstances. Several were generous with all three.

Davis, California
February, 1965

CONTENTS

COMING OF AGE
IN AMERICA

I

ADOLESCENCE
in an
OPEN SOCIETY

What is most extraordinary about youth today is that adults everywhere should be so worried about it. I do not mean to suggest that this concern is groundless; on the contrary. A great many young people are in very serious trouble throughout the technically developed and especially the Western world. Their trouble, moreover, follows certain familiar common patterns; they get into much the same kind of difficulty in very different societies. But it is nevertheless strange that they should. Human life is a continuous thread which each of us spins to his own pattern, rich and complex in meaning. There are no natural knots in it. Yet knots form, nearly always in adolescence. In American, British, European, Japanese, Australasian, and at least the more privileged Soviet youth, puberty releases emotions that tend toward crisis. Every major industrial society believes that it has a serious youth problem.

Adolescence is both a stage and a process of growth. As such it should proceed by doing what comes naturally. Instead, there is a widespread feeling that it cannot be allowed to proceed without massive intervention. The young disturb and anger their elders, and are themselves angered and disturbed, or repelled and depressed, at the thought of becoming what they see their elders to be. Adults observe and condemn the "teen-age tyranny" of "the adolescent society," over which they seek to establish and maintain hegemony by techniques of infiltration and control.

Adolescents are among the last social groups in the world to be given the full nineteenth-century colonial treatment. Our colonial administrators, at least at the higher policy-making levels, are usually of the enlightened sort who decry the punitive expedition except as an instrument of last resort, though they are inclined to tolerate a shade more brutality in the actual school or police station than the law allows. They prefer, however, to study the young with a view to understanding them, not for their own sake but in order to learn how to induce them to abandon their barbarism and assimilate the folkways of normal adult life. The model emissary to the world of youth is no longer the tough disciplinarian but the trained youth worker, who works like a psychoanalytically oriented anthropologist. Like the best of missionaries, he is sympathetic and understanding toward the people he is sent to work with, and aware and critical of the larger society he represents. But fundamentally he accepts it, and often does not really question its basic values or its right to send him to wean the young from savagery.

Like the missionary among his natives, the youth worker finds the young in no virgin state. By the time he gets there it is too late for that. "Youth cultures" vary from the more flamboyant forms of delinquency to the conservative eroticism of the college fraternity. But all of them have been altered by continuous interaction with the adult world; the youngsters, unlike natives of a primitive tribe, have never known anything else and have no traditions wholly their own. The idols of the "teen-age" culture are the entertainers who use their "teen-age" clientele to make it as disk jockeys, on TV, or within the residually "teen-age" enclave of the B-movie. The explicit values of the juvenile gang are taken from the adult world; they, too, covet status and success, and do not imagine that these could be conceived in terms more compelling than those they find familiar. The worst off, perhaps, are the traders and interpreters: the big men on campus, the boys who wear the sports jackets clothing man-ufacturers are trying to introduce to the "teen-age" market, the occasional gang leader who, at seventeen, is already working up the memoirs of his reformation, as told to the youth worker or his parish priest. In any society, marginal individuals have especially severe problems.

The economic position of "the adolescent society," like that of other colonies, is highly ambiguous. It is simultane-ously a costly drain on the commonwealth and a vested interest of those members of the commonwealth who earn their living and their social role by exploiting it. Juvenile delinquency is destructive and wasteful, and efforts to con-trol and combat it are expensive. Schooling is even more expensive. Both undertakings are justified on the assumption that youth must be drawn into the social order if the social order is to continue, and this is self-evident. But both act as agents of society as it now is, propagating its values and assumptions among a youth often cynical and distrustful but ignorant of the language or the moral judgments in terms of which its complaints might be couched. Neither the youth agency nor the school is usually competent or sufficiently independent to help adolescents examine the sources of their pain and conflict and think its meaning through, using their continuing experience of life to help them build better social arrangements in their turn. This, in a democracy, ought clearly to be among the most fundamental functions of citizenship education; in a public school system geared and responsive to local political demands and interests it may well be impossible. Official agencies dealing with youth vary enormously in the pretexts and technics with which they approach their clientele, from those of the young worker attached to a conflict gang to those of the Cit Ed teacher in the academic track of a suburban high school. But they all begin, like a Colonial Office, with the assumption that the long-term interests of their clientele are consistent with the present interests of their sponsor.

Like other colonial peoples, adolescents are economically dependent on the dominant society, and appear in its accounts as the beneficiaries of its philanthropy. Like them also, adolescents are partly dependent because of their immature stage of development, but even more because of restrictions placed upon them by the dominant society. In the United States at present, one of the most serious sources of difficulty for adolescents is that few can find jobs. There are not many jobs for "boys" any more: delivery, elevator, messenger, and house have all largely disappeared in the wake of automation and the decline of small business and the Sahib. Even when these jobs were not worth doing they provided the adolescent with some money and a valid social role. Their disappearance has left him with no legitimate role except that of high school student, which provides no income and no independence. If he leaves school before graduation he is almost certain to be unemployed for months before getting one of the few dead-end unskilled or semi-

skilled jobs available to him; he faces a lifetime of substand-
ard living and sporadic unemployment. Wide recognition
of this fact has led to stepped-up efforts to keep adolescents
from dropping out of school; we are less willing to recognize
that they may, quite literally, have no business there. In any
case, until they are old enough for the Army, they have
none, and are permitted none, anywhere else.

Nevertheless, "teen-agers" do have money, about ten bil-
lion dollars a year of it, though this comes to only about ten
dollars a week as an average. They scrounge it from home
or earn it at odd times, and this, too, contributes to their
colonial status. The "teen-age" market is big business. We
all share an economic interest in the dependency of the
"teen-ager." The school is interested in keeping him off the
streets and in its custody. Labor is interested in keeping him
off the labor market. Business and industry are interested
in seeing that his tastes become fads and in selling him
specialized junk that a more mature taste would reject.
Like a dependent native, the "teen-ager" is encouraged to
be economically irresponsible because his sources of income
are undependable and do not derive from his personal qualities. He can be very responsible in buying things that are
closely related to his real skills and interests and his evolving
sense of himself: sporting equipment, used cars, the things
that mean something to him. But he cannot easily work out
an entirely personal and responsible pattern of economic
behavior because he has no serious economic status; he is
treated like a plantation worker whose benevolent master
allows him a few dollars to take into town on Saturday
afternoon, though they both know he will only spend it
foolishly.

Other forms of colonialism are dead or dying. A technically developed society has no use for a pool of unskilled

labor which at its cheapest is far costlier than machinery and which nevertheless cannot afford to buy machine products. By one of these strokes of precious insight that the sociology of knowledge has led us rather to expect, the Western world began to perceive colonialism as immoral almost as soon as it became patently unprofitable. The missionary spirit and the White Man's Burden have yielded to the anthropologist's relativism and the Common Market. Why has the "teen-ager" then remained, so stubbornly, the object of colonial solicitude?

Primarily because we are dependent on him, too. Disorderly as it is, our house needs an heir. The colonial analogy is defective at a crucial point. The essence of the "teen-ager's" status is that he is in transition; the essence of the native's status is that he is not supposed to be. The maintenance of a colonial system requires that the native accept enough of the dominant culture to meet its schedules, work for payment in its smaller currency, desire and consume its goods, and fight in its armies; and so far the analogy holds for the "teen-ager." But the native is not expected—indeed, not usually permitted—to actually "pass"; he is never granted full membership in the dominant culture, and the dominant culture does not depend for its survival on his ultimate willingness to accept it.

But every society depends on the succession of generations, and adults usually assume that this means that their values and life style should be transmitted to the young. Youth cannot be allowed to "go native" permanently; some writers and artists may be allowed to live as beachcombers and to go on negotiating with other adults in beat and jive as if it were pidgin, but the rest have to grow up to be like their elders. When adults observe that a large proportion of youth is becoming threateningly unfamiliar and uncongenial, there is said to be a youth problem, and deliberate efforts are made to induce or compel the young to accept and participate in the dominant culture.

At this point, therefore, the position of youth is less that of a colonized native than it is that of a minority group that is gaining status and being assimilated. The plight of the adolescent is basically similar to that of an emigrant in that he can neither stay what he was nor become what he started out to be. Minority-group status occurs, and is recognized as such, only in societies that are abandoning a colonial stance and accepting the position that the lesser breeds over whose destinies they have assumed control are to be brought *within* the law and ultimately to be treated as equals. In the United States, this position has been part of our ideology from the beginning; our true colonial subjects have been the Negroes, who have actually been native Americans for a century but who are only now being taken really seriously as citizens.

The "Negro problem" and the "youth problem" have many features in common. In one fundamental way, however, they are in sharp contrast. The "Negro problem" is exacerbated by the urgency with which Negroes seek the integration to which they are legally and morally entitled. But only those youth who resist integration into the ordinary folkways of our life are regarded by adults as a problem; those who accept the world in which they live and work or scheme to make it within the prevailing framework of values and practices are thought to be doing fine; they are taken as a model. Apart from the Black Muslims, who have made up a version of Islam suited to their present emotional needs as insulted Americans, most Negroes seek equal status in the larger society. So do most young people, ultimately. But, meanwhile, many behave in such a way as to frighten adults into fearing that they will never accept or qualify themselves for what American life has to offer.

As Paul Goodman points out in the last chapter of *Growing Up Absurd*,[1] we rarely finish our revolutions; we manage to avoid the moral issues that occasion them by devising technical solutions to the immediate problems they present. This is what we are trying to do with our youth and Negro "problems"; we may succeed. But our habitual evasion of moral issues by turning them into empirical problems is more likely to make things a little worse for youth. The absence of ethical clarity, the overriding commitment of our culture to working compromises, even when they weaken the whole fabric of individual experience, create the situation youth protest against, surrender to, or seek to escape by finding a personally meaningful style of life even if it be destructive or nihilistic.

Erik Erikson—in my judgment the most astute and perceptive living student of human growth and development—in an article entitled "Youth: Fidelity and Diversity,"[2] stresses that adolescents must experience both these in order to become themselves. Fidelity, he defines as "the strength of disciplined devotion. It is gained in the involvement of youth in such experiences as reveal the essence of the era they are to join—as the beneficiaries of its tradition, as the practitioners and innovators of its technology, as renewers of its ethical strength, as rebels bent on the destruction of the outlived, and as deviants with deviant commitments."

It would seem, then, that societies that are passing from colonialism to a period in which they recognize and accept

[1] New York: Random House, 1960.
[2] In *Daedalus*, Winter 1962: an entire issue devoted to the topic *Youth: Change and Challenge*.

as constituents a variety of minority groups ought to provide specially good opportunities for growing up. At such a time, there are many different ways to express fidelity in action. There is, or should be, opportunity for real social action and political commitment; for trying out roles and experimenting with new causes and foci for loyalty. Indeed, in one instance, it has turned out so. The Freedom Riders' buses, I believe, are carrying their Negro passengers to suburbia; but they are certainly carrying both them and their white fellow travelers a long way toward self-realization as well. The issue seems almost ideally suited to the needs of the better sort of American youth today; it is fundamental to human dignity, involves real sacrifice and personal danger freely undertaken in comradeship. Yet it is legitimate, and does not alienate youth from the expressed values of the larger society as a continued struggle for "Fair Play for Cuba," for example, would. Few revolutionaries in history have enjoyed the comfort, as the cudgels of the police descend, of knowing that the Supreme Court was behind them and moving along with all deliberate speed.

Few other American youngsters seems to have found so relevant a focus for fidelity. "The strength of disciplined devotion" that innovators, renewers, and committed deviants need is gained only through "involvement of youth in such experiences as reveal the essence of the era they are to join" if such strength already colors those experiences. In our era it doesn't, not predominantly anyway. Examples of individual integrity can still be uncovered, but they hardly set the prevailing tone of our life. The essence of our era is a kind of infidelity, a disciplined expediency.

This expediency is not a breach of our tradition, but its very core. And it keeps the young from getting much out

of the diversity that our heterogeneous culture might otherwise provide them. This kind of expediency is built into
the value structure of every technically developed open
society; and it becomes most prevalent when the rewards of
achievement in that society appear most tempting and the
possibilities of decent and expressive survival at a low or
intermediate position in it least reliable. Being different,
notoriously, does not get you to the top. If individuals must
believe that they are on their way there in order to preserve
their self-esteem they will be under constant pressure, initially from anxious adults and later from their own aspirations, to repudiate the divergent elements of their character
in order to make it under the terms common to mass culture.
They choose the path most traveled by, and that makes all
the difference.

To anyone who is concerned about what his life means,
this pressure is repugnant. "Every human being is of supreme
value," writes Rebecca West in *Black Lamb and Grey Falcon*, "because his experience, which must be in some measure
unique, gives him a unique view of reality; and the sum of
such views is needed if mankind is ever to comprehend its
destiny."[3] The abandonment of this quest is what really
appalls us; this is what we mean when we deplore that we
live in an age of conformity. But this is too simple. Conformity is a very useful economy when what the individual
conforms to grows out of and expresses the meaning of his
own experience. If we are to make sense of ourselves and
the world we live in, most of our behavior must express the
pattern of our growth in the symbols and through the roles
available in our culture. Patterns, however original, are partly

[3] New York: The Viking Press, 1940.

composed of repetitive and traditional elements; and symbols, to be intelligible, must be held in common. The proverbial Englishman, by dressing for dinner in the jungle, expressed his conviction that he was still an Englishman who knew where his home was and that it was far away. On ceremonial occasions, officials of the new African nations array themselves in the magnificent costumes of their culture; while conducting the daily business of the state they assert, by wearing a conventional business suit, their membership in the dowdy bureacracy of contemporary statecraft. Both modes of dress are, in a sense, conforming, but neither is a form of self-denial; each is appropriate to, and expressive of, the actual meaning of the occasion for which it is worn.

What is immeasurably destructive is rather the kind of conformity that abandons the experience of the individual in order to usurp a tradition to which he does not belong and to express a view of life foreign to his experience and, on his lips, phony. For an adult this is self-destructive; for an adolescent it is the more pitiful and tragic, because the self that is abandoned is still immanent and further growth requires that it be nurtured and continuously clarified and redefined. A pregnant woman may recover, more or less, from abortion; the foetus never does.

For nearly a decade, sympathetic adults have been complaining that contemporary youth is apathetic and conforming, until new cults of nonconformity have arisen to give us what we now want and to exploit the new opportunities created by our wanting it. Many a bright young man has concealed himself strategically behind a beard and a uniform "beat" costume ill suited to his nature; and who can deny that the managers of the Hiltons of tomorrow may gain useful experience in the coffee houses of today. But actual autonomy, when it can be found, looks and sounds different.

For example, Mr. Bond: a healthy-looking, jolly, crew-cut young undergraduate from Ohio State:[4]

BOND: In my mind, to really do something, you've got to have a skill. It takes more than just aspirations. And you've got to have a certain amount of specific skill that you can offer. I'm talking in terms of humanitarian endeavor, if you want. So, therefore, being realistic, I wanted to get into something that I could deal with, if you want, physically or tangibly. The ministry or medicine, it came down to that. In the ministry, I was dealing with things that were too intangible and just didn't seem that I could grasp ahold of them. I didn't know what I was doing exactly. I wasn't sure of myself. With medicine, I'm sure I've got something whereby I can truly help people, and I'd like to apply it on the largest scale I can.

INTERVIEWER: You didn't think of playing the organ, by any chance?

BOND: No. You're talking about Schweitzer now. No. Schweitzer. I've read all of his books and such, but I'll say that I'm not going to pattern myself after Schweitzer or any other man, because I don't intend to do the exact kind of work he's done. I like to be the organizational type in WHO or something like that, if you want. A man in WHO working, I think, can accomplish more than Schweitzer . . . Schweitzer has become quite a symbol. He has, there's

[4] All the following excerpts are quoted from recorded interviews obtained by Carl Nordstrom and myself in the course of an investigation, supported by the Co-operative Research Division of the United States Office of Education, of "Why Successful Students in the Natural Sciences Abandon Careers in Science," and reported to that office in June 1961. A nonstatistical summary, including many interview excerpts, was also published under the title "Why Students Leave Science," by myself, in *Commentary*, August 1961, pp. 144–155.

no doubt about it. A young man, you like to think—at least I do—"What can I do with my life, which I consider to be really valuable?" And at the end of fifty years of living, I want to say, "Now what have I accomplished?" in certain terms. And to me, service is the biggest concept. It really is. Along with, of course, in the end, I'm trying to achieve personal happiness. Let's not get away from that. And this is just my definition of the way I'm going to achieve it. . . . I'm going to medical school in four years, and then I'd possibly like to do traveling for maybe four years or so. I'm serious. Just on an adventure kick, if you want, and then settling down for thirty years to some specific application of what I know.

INTERVIEWER: Won't you also have to take your internship or residency?

BOND: Surely, but I can also tie this in with a romantic adventure somewhere. Because I can very easily possibly go to a foreign land, and, actually, this could help me in doing what I want to do, if you use it that way.

. . . . .

Science is not an end in itself to me. It's merely, once you go far enough in science, I think that you do have to jump again to other questions, because I think science stops, and, if you want, philosophy and a lot of other questions begin to pick up a little bit. And I couldn't. I think you could say that I'm a scientifically-trained person with goals that are strictly not scientific research, but an application of science to man, so I guess you would call me, well, a humanist.

. . . . .

When I have, for example, a course which makes me think in my own terms, and new ideas, I do extra reading and everything. Well, for science, I just read the syllabus, and I memorize the muscles and such. So, independence of thought; if one just took science courses, I'd feel like he was just regurgitating. Until you reach the state, now . . . that might take me toward research eventually, way further on, that you know science so well there's no more regurgitating. From there, it's newness; and if I could find newness in science there'd be a real challenge.

· · · · ·

INTERVIEWER: Is there anything of a more general kind you would care to add?

BOND: No. This has been interesting though. It's been very interesting to be able to sit and analyze. I've thought about this . . . or else I would have switched out of the curriculum of science which I'm now in. And I couldn't go ahead and be a doctor. I'd become a philosopher, but to me being a philosopher all your life isn't achieving what I'd like to achieve very generally. There is a temptation for a young man, I think, once you begin to be exposed to thinking and to new thoughts and to philosophy and to more general readings, and Tillich and a few others, to want to do more thinking and less learning of facts. Original thought. And I'd like with science to lead an original life. Not a life stereotyped on Schweitzer.

INTERVIEWER: Like your own?

BOND: Yes, that's right; like my own. And it's not a life that's so set up that it's rigid to begin with. It's very general. I can't tell exactly what fate is going to take me into, but I can only define things as I clearly see them now. They may change in the future.

Or Mr. Grant, a young Westerner, tall in the saddle:

GRANT: Well, my personal reason for my own changes were, well, originally, when I wanted to come to Stanford, I wanted to come to Stanford because, though at the time I thought I wanted a scientific or technical education, I did want to come to a university where I could get a good, some good liberal education; and as I got here, I discovered I was more interested in what they were teaching in the liberal field than what I was getting in my scientific field. And then, at the start of my junior year, when I should have been maturing in my views toward scientific education, I found that other students who I knew were maturing in it more and taking it more—of a kind of attitude you were supposed to take. But myself, I still had the desire to—oh, more towards ideas in philosophy and political science and my . . . as far as a career is based, when I changed, I threw away virtually a set career and a job in companies I could have gone to work for, knowing that what I was going to study now was what I wanted to study. I'd just take a chance on what I'd find. I figured I'd find my place.

· · · · ·

Another thing, my experience in summer work, which was in construction and very closely related to the field I would have gone into, I consider more valuable from a practical standpoint, in the way you figure out things than the way they go at it in the classroom situation. And these friends of mine, they were also engineers, they just took to this in a way that was foreign to my nature because I've seen too many people—young engineers in jobs, I've worked with them—who come out and know it right out of the books but don't have the slightest idea how to get a job done. And I've turned away from this and I knew I could never be that way and I began to kind of re-examine what I really wanted; I found that engineering wasn't really what I wanted. I've always, ever since I've been here, I've always entertained the thought of shifting over into political science or philosophy. So finally I decided it was time to get out . . . I'd rather get the kind of education that would do me . . . that I'd feel would do me the most good in the long run, and that is a broader, liberal education.

INTERVIEWER: Yes. Do you what sort of good?

GRANT: Just being more (Pause) . . . this is the question, because the things that I figure are . . . have come to figure are least important is the economic angle, because I figure that if I can get the liberal education, why, I can make a living anyway; if you've got a college degree, you stand a reasonably good chance of making a living. I'm not out to get rich in this world, because there's so much of this world that I don't understand and want to find out about; and I don't think you find it in math books or engineering books. And I know I'll probably never find it, and I know it's very, very easy to think about these things; that you . . . the same criticism that I apply to engineering applies to liberal education. It's very easy to be all involved with these ideas while you're in school, but I can sit around in a discussion and talk about these ideas and philosophies and different things, and you can walk right out, and never think about them again. I'm just more interested in the ideas of politics and political action and theories of government and the way men are, the way men work, why men do things, than I am in building roads for men to drive on. That's it. It's a great way to make a living—to be outside and whatnot—and it's a challenge, but people are a greater challenge. . . . Apparently that's . . . that's something . . . what do people in this country really need, and what do they really want? It seems like all they're really interested in is a swimming pool and a boat to take out on weekends. Looks like that. Now, maybe this is right and maybe this is wrong, but still, I think the very fact that we do have our high standard of living and we *are* the leading country in the world obligates us to some concern over the other peoples in the world, and there are so many other people who do not feel this way . . . I think this obligates to concern over the rest of the world even if we weren't faced with the challenge of the East—Russian ideology . . . I don't have any false illusions about going out on any big campaign of any ideal, and that's just it. I'd like to try and sell these ideas or try to influence a few people, but yet, I really don't know whether my ideas are as yet that important or that good; and if I should come to the conclusion that I did have some ideas that could be of some use, I really don't know how I could go about trying to spread them . . . I came here myself because I know the only way . . . to get a college education is the way to make a better living . . . I mean, I have to get out and work to make money to come to school, but I don't think that everybody in this world is going to be able to get rich and I think that what we do have now —our living standard is high enough that nobody is really suffering from much want in this country, where a lot of other places, a lot of people are . . . This way, I don't . . . at the present time have the same connections and ins, but I think I'll find what I'm more interested in here. I don't know where it'll lead me; lead me more along the lines I'm more interested in following.

Mr. Bond, Mr. Grant, and a few others like them hint at the qualities some of our youth still display. But they are uncommon; another of our subjects, Mr. Rabinow, seems more in keeping with the spirit of our age.

RABINOW: Well, I've had opportunities, see. I work after school. I work for a big chemical company, and I see what most research scientists are expected to do. Only Ph.D. chemists do actual research. The way they set it up is most of it is dull, routine activity.[5] Most scientific research, that *is* the nature of scientific research. I mean, once in a while you come up with an idea, I mean, that's the fascinating

[5] The phrase "dull, routine activity" occurs in one of the test-instruments used in the study, which Mr. Rabinow was discussing at this point. He is quoting, not perseverating.

part, but then to go through the synthesis and the library work, I mean, that's actually a big part of science, really, and that is dull and routine; and, I mean, people, I mean— I don't know, maybe a lot—I suppose there would be people that are taken in by thinking that there isn't much leg work and library work to it, but especially in science now, the literature output's so great, so it is pretty dull and routine most of the time . . . I suppose everybody says Hollywood-type scientists are something glorious, and that's not really true.

. . . . .

The way they work it at _____, where I work . . . at least, the way it seems to me at my level. Certain research is done along medicinal purposes, and they get up in the literature and somebody up in the—usually the Board of Directors, they don't know much about scientific research, and they decide, well, some other company is coming out with some product—let's say, right now, the big thing is psychic energizers. Well, we have to come up with something too; so, therefore, they tell the director of research, therefore, tells his different heads that "we need a psychic energizer!" And, therefore, whether you're interested in this type of work or not, you go down and get all the information you can on psychic energizers: go to lectures, do research work and try to test it out and, I mean, this is really the . . . administration is the big thing in what you do.

I know I like a certain kind of recognition when I do a certain type of work. See, the work I do is nothing, really —I mean, to be recognized, but on my level, naturally, there isn't any. But even on the higher levels it's always emphasized—one man never gets the credit; it's always four or five men have done it. Usually the—I know this would bother me—I mean, the—usually the research director gets his name on it even though he had nothing to do with it, and then other people, you know, sometimes the vice president, they might stick his name on there, too, to show, you know, sort of a dedication to a symphony or something to your patron sort of kind of thing, and I just don't feel that this is right . . . In other words, you know, apple-polishing is very prevalent if you want to get somewhere, you've got to be able to toe the line and show them that, you know, you're with them—very little dissension. Everybody's very smooth and calm. No arguments, no fights.

I finally asked Mr. Rabinow whether the things that he expressed such strong dissatisfaction about in scientific work seemed to him likely to spoil his life-work for him.

No, I've sort of become resigned to the fact . . . let's say that I'm not particularly satisfied with my work now, but . . . well, after I get out of graduate school [Mr. Rabinow is still an undergraduate] if I go back into industry, I don't feel that it'll be—I don't expect—let's say, I *hope* it will be different but I don't expect it to be much different from now. I mean, the work that I'll be doing will be different, but as far as general attitude, the company, I don't think will be different. [Mr. Rabinow's company, in fact, has since been prosecuted for collusive practices.] This is the way it is.

• • • • •

It's really hard for me to say exactly why, the general question, why I chose science. I never had a chemistry set. When I wanted to do some things, I couldn't do it at my house. I mean, my parents couldn't see it, you know. I did fool around a little bit, but right away they were on my back for fooling around. Once I even developed some pictures, and this annoyed my father because of the acetic acid smell—he didn't like it, so that was the end of that . . . I don't know, I was just curious about different things, and I thought that in science you have the opportunity, really, to see a lot of different things . . . really, you need extensive training. I try to tell myself, from the way I talk, I try to tell myself that the thing I'm looking after in life is not a lot of money. That's the way I feel. (*Pause*) I feel that I just want to make, naturally, a comfortable living and then devote myself to, oh, reading and learning and things . . . That's what I like to do . . . I also enjoy, well, working with my hands. I enjoy that, and not as a hobby, but more as a career. I rather enjoy that. And science lends itself most to that . . . I rather like to work with my hands. It fascinates me, and I get pleasure out of it. That's another reason why, well, where I worked I moved. Aside from the human factors involved, associates, where I worked before I liked much better than down here . . . I mean, at least there you did something, you made something, you had something to show for your work; here it's just . . . I don't really care what I do. I just do it and get paid and that's it.

· · · · ·

Anyway, it's remarkable the way things fit in when I look back, because I wasn't . . . I was planning on going to college, see, but not full-time day school. I never thought I could do it. 'Course, I had to work, I mean, I had to support myself, and had to support my mother also; I mean, it was just, . . . I couldn't do it. But I got this job, this work . . . I don't know what you want to call it: God, fate, whatever you believe in, but through high school I got this job where I work now, and when I started to work there it just so happened, well, I mean they had students working there who were working nights and going to full-time day school, and they said, "Well, why don't *you* do this?" and I said, "Why not?" . . . and I started to go to day school, that I had originally planned on going to night school. And everything worked out for the best (*Sotto voce, words lost*) best of all possible worlds.

All three of these young men illustrate, articulately and

with exceptional self-consciousness, the later stages of the adolescent quest for identity. None of them finds real affirmative support in the culture for the kind of person he wishes to become. Mr. Bond and Mr. Grant, to be sure, are very much rooted in their culture, and draw on it easily for their strengths. The dignity, self-confidence, and unquestioned assumption that the individual is significant in himself are certainly parts of our heritage; Bond and Grant learned these by growing up American just as they learned that they would have to pay heavy taxes on this portion of their heritage unless they repudiated it. Being American taught them to lay claim to themselves, but this is only half the proposition. They have no corresponding feeling that in claiming their right of self-determination they are asserting and celebrating their membership in a society of equals. Jefferson, no doubt, would have seen these boys as patriots, but he has been dead a long time. The social institutions of a free-ish country, including its universities, have, of course, made Bond and Grant what they are, and helped them toward what they are becoming. But those institutions have also taught them better than to expect present confirmation. Like OSS men dropped into enemy territory, Bond and Grant know that they are carrying out the mission of their nation, and that, if they get caught, their nation, responding to other values in itself, will deny them. "When I should have been maturing in my views toward my scientific education, I found that other students who I knew were maturing in it more and taking it more—of a kind of attitude you were supposed to take."

What is happening to Rabinow is uglier. If his values were fundamentally different from those of Bond and Grant, if he were less sensitive or more stupid, if he had never glimpsed what they hope to explore, we could not use his comments to define our problem. But he seeks the same fulfillment they do; he is merely more passive, more marginal, and more, as we say, realistic. Rabinow is pretty close to a paradigm of maturity; he defers to the facts, accepts his responsibilities, wants to make something more of himself than his parents did, and is highly considerate of his mother. As a Brooklyn Jew he cannot afford to work with his hands or take too many chances.

There is great pathos, and potential misery, in Rabinow's acceptance of how his responsibilities are to be defined, of how he is to learn what he has to do. *He already knows what he wants;* and it has much in common with what Bond and Grant want. "I try to tell myself, from the way I talk, I try to tell myself that the thing I'm looking after in life is not a lot of money. That's the way I feel. (*Pause*) I feel that I just want to make, naturally, a comfortable living and then devote myself to, oh, reading and learning and things." But when he tries to tell himself, why does he fail?

Through passivity, in part. What he lacks is a sense of personal authority, even over himself. This is no Sammy running; Rabinow is driven by humility rather than ambition. He is so democratic that he is trying to earn his own birthright. If he were merely a climber trying to get what he wants by techniques too crude to work, he would probably learn in time; he would not be at odds with himself. Such people are likely to be comical at the beginning of their careers and either tragic or majestic at the end of them; they risk losing their races, not themselves. Rabinow's risk is much greater. His name was submitted to our study by his department chairman as one of the most promising chemistry majors currently enrolled in the department, and he is indeed responding by "taking it more—of a kind of attitude you are supposed to take."

It is easy to say that Rabinow is a victim of his own conformity, but this is not a very illuminating slogan. Conformity, like nuclear warfare, does not become less probable or
less disastrous simply because people inveigh against it. Evils
do not disappear because people disapprove of them, unless
the conditions at their root are changed. Conformity, however pandemic, is not at the root of anything; it is a symptom
of certain prevalent social conditions. These conditions,
unfortunately, are by no means disorders. They are the
normal processes, and express the cherished values, of life in
an open, urban, technically developed society.

Open, urban, technically developed societies favor the
kinds of terms that Rabinow has come to accept. To Bond
and Grant, such societies are more likely to prove an inhospitable wilderness. Rabinow is right in taking this for
granted; but he is weakened by a failure of nerve that keeps
him from quite realizing that there are technics for keeping
body and soul together in an inhospitable wilderness; for
more than survival, for living a rich and bounteous life.

This kind of scouting is appropriate to and an integral
part of adolescence. A boy who has never experienced it, at
least vicariously by sympathy and affection for the kind of
boy who has, may never become quite a man. But, what is
more to the present point, the society that prefers the kind
of man who has never examined the meaning of his life
against the context in which he lives is bound to believe that
it has a youth problem. For its own sake, and the sake of its
social future, one can only pray that it really does have.

Adolescents have very low status in our society, and
serious questions about their role in it tend to turn into
inquiries as to whether they are receiving adequate custodial
service from their teachers, jailers, and social workers. Since,
in fact, they usually are not, this is a fairly important ques-

tion, and a recurrent one. When we go beyond this, however, into the basic question of why their status is low, and
why they are so consistently disparaged and prevented from
forming a conception of themselves strong enough to resist
disparagement, we must deal with far more fundamental
issues. At bottom, I suggest, is nothing less than the question
of what it costs in individual freedom and dignity to provide
justice and equality in a mass society. Americans hate facing
this question more than any other; technicians as good as
ourselves ought to be able to arrange to enjoy all those good
things without limit. This book is about what happens to
our young people as we try it.

2

The

CRADLE

of

LIBERTY

Not far from Los Angeles, though rather nearer to Boston, may be located the town of Milgrim, in which Milgrim High School is clearly the most costly and impressive structure. Milgrim is not a suburb though it is only fifty miles from a large and dishonorable city and a part of its conurbation. Comparatively few Milgrimites commute to the city for work. Milgrim is an agricultural village which has outgrown its nervous system; its accustomed modes of social integration have never even begun to relate its present, recently acquired inhabitants to one another. So, though it is not a suburb, Milgrim is not a community either.

Milgrim's recent, fulminating growth is largely attributable to the extremely rapid development of light industry in the outer suburbs, with a resulting demand for skilled labor.

But recent demographic changes in the area have produced a steady demand for labor that is not so skilled. In an area not distinguished for racial tolerance or political liberalism, Milgrim has acquired, through no wish of its own, a sizable Negro and Puerto Rican minority. On the shabby outskirts of town, a number of groceries label themselves Spanish-American. The advanced class in Spanish at Milgrim High School makes a joyful noise—about the only one to be heard.

Estimates of the proportion of the student body at Milgrim who are, in the ethnocentric language of demography, non-White, vary enormously. Some students who are clearly middle-class and of pinkish-gray color speak as if they were besieged. But responsible staff members estimate from 12 to 30 percent. Observations in the corridors and lunchrooms favor the lower figure. They also establish that the non-Whites are orderly and well behaved, though somewhat more forceful in their movements and manner of speech than their light-skinned colleagues.

What is Milgrim High like? It is a big, expensive building, on spacious but barren grounds. Every door is at the end of a corridor; there is no reception area, no public space in which one can adjust to the transition from the outside world. Between class periods the corridors are tumultuously crowded; during them they are empty; but they are always guarded with teachers and students on patrol duty. Patrol duty does not consist primarily in the policing of congested throngs of moving students, though it includes this, or the guarding of property from damage. Its principal function is the checking of corridor passes. Between classes, no student may walk down the corridor without a form, signed by a teacher, telling where he is coming from, where he is going, and the time, to the minute, at which the pass is valid. A student caught in the corridor without such a pass is taken to the office where a detention slip is made out against him, and he is required to remain at school for two or three hours after the close of the school day. He may do his homework during this time, but he may not leave his seat or talk.

There is no physical freedom whatever at Milgrim. That is, there is no time at which, or place in which, a student may simply go about his business. Privacy is strictly forbidden. Except during class breaks, the toilets are kept locked, so that a student must not only obtain a pass but find the custodian and induce him to unlock the facility. My mother, who had a certain humor about these matters unusual in her generation, had a favorite story about a golfer who, in a moment of extreme need, asked his caddy to direct him to the nearest convenience. The poor boy, unfortunately, stuttered; and the desperate golfer finally interrupted him, sadly, saying, "Never mind, now, son; I've made other arrangements." How often this occurs at Milgrim I do not know, but when it does, the victim is undoubtedly sent for detention.

Milgrim High's most memorable arrangements are its corridor passes and its johns; they dominate social interaction. "Good morning, Mr. Smith," an attractive girl will say pleasantly to one of her teachers in the corridor. "Linda, do you have a pass to be in your locker after the bell rings?" is his greeting in reply. There are more different kinds of washrooms than there must have been in the Confederate Navy. The common sort, marked just "Boys" and "Girls," are generally locked. Then, there are some marked "Teachers, Men" and "Teachers, Women," unlocked. Near the auditorium are two others marked simply "Men" and "Women," intended primarily for the public when the auditorium is being used for some function. During the school day a cardboard sign saying "Adults only" is added to the legend on these washrooms; this is removed at the close of the school day. Girding up my maturity, I used this men's room during my stay at Milgrim. Usually it was empty; but once, as soon as the door clicked behind me, a teacher who had been concealed in the cubicle began jumping up and down to peer over his partition and verify my adulthood.

He was not a voyeur; he was checking on smoking. At most public high schools students are forbidden to smoke, and this is probably the most common source of friction with authority. It focuses, naturally, on the washrooms which are the only places students can go where teachers are not supposed to be. Milgrim, last year, was more liberal than most; its administration designated an area behind the school where seniors might smoke during their lunch period. Since, as a number of students explained to me during interviews, some of these students had "abused the privilege" by lighting up before they got into the area, the privilege had been withdrawn. No student, however, questioned that smoking *was* a privilege rather than a right.

The concept of privilege is important at Milgrim. Teachers go to the head of the chow line at lunch; whenever I would attempt quietly to stand in line the teacher on hall duty would remonstrate with me. He was right, probably; I was fouling up an entire informal social system by my ostentation. Students on hall patrol also, when relieved from duty, were privileged to come bouncing up to the head of the line; so did seniors. Much of the behavior Milgrim depends on to keep it going is motivated by the reward of getting a government-surplus peanut butter or tuna fish sandwich without standing in line for it.

The lunchroom itself is a major learning experience which

must make quite an impression over four years' time. There are two large cafeterias which are used as study halls during the periods before and after the middle of the day—the middle three or four are lunch shifts. The food, by and large, is more tempting than the menu; it tastes better than it sounds. The atmosphere is not quite that of a prison, because the students are permitted to talk quietly, under the frowning scrutiny of teachers standing around on duty, during their meal—they are not supposed to talk while standing in line, though this rule is only sporadically enforced. Standing in line takes about a third of their lunch period, and leaves plenty of time for them to eat what is provided them. They may not, in any case, leave the room when they have finished, any more than they may leave class in the middle. Toward the end of the period a steel gate is swung down across the corridor, dividing the wing holding the cafeterias, guidance offices, administrative offices, and auditorium from the rest of the building where the library and classrooms are. Then the first buzzer sounds, and the students sweep out of the cafeteria and press silently forward to the gate. A few minutes later a second buzzer sounds, the gate is opened, and the students file on to their classrooms.

During the meal itself the atmosphere varies in response to chance events and the personality of the teachers assigned supervisory duty, especially in the corridor where the next sitting is standing in line. The norm is a not unpleasant chatter; but about one teacher in four is an embittered martinet, snarling, whining, continually ordering the students to stand closer to the wall and threatening them with detention or suspension for real or fancied insolence. On other occasions, verbal altercations break out between students in the cafeteria or in line and the *student* hall patrolmen. In one of these that I witnessed, the accused student, a handsome, aggressive-looking young man, defended himself in the informal but explicit language of working-class hostility. This roused the teacher on duty, who walked over toward the boy and, silently but with a glare of contempt, beckoned him from the room with a crooked and waggling finger and led him along the corridor to the administrative office: the tall boy rigid in silent protest; the teacher, balding and duck-bottomed in a wrinkled suit, shambling ahead of him. The youth, I later learned, was suspended for a day. At some lunch periods all this is drowned out by Mantovani-type pop records played over the public address system.

What adults generally, I think, fail to grasp even though they may actually know it, is that there is no refuge or respite from this: no coffee break, no taking ten for a smoke, no room like the teachers' room, however poor, where the youngsters can get away from adults. High schools don't have club rooms; they have organized gym and recreation. A student cannot go to the library when he wants a book; on certain days his schedule provides a forty-five-minute library period. "Don't let anybody leave early," a guidance counselor urged during a group testing session at Hartsburgh, an apparently more permissive school in our sample. "There really isn't any place for them to go." Most of us are as nervous by the age of five as we will ever be; and adolescence adds to the strain; but one thing a high school student learns is that he can expect no provision for his need to give in to his feelings, or to swing out in his own style, or to creep off and pull himself together.

The little things shock most. High school students—and not just, or even particularly, at Milgrim—have a prisoner's sense of time. They don't know what time it is outside. The research which occasioned my presence at Milgrim, Hartsburgh, and the other schools in the study required me to interview each of twenty-five to thirty students at each school three times. Just before each interview, the student was given a longish description of an episode at a fictitious high school to read as a basis for our subsequent discussion, and I tried to arrange to be interviewing his predecessor while he was reading the descriptive passage. My first appointment with each student was set up by the guidance counselor; I would make the next appointment directly with the student and issue him the passes he needed to keep it. The student has no *open* time at his own disposal; he has to select the period he can miss with least loss to himself. Students well adapted to the school usually pick study halls; poorer or more troublesome students pick the times of their most disagreeable classes; both avoid cutting classes in which the teacher is likely to respond vindictively to their absence. Most students, when asked when they would like to come for their next interview, replied, "I can come any time." When I pointed out to them that there must, after all, be some times that would be more convenient for them than others, they would say, "Well, tomorrow, fourth period," or whatever. *But hardly anyone knew when this would be in clock time.* High school classes emphasize the importance of punctuality by beginning at regular but uneven times like 10:43 and 11:27, which are, indeed, hard to remember; and the students did not know when this was.

How typical is all this? The elements of the composition—the passes, the tight scheduling, the reliance on threats of detention or suspension as modes of social control—are nearly universal. The complete usurpation of any possible *area* of student initiative, physical or mental, is about as universal. Milgrim forbids boys to wear trousers that end more than six inches above the floor, and has personnel fully capable of measuring them. But most high schools have some kind of dress regulation; I know of none that accepts and relies on the tastes of its students. There are differences, to be sure, in tone; and these matter. They greatly affect the impact of the place on students.

Take, for comparison and contrast, Hartsburgh. Not fifteen miles from Milgrim, it is an utterly different community. It is larger; the school district is more compact and more suburban, more of a place. First impressions of Hartsburgh High are almost bound to be favorable. The building, like Milgrim, is new; unlike Milgrim, it is handsome. External walls are mostly glass which gives a feeling of light, air, and space. There is none of the snarling, overt hostility that taints the atmosphere at Milgrim. There are no raucous buzzers, no bells of any kind. Instead, there are little blinker lights arranged like the Italian flag. The green light blinks and the period is over; the white light signals a warning; when the red light blinks it is time to be in your classroom. Dress regulations exist but are less rigorous than at Milgrim. Every Wednesday, however, is dress-up day; boys are expected to wear ties and jackets; the girls, dresses rather than skirts and sweaters. On Wednesday the school day ends with an extra hour of required assembly and, the students explain, there are often outside visitors for whom they are expected to look their best.

Students at Hartsburgh seem much more relaxed than at Milgrim. In the grounds outside the main entrance, during lunch period, there is occasional horseplay. For ten minutes during one noon hour I watched three boys enacting a mutual fantasy. One was the audience who only sat and laughed, one the aggressor, and the third—a pleasant, inarticulate varsity basketball player—was the self-appointed victim. The two participants were portraying in pantomine old, silent-movie-type fights in slow motion. The boy I did not know would slowly swing at Paul, who would sink twisting to the ground with grimaces of anguish; then the whole sequence would be repeated with variations, though the two boys never switched roles. In my interviews with Paul I had never solved the problems arising from the fact that he was eloquent only with his arms and torso movements, which were lost on the tape recorder, and it was a real pleasure to watch him in his own medium. This was a pleasure Milgrim would never have afforded me. Similarly, in the corridors at Hartsburgh I would occasionally come upon couples holding hands or occasionally rather more, though it distressed me that they always broke guiltily apart as they saw me or any other adult. One of my subjects, who had completed the preliminary readings for his interview and was waiting outside for me to finish with the previous subject, was dancing a little jig by himself in the corridor when I got to him. This is all rather reassuring.

It is also contrary to policy. There is a regulation against couples holding hands and they are punished if caught by the kind of teacher who hates sexuality in the young. The air and space also, subtly, turn out to be illusions if you try to use them. Hartsburgh High is built around a large landscaped courtyard with little walks and benches. I made the mistake of trying to conduct an interview on one of these benches. When it was over we could not get back into the building except by disturbing a class; the doors onto this inviting oasis can only be opened from the inside, so nobody ever goes there. Since the courtyard is completely enclosed by the high school building this affords no additional protection from intruders; but it does sequester a possible place of informal refuge. The beautiful glass windows do not open enough to permit a body to squirm through and consequently do not open enough to ventilate the rooms, in which there are no individual controls for the fiercely effective radiators. Room temperature, at Hartsburgh, is a matter of high policy.

Teachers do not hide in the washrooms at Hartsburgh, but the principal recently issued to all students a letter warning that any student caught in the vicinity of the school with "tobacco products" on him would be subject to suspension; students were directed to have their parents sign the letter as written acknowledgment that they were aware of the regulation and return it to school. Staff, of course, are permitted to smoke.

A former teacher, promoted to assistant principal, is now a full-time disciplinarian, but students are not dragged to his office by infuriated teachers as sometimes happens at Milgrim. Instead, during the first period, two students from the school Citizenship Corps go quietly from classroom to classroom with a list, handing out summonses. The air at Hartsburgh is less rancorous and choleric than at Milgrim, and there seem to be more teachers there who like teaching and like kids. But the fundamental pattern is still one of control, distrust, and punishment.

The observable differences—and they are striking—are the result almost entirely, I believe, of structural and demographic factors and occur despite very similar administrative purposes. Neither principal respected adolescents at all or his staff very much. Both were preoccupied with good public relations as they understood them. Both were inflexible. But their situations are different.

At Milgrim there is a strong and imaginative district superintendent who takes cognizance of educational problems. He likes to have projects going on that place the district in the national eye, particularly in research and guidance. Guidance officers report through their chairman directly to him, not to the building principal; and the guidance staff is competent, tough, and completely professional. When wrangles occur over the welfare of a student they are likely to be open, with the principal and the guidance director as antagonists; both avoid such encounters if possible, and neither can count on the support of the district office; but when an outside force— like an outraged parent—precipitates a conflict, it is fought out. At Hartsburgh, the district superintendent is primarily interested in keeping a taut ship with no problems. To this end, he backs the authority of the building principal whenever this might be challenged. The guidance office is rudimentary and concerned primarily with college placement and public relations in the sense of inducing students to behave in socially acceptable ways with a minimum of fuss.

In these quite different contexts, demographic differences in the student bodies have crucial consequences. At Milgrim, the working-class students are not dominant—they have not got quite enough self-confidence or nearly enough social savvy to be—but they are close enough to it to be a real threat to the nice, college-bound youngsters who used to set the tone of the place in their old elementary or junior high school and who expect to go on dominating the high school. The working-class influx has left many middle-class students feeling engulfed by the rising wave of lower-status students, as they see it; while the lower-status students, many of whom are recent migrants and even high school transfers from the city, can remember schools in which they felt more at home.

The result is both to split and to polarize student feeling about the school, its administration, and other students. Nobody likes Milgrim High. But the middle-class students feel that what has ruined it is the lower-class students and that the punitive constraint with which the school is run is necessary to keep them in line. In some cases these middle-class students approach paranoia; thus, one girl, in commenting on the mythical high school described in our research instrument, said, "Well, it says here that the majority of the students are Negro—about a third!" (The actual statement is "about a fifth.")

The working-class students are hard-pressed, but being hard-pressed they are often fairly realistic about their position. If the Citizenship Corps that functions so smoothly at Hartsburgh went about its duties as smugly at Milgrim, actually turning people in and getting them in trouble, they would pretty certainly receive some after-school instruction in the way social classes differ in values and in the propensity for nonverbal self-expression. At Milgrim, the working-class kids know where they stand, and stand there. They are exceptionally easy to interview, for example, because it isn't necessary to be compulsively nondirective. Once they sense that they are respected, they respond enthusiastically and with great courtesy, but they do not alter their position to give the interviewer what they think he wants, or become notably anxious at disagreeing with him. They are very concrete in handling experience, not given to generalization. Most of them seem to have liked their elementary school and they share the general American respect for education down to the last cliché—then one will add, as an afterthought, not bothering even to be contemptuous, "Of course, you can't respect *this* school." They deal with the situation it presents them with in correspondingly concrete terms. Both schools had student courts last year, for example, and Hartsburgh still does, though few students not in the Citizenship Corps pay much attention to it. Student traffic corpsmen give out tickets for corridor offenses, and the culprits are brought before an elected student judge with an administrative official of the school present as adviser. But Milgrim had a student court last year that quickly became notorious. The "hoody element" got control of it, and since most of the defendants were their buddies, they were either acquitted or discharged on pleas of insanity. The court was disbanded.

The struggle at Milgrim is therefore pretty open; though none of the protagonists see it as a struggle for freedom, or could define its issues in terms of principle. The higher-status students merely assent to the way the school is run, much as middle-class white Southerners assent to what the sheriff's office does, while the lower-status students move, or get pushed, from one embroilment to the next without ever quite realizing that what is happening to them is part of a general social pattern. At Hartsburgh there aren't very many lower-status students, and those that there are can easily be dismissed by their middle-class compeers, who set the tone, as a "hoody element." There are not enough of these and they are not sufficiently aggressive to threaten the middle-class youngsters or their folkways, but, for that same reason, they do not force the middle-class youngsters to common cause with the administration. The administration, like forces of law and order generally in the United States, is accepted without deference, as a part of the way things work. In America, one doesn't expect authority to be either intelligent or forthright; it looks out for its own interests as best it can. Reformers and troublemakers can only make it nervous and therefore worse; the best thing is to take advantage of it when it can help you and at other times to go on living your own life and let it try to stop you.

This is what the Hartsburgh students usually do and, on the whole, the results are pleasant. The youngsters, being to some degree Ivy, do not constantly remind the teachers, as the Milgrim students do, that their jobs have no connection with academic scholarship. Many of the teachers, for their part, act and sound like college instructors, do as competent a job, and enjoy some of the same satisfactions. The whole operation moves smoothly. Both Milgrim and Hartsburgh high schools are valid examples—though of very different aspects—of American democracy in action. And in neither could a student learn as much about civil liberty as a Missouri mule knows at birth.

What is learned in high school, or for that matter anywhere at all, depends far less on what is taught than on what one actually experiences in the place. The quality of instruction in high school varies from sheer rot to imaginative and highly skilled teaching; but classroom content is often handled at a creditable level and is not in itself the source of much difficulty. Generally speaking, both at Milgrim and Hartsburgh, for example, the students felt that they were receiving competent instruction and that this was an undertaking the school tried seriously to handle. Throughout our sample of nine schools—though not necessarily in each of them—more than four-fifths of our pretest sample, aggregating nearly one thousand students, agreed that the following statements applied to their school:

> There are teachers here who, when they tell you your work is well done, you know it is good.

> Many of the teachers know a great deal about things other than what they cover in their subject in class.

> Some teachers surprise you by getting you interested in subjects you'd never really thought of before.

But important as it is to note that students generally recognize academic quality in the schools, and particularly the contributions of exceptional teachers, serious questions remain as to how the school affects the students' conception of either academic mastery or of themselves. For more than 80 percent also agree that:

You have to be concerned about marks here; that is, if you are going to get anywhere and be anything.

The school doesn't expect students to wear expensive clothes, but they do have to be neat and clean. Clothes that are too sporty or sexy are "out."

The student newspaper here is pretty careful not to report things in such a way that they might make trouble for the school with other people.

Keeping everybody quiet when they're in the library is a regular cause with the librarians here.

A girl who went too far here and got into trouble would be suspended or expelled.

In my judgment, the kind of tutelage and status that the high school assigns students affects their lives and subsequent development far more crucially than the content and quality of formal instruction. What is learned most thoroughly by attendance at Milgrim or Hartsburgh is certain core assumptions that govern the conditions of life of most adolescents in this country and train them to operate as adult, if not as mature, Americans. The first of these is the assumption that the state has the right to compel adolescents to spend six or seven hours a day, five days a week, thirty-six or so weeks a year, in a specific place, under the charge of a particular group of persons in whose selection they have no voice, performing tasks about which they have no choice, without remuneration and subject to specialized regulations and sanctions that are applicable to no one else in the community nor to them except in this place. So accustomed are we to assuming that education is a *service* to the young that this statement must seem flagrantly biased. But it is a simple statement of what the law provides. Whether this provision is a service or a burden to the young—and, indeed, it is both, in varying degrees—is another issue altogether. Compulsory school attendance functions as a bill of attainder against a particular age group, so the first thing the young learn in school is that there are certain sanctions and restrictions that apply only to them, that they do not participate fully in the freedoms guaranteed by the state, and that, *therefore, these freedoms do not really partake of the character of inalienable rights*.

When services are to be provided to an individual whom the law respects as it does the agency providing the services the normal legal instrument is, of course, a contract, which defines the rights and obligations of both parties and provides each with legal remedies against the contract's breach.

Compulsory school attendance, however, is provided by a law which recognizes no obligation of the school that the students can enforce. He cannot petition to withdraw if the school is inferior, does not maintain standards, or treats him brutally. There are other laws, certainly, that set standards for school construction and maintenance, the licensing of teachers, technics of discipline, and so forth; and proceedings under these may be invoked if the school does not abide by them. But they do not abate the student's obligation to attend the school and accept its services. His position is purely that of a conscript who is protected by certain regulations but in no case permitted to use their breach as a cause for terminating his obligation.

Of course not. The school, as schools continually stress, acts *in loco parentis;* and children may not leave home because their parents are unsatisfactory. What I have pointed out is no more than a special consequence of the fact that students are minors, and minors do not, indeed, share all the rights and privileges—and responsibilities—of citizenship. Very well. However one puts it, we are still discussing the same issue. The high school, then, is where you really learn what it means to be a minor.

For a high school is not a parent. Parents may love their children, hate them, or, like most parents, do both in a complex mixture. But they must, nevertheless, permit a certain intimacy and respond to their children as persons. Homes are not run by regulations, though the parents may think they are, but by a process of continuous and almost entirely unconscious emotional homeostasis, in which each member affects and accommodates to the needs, feelings, fantasy life, and character structure of the others. This may be, and often is, a terribly destructive process; I intend no defense of the family as a social institution. Salmon, actually, are much nicer than people: more dedicated, more energetic, less easily daunted by the long upstream struggle and less prudish and reticent about their reproductive functions, though inclined to be rather cold-blooded. But children grow up in homes or the remnants of homes, are in physical fact dependent on parents, and are too intimately related to them to permit their area of freedom to be precisely defined. This is not because they have no rights or are entitled to less respect than adults, but because intimacy conditions freedom and growth in ways too subtle and continuous to be defined as overt acts.

Free societies depend on their members to learn early and thoroughly that public authority is *not* like that of the family; that it cannot be expected—or trusted—to respond with sensitivity and intimate perception to the needs of individuals but must rely basically, though as humanely as possible, on the impartial application of general formulae. This means that it must be kept functional, specialized, and limited to matters of public policy; the meshes of the law are too coarse to be worn close to the skin. Especially in an open society, where people of very different backgrounds and value systems must function together, it would seem obvious that each must understand that he may not push others further than their common undertaking demands or impose upon them a manner of life that they feel to be alien.

After the family, the school is the first social institution an individual must deal with—the place in which he learns to handle himself with strangers. The school establishes the pattern of his subsequent assumptions as to which relations between the individual and society are appropriate and which constitute invasions of privacy and constraints on his spirit—what the British, with exquisite precision, call "taking a liberty." But the American public school evolved as a melting pot, under the assumption that it had not merely the right but the duty to impose a common standard of genteel decency on a polyglot body of immigrants' children and thus insure their assimilation into the better life of the American dream. It accepted, also, the tacit assumption that genteel decency was as far as it could go. If America has generally been governed by the practical man's impatience with other individuals' rights, it has also accepted the practical man's respect for property and determination to protect it from the assaults of public servants. With its contempt for personal privacy and individual autonomy, the school combines a considerable measure of Galbraith's "public squalor." The plant may be expensive—for this is capital goods; but nothing is provided graciously, liberally, simply as an amenity, either to teachers or students, though administrative offices have begun to assume an executive look. In the schools I know, the teachers' lounges are invariably filled with shabby furniture and vending machines. Teachers do not have offices with assigned clerical assistance and business equipment that would be considered satisfactory for, say, a small-town, small-time insurance agency. They have desks in staffrooms, without telephones.

To justify this shabbiness as essential economy and established custom begs the question; the level of support and working conditions customarily provided simply defines the status of the occupation and the value the community in fact places on it. An important consequence, I believe, is to help keep teachers timid and passive by reminding them, against the contrasting patterns of commercial affluence, of their relative ineffectiveness; and to divert against students their hostilities and their demands for status. Both teachers and students, each at their respective levels, learn to regard the ordinary amenities and freedoms of middle-class life as privileges. But the teacher has a few more of them. He hasn't a telephone, but he may make calls from a phone in the general office, while, in some schools, the public pay phone in the hallway has a lock on it and the student must get a key from the office before he can dial his call. Where a hotel or motel, for example, provides in its budget for normal wear and tear and a reasonable level of theft of linens and equipment and quietly covers itself with liability insurance, the school—though it may actually do the same thing—pompously indoctrinates its students with "respect for public property," "good health habits," and so forth before it lets them near the swimming pool. In a large city, the pool may have been struck out of the architect's plans before construction began, on the grounds that it would be unfair to provide students in a newer school with a costly facility that students in older schools do not have.

If the first thing the student learns, then, is that he, as a minor, is subject to peculiar restraints, the second is that these restraints are general, and are not limited to the manifest and specific functions of education. High school administrators are not professional educators in the sense that a physician, an attorney, or a tax accountant are professionals. They are not practitioners of a specialized *instructional* craft, who derive their authority from its requirements. They are specialists in keeping an essentially political enterprise from being strangled by conflicting community attitudes and pressures. They are problem-oriented, and the feelings and needs for growth of their captive and disfranchized clientele are the least of their problems; for the status of the "teenager" in the community is so low that even if he rebels the school is not blamed for the conditions against which he is rebelling. He is simply a truant or juvenile delinquent; at worst the school has "failed to reach him." What high school personnel become specialists in, ultimately, is the *control* of large groups of students even at catastrophic expense to their opportunity to learn. These controls are not exercised primarily to facilitate instruction, and, particularly, they are in no way limited to matters bearing on instruction. At several schools in our sample boys had, for example, been ordered by the assistant principal—sometimes on the complaint of teachers—to shave off beards. One of these boys, who had played football for the school all season, was told that, while the school had no legal authority to require this, he would be barred from the banquet honoring the team unless he complied. Dress regulations are another case in point.

Of course these are petty restrictions, enforced by petty penalties. American high schools are not concentration camps; and I am not complaining about their severity but about what they teach their students concerning the proper relationship of the individual to society. The fact that the restrictions and penalties are petty and unimportant in themselves in one way makes matters worse. Gross invasions are more easily recognized for what they are; petty restrictions are only resisted by "troublemakers." What matters in the end, however, is that the school does not take its own business of education seriously enough to mind it.

The effects on the students of the school's diffuse willingness to mind everybody's business but its own are manifold. The concepts of dignity and privacy, notably deficient in American adult folkways, are not permitted to develop here. The high school, certainly, is not the material cause of this deficiency, which is deeply rooted in our social institutions and values. But the high school does more than transmit these values—it exploits them to keep students in line and develop them into the kinds of people who fit the community that supports it.

A corollary of the school's assumption of custodial control of students is that power and authority become indistinguishable. If the school's authority is not limited to matters pertaining to education, it cannot be derived from educational responsibilities. It is a naked, empirical fact, to be accepted or controverted according to the possibilities of the moment. In this world power counts more than legitimacy; if you don't have power it is naïve to think you have rights that must be respected; wise up. High school students experience regulation only as control, not as protection; they know, for example, that the principal will generally uphold the teacher in any conflict with a student, regardless of the merits of the case. Translated into the high school idiom, *suaviter in modo, fortiter in re* becomes "If you get caught, it's just your ass."

Students, I find, do not resent this; that is the tragedy. All weakness tends to corrupt, and impotence corrupts absolutely. Identifying, as the weak must, with the more power-ful and frustrating of the forces that impinge upon them, they accept the school as the way life is and close their minds against the anxiety of perceiving alternatives. Many students like high school; others loathe and fear it. But even these do not object to it on principle; the school effectively obstructs their learning of the principles on which objection might be based; though these are among the principles that, we boast, distinguish us from totalitarian societies.

Yet, finally, the consequence of submitting throughout adolescence to diffuse authority that is not derived from the task at hand—as a doctor's orders, or the training regulations of an athletic coach, for example, usually are—is more serious than political incompetence or weakness of character. There is a general arrest of development. An essential part of grow-ing up is learning that, though differences of power among men lead to brutal consequences, all men are peers; none is omnipotent, none derives his potency from magic but only from his specific competence and function. The policeman represents the majesty of the State, but this does not mean that he can put you in jail; it means, precisely, that he can-not—at least not for long. Any person or agency responsible for handling throngs of young people—especially if it does not like them or is afraid of them—is tempted to claim diffuse authority and snare the youngster in the trailing remnants of childhood emotion, which always remain to trip him. Schools are permitted to infantilize adolescence and control pupils by reinvoking the sensations of childhood punishment, effective because it was designed, with great unconscious guile, to dramatize the child's weakness in the face of authority. In fact, they are strongly encouraged to do so by the hostility to "teen-agers" and the anxiety about their conduct that abound in our society.

In the process, the school affects society in two complementary ways. It alters individuals: their values, their sense of personal worth, their patterns of anxiety and sense of mastery and ease in the world on which so much of what we think of as our fate depends. But it also performs a Darwinian function. The school endorses and supports the values and patterns of behavior of certain segments of the population, providing their members with the credentials and shibboleths needed for the next stages of their journey, while instilling in others a sense of inferiority and warning the rest of society against them as troublesome and untrustworthy. In this way, the school contributes simultaneously to social mobility and social stratification. It helps to see to it that the kinds of people who get ahead are those who will support the social system it represents; while those who might, through intent or merely by their being, subvert it are left behind as a salutary moral lesson.

This leads immediately to two questions: what patterns of values are developed and ratified through the experience of compulsory school attendance, and what kinds of people and what social groups do succeed best in school and find most support there? The issue of bias in the schools is old and familiar; but it cannot be stated as a simple tendency of the schools to favor the "economically advantaged" over the "culturally deprived." The school's bias is both more and less diverse than this statement suggests. The school quite often—indeed, traditionally—supports the respectable and ambitious poor against the presumptions of the privileged; its animus is directed against youngsters who possess certain common features regardless of the widest possible variation in status and income. In the next chapter, I shall present some of the evidence derived from our research that bears on the first of these questions: what values does the school convey and support? In chapters 4 and 5, drawing partly from published sources and partly from my own observations, I will examine the second: what are the people like who fare well in school in contrast to those who fare badly, what social groups and what folkways are thereby favored, and how does the resulting educational bias influence the structure of society?

3

The

STRUCTURE

of

STUDENT VALUES

To provide all our subjects with a common basis for discussion of issues and value-conflicts that arise in high school life, my colleague Carl Nordstrom and I invented an imaginary high school, which we called LeMoyen High School, and made up a series of six narrative episodes about it. These little stories are genuinely serial; they involve the same characters in different situations that become more complicated as the series continues. Each episode is typed up as a separate document and given to the student to read. With it he receives also a set of nine cards, each of which bears a comment or other item relating to the narrative episode. The directions for using the cards are standard for all six episodes, except for minor changes according to the nature of the items on the cards.

Please read *all the cards* through thoughtfully. Then, having read them through:

1. Select the *three* cards which, you feel, represent the *best* comments on the situation described.
2. From these three, select the *one* comment which, you feel, would be best of all.
3. Returning to the cards remaining, select the *three* cards which, you feel, represent the *worst* comments on the situation described.
4. From these three, select the *one* comment which, you feel, is the *worst* of all.

These directions result, of course, in a symmetrical forced-choice distribution of the cards into a 1-2-3-2-1 distribution, from the one best to the one worst. Each student taking part in the research procedure was given *two* episodes with their respective sets of cards, told to read and sort them consecutively, and then to report to me that he had finished so that I could record his card-choices. The distribution of cards forms the basis of my interviews with students as well as the basis for certain subsequent statistical analyses that are still under way and that are intended to identify students with highly similar value-structures who may have attended any of the nine different schools, and to reveal the pattern of values that they hold in common.

In the interviews I asked each subject to discuss his reasons for choosing each of the cards he had rated as good or bad comments—all the cards in the episode, that is, except the three he had left in the middle. I asked each subject, after he had discussed all six of his card-choices, if there were pertinent issues that the comments on the cards had not touched on sufficiently. Most of the interviews were private; in about a fourth, two students who were working on the same episode would discuss their card-choices jointly with each other and with me. Students were paid two dollars for each session, or eight dollars for the entire series, including the pretest. Students invited to participate were clearly informed that they need not do so; but only one declined, while two others withdrew before completing their third session.

I have included here in the body of the text only those portions of the series of six episodes, with their cards, that are needed to illustrate and clarify my discussion; the entire set of instruments is included in the Appendix. I have also rearranged them from the order in which they were presented to the research subjects, so as to present more clearly and logically the inferences we drew from the entire series. This results, occasionally, in the appearance in the episode of a character unknown to the reader but whom research subjects had encountered at an earlier session.

The episode with which I shall begin is actually fourth in the order in which these were presented to our subjects. This episode, which is called "The King's Visit," begins:

> Several weeks ago, the Governor wrote to the principal of LeMoyen High School to tell him about the impending visit to Capital City of the King of a country not unlike Denmark and of the King's notable interest in spirited young people. He also informed the principal of the King's expressed desire to meet with some interesting and representative high school students during his visit. The Governor then went on to say that he had selected LeMoyen as one of the ten high schools chosen from throughout the state which were to pick several students to meet with the King when he visits the Governor at the Executive Mansion. The Governor added that the King speaks English fluently, and then concluded with the suggestion that such young people as were to be chosen should be persons to whom the school could point with pride as expressing what was finest and best about their school.

The next, and final, paragraph goes on to tell how the student nominations will be processed, making it clear that they will be advisory, with final decision left to the principal of LeMoyen High School. The paragraph was included to make the story consistent with actual high school practice on most issues nominally falling within the province of student government but affecting the school's public relations.

How did the subjects respond to "The King's Visit"? For this episode, the nine cards given them to sort describe fictitious students whom they may include, ignore, or reject. The actual distributions made by 246 subjects are given below.

TABLE I

Student selections of fictitious candidates for
"The King's Visit"
(*in descending order of popularity*)

N = 246

Name	Best	Good	Neutral	Poor	Worst
Karen Clarke	109	91	35	9	2
Elfrieda Eubanks	60	116	57	12	1
Bernstein Sisters	36	70	104	30	6
Nicky Galetti	9	52	119	56	10
The Combo	10	49	113	60	14
Nancy Harris	0	41	123	68	14
Scott Cowen	10	31	87	90	28
Johnny Adams	9	26	64	106	41
Eric Pratt	3	16	36	61	130
Pure chance*	27	55	82	55	27

* I.e., the way *any* one of the cards might be assumed to have been distributed if it had been subjected to no selection at all.

Karen Clarke

Karen Clarke will be giving the valedictory at graduation for this year's class. As she should. Always well groomed and polite, she is completely in command of herself in any situation. She is the perfect model of what a high school student ought to be. Her work is neat, correct, and unlike that of so many other students, in on time. It really has to be, because her dad, Mr. Clarke, teaches here and he makes sure Karen doesn't get any special favors. He makes certain that she stands up for herself and does her work. In student activities she is Treasurer of the Senior Class. She is also a teacher's aide for Mr. Pottitone's chemistry laboratory and a member of the Ethics Committee of the Student Government. Where others are concerned, Karen always tries to be helpful. She wants to go to a good college like Vassar or Smith, and plans everything she does carefully, with this in mind. At LeMoyen everybody feels that she has a real chance to get into the kind of college she would like to go to.

Elfrieda Eubanks

Elfrieda Eubanks is so sweet you couldn't help liking her, and everybody at LeMoyen does. She's president of the Girls' Athletic Association and a sure thing for the Chamber of Commerce's best All-Around Girl award this spring. Elfrieda is tall, slender, and very graceful. She has a beautiful voice and sings regularly at several local churches. A better-than-average student, she's also a volunteer nurse's aide at the hospital, chairman of the school hostess club, and LeMoyen's number one cheerleader. She dances beautifully, too. One thing you can say about Elfrieda, she's always smiling, always a good guy, no matter what. That's what makes her so popular. Even her twin brother, Grant, who was the best basketball player LeMoyen had until Kevin McGuire came along, isn't as popular as Elfrieda, and that's saying something.

Either Karen Clarke or Elfrieda Eubanks is the first choice of 69 percent of our subjects; *both* girls are included among the top three choices a bit over three-fourths as often as they would have been if every student had picked one of them first and had included the other among his two second choices. Only two students thought Karen would be the worst choice, and only one thought Elfrieda would be; they were placed in one of the last two categories only 7 percent as often as they might have been if every student had rejected them. If the Bernstein sisters are added on, they, Karen, and Elfrieda account for 84 percent of first choices.

Why were these people—and particularly Karen and Elfrieda—chosen? Nearly all the students said in their interviews that the important thing was to pick somebody who would "make a good impression on the King." From the outset, they defined the situation as a *problem*—and a problem in the establishment of good public relations. But the story makes it clear that the visit is *not* a public relations gimmick, or a pseudo-event planned by the King's hosts. The King himself originated the suggestion, and is known to prefer "spirited" young people; and while the young people selected are to represent what is "finest and best" about the school, the research-subjects were left completely free to decide what characteristics were "finest and best." But they set aside at the outset any possibility that the King might actually have a serious interest in youth and might prefer challenging young people to those who would impress him favorably. Some students explained this position very realistically; the proposed meeting would be too brief and superficial for him to get to know his visitors anyway, and the school administration would certainly insist on sending well-mannered, socially graceful youngsters. But, more often, they simply assumed that what was "finest and best" meant what would make a good impression.

But what did they think would? The most important thing was good social technique. You had to have somebody who "would know how to talk to the King." Karen Clarke would; she was very active and successful in school, and had lots of experience putting strangers at their ease. Furthermore, the card that describes her said "she is the perfect model of what a high school student ought to be." In my experience, few American high school students have any sense of irony. The research subjects also liked Karen for being exceptionally well organized: "Karen doesn't get any special favors . . . and plans everything she does carefully." Most of the students who picked her answered "yes" when asked whether they thought they would like this paragon personally.

Elfrieda, too, would have these skills and graces, and in addition, sweetness and warmth. Both these girls were seen as "well rounded" and "good mixers." Our research subjects also stress that, being very much involved in the school, Karen and Elfrieda would know a lot about it so that their conversation would be well informed. They were, in short, experts on high school life and the "teen-age" condition; they would be what the students called "representative."

The students' response to Elfrieda consistently showed one very curious feature. The references on her card-description to her brother Grant Eubanks and to Kevin McGuire concern the characters in episode two, "The LeMoyen Basketball Team," which we had given to our research subjects at the preceding session—usually not more than two days earlier and sometimes just the day before. I have deferred discussing this episode until our mode of analysis becomes more familiar, because the students' responses to it are more ambiguous and perhaps more subtle; certainly, they were harder to follow. But the episode hinges on the effort of Elfrieda's brother Grant to sponsor McGuire, a newcomer to town and an excellent basketball player whom Eubanks had previously

known, for inclusion on the school team. Both the Eubankses and the McGuires are portrayed as upper-middle-
class people; but the Eubankses are Negro, the McGuires
white.

I shall return to the issues this episode calls forth in discussion a little later in this chapter. At this point, I wish
merely to note that hardly any one of the respondents who
selected Elfrieda as a King's visitor recalled that she was
Negro. In part this is undoubtedly because the students
regarded the research as "testing" and the episodes as tests,
and they have been trained for a decade to treat every test
as a separate event. But it cannot be just that; they did often
remember that Karen Clarke's father had been mentioned in
the first episode; and they even remembered one character
who plays a central part in the last episode as the same
boy who had figured largely in the first, though he had not
been mentioned in between.

Nobody withdrew Elfrieda on being reminded of her
race; and a minority cited this as added reason for sending
her, so that the King would learn, as part of his good impression, that there was no racial discrimination at LeMoyen.
Many of our subjects undoubtedly did not care whether
Elfrieda was Negro or not. But this curious amnesia suggests
that the research-subjects' failure to notice her race was
something more than indifference. The idea of a family of
highly successful Negroes who were the acknowledged
social leaders of the school just did not sink in. It was either
too implausible to consider seriously, or so ghastly that it
turned Elfrieda white overnight.

Mill and Jill Bernstein

Mill and Jill Bernstein are two of the craziest kids you
can imagine, crazy in a great way, that is. While they aren't
really twins they look so much alike that they might as

well be. It really gets you, you never know which one you're talking to, and they are always pulling gags on people that way. They've got so much talent they can do anything, and almost do. They both play instruments in the band, they have their own vocal duet, and they are really wonderful with their mimicry. They are a must at any party because they usually make it go. At LeMoyen, they're for the school all the way, the real boosters. They're the in-everything girls, cheerleading, the school paper, debating, the works. They also run everything; they should, too, because they get things done. Right now Mill is organizing the Senior Class trip, and Jill is chairing the Junior Clambake Committee. LeMoyen has a lot to thank Mill and Jill for, and it's going to remember them for a long time.

The Bernstein sisters did not fare nearly as well as Karen and Elfrieda; where Karen was chosen as first more often than she was disposed of in any other manner, and Elfrieda was usually included among the two next best people to send, the Bernstein sisters were left in the middle as trivial. Nevertheless, they were sent to the King just three times as often as they were deliberately excluded, whereas everyone else, except Karen and Elfrieda, is rejected slightly more often than he or she is chosen. Those who picked them often said that they would be lots of fun and exactly what the King must be looking for if what he liked was "spirited young people." They, too, were well rounded, and would certainly know how to talk to the King; there was a slight risk that they might pull some sort of joke that went too far, but our subjects seldom thought this was a great risk; Mill and Jill would have too much social savvy for that. Beneath their informal, jocular style the Bernstein sisters were perceived as very serious young women, indeed, who would know how to leave the King purring and satisfied.

Nicky Galetti

For the past three years the right side of the line of the
LeMoyen football team has been practically impregnable.
The reason is right tackle, Nicky Galetti, two hundred and
twenty pounds of solid bone and muscle. Nicky is a great
team man, hard-working and loyal, and never an angry
word. This year Nicky played every minute of every
game, except for the last two in the game with City High.
It was really Nicky's game, and against LeMoyen's traditional foes, too. Nicky led the offense, and on defense, he
was, as usual, the key man. Unfortunately, LeMoyen's
backfield was weak this year, and the game was scoreless
until the last few minutes, when Nicky blocked a City
punt. Joe White recovered it for a touchdown. Everybody
felt that it was too bad that it wasn't Nicky, just so he
could have scored at least once. When the coach took him
out a few minutes later, the stands went mad cheering for
him—a great team man if there ever was one.

Our subjects' response to Nicky Galetti is also, I think, very
interesting. Through most of this work I complain of the
devotion adolescents in a mass society show to averageness
and well-roundedness. Nicky, however, has the kind of
averageness that does not thrive—the Nicky Galettis just get
lost. I did not, under our methodology, discuss with our
subjects why they left the cards they did in the middle,
residual category. But the people who rejected Nicky generally did so on the grounds that he was just a big nothing.
They were kindly about him; he was a nice boy, but he
would have nothing to talk to the King about; he wasn't
well rounded at all, and was interested only in football.
Those who accepted him said, in effect, that the delegation
ought to include a boy, and Nicky was the least offensive
boy described; athletics were important in school, and the

delegation, in order to be representative, might well include an athlete. The card describing Nicky, however, is placed at either end—as best or as worst—less often than any other card and only a third as often as it would have been by chance. Nicky just doesn't register much.

The reader will already have noticed that the girls described on our cards are included in the delegation much more often than the boys and that Nicky, dull as he is, is the most acceptable of the boys. Is this a real sex bias, or is it an artifact built into the instrument? When I asked subjects who had classically picked Karen first and Elfrieda and the Bernstein sisters as their two second choices whether they considered and accepted the fact that the King would then learn nothing new about how American high school *boys* acted or how they saw their life in school, they almost invariably said either that they had not thought it important or, more often, that this had occurred to them and they regretted it, but that there was nothing they could do about it because all the boys described seemed to them more or less inappropriate to send, if not downright obnoxious. The subjects, then, are unaware of any sex bias and may have none; if we had described a male equivalent of Karen—a happy, politically competent officer in the General Organization and a cheerleader, they might have picked him enthusiastically. But it has been rather consistently observed by many investigators that girls generally fare better in school than boys of the same aptitude, and are also more likely to be regarded as apt. Girls make better grades, are less often and less severely punished, and adapt more readily to school routines. In this sense, a boy like Karen would have been a phonier idea in the first place—though there are such—while Nicky, as both a plodder and an athlete, threatens nobody; he is both passive and mutely, safely male.

Ronnie, Big Joe and Pink

Ronnie, Big Joe and Pink have just cut their second platter. Known as the Combo, they play and sing with a fast, easy beat that's sometimes subtle and sometimes frantic. It's easy to like, too. The Combo is so good, actually, that it was featured on a coast-to-coast TV network last month. About the members of the Combo, well, they're not just ordinary: Big Joe, Joe White, that is, is the first Negro ever to be elected president of the school honor society. Pincus Peabody is going to a music school in New York on a scholarship next year. He's quite a composer and works up the arrangements for the Combo. He can write in the classical mood also, and is the composer of the violin sonatina Nancy Harris is planning to play at graduation. One can't say too much for Ronnie, though, except that he organized the Combo and writes the lyrics. And really, the lyrics are great; they have a twist to them that gives them class, something like the Kingston Trio, and still it's different.

Our subjects distributed the card describing the jazz Combo—Ronnie, Big Joe and Pink—in a pattern almost identical to the way they treated Nicky. Their comments, of course, were quite different. The Combo's claim to consideration—like Nicky's, only more so—is based on *specialized competence*. Both Nicky and the Combo are described as excelling in activities to which "teen-agers" are thought to attach great importance. But our respondents treated this excellence quite ambivalently. They were looking for excellence and expertise, to be sure; but the expertise they wanted was impersonal, social technique. If they included Nicky or the Combo, it was because they thought the King should get a chance to see what a wide *range* of activities go on in a high school. If they were excluded from the delegation, as they rather more often were, it was because they were "not well rounded," and could only talk to the King about one thing, football or jazz as the case might be, and suppose he wasn't interested in that? The subjects refused to consider that the King might really be interested in the young people themselves or in what their consciousness of their craft had meant to them and contributed to their distinction as people. "Well-roundedness" and knowing how to be effective in a social group were, if not "finest and best" in themselves, qualities that our subjects thought indispensable to gaining acceptance and recognition for any others.

Nancy Harris

Nancy Harris is a violinist. This year she has been accorded the signal honor of being first violinist and concert master of the all-state orchestra. She has also performed as soloist for several of the local symphony orchestras. Nancy is gifted with artistic sensibility and quickness in all things. She is a very good student, and still manages to keep her course work up while practicing three or four hours a day. Unfortunately, her schedule does not allow her much opportunity for social activity, which is too bad because she is really an attractive young lady who, with a little effort, could easily be very popular. But her enthusiasms are more for things than for people and she prefers artistic creation to success with her fellow students.

This attitude becomes more apparent in the subjects' response to Nancy Harris. Just half the subjects ignore her by leaving her card in the middle pile—more frequently than any other card of the nine—she is actively rejected twice as often as she is accepted, and no one at all puts her first. Though she is described as a gifted and experienced concert violinist, subjects tend to dismiss her because "she wouldn't know what to say to the King"—she wouldn't know how to talk to him. They see her devotion to her career as self-centered. Her card states that "her enthusiasms are more for things than for people and she prefers artistic creation to success with her fellow students." Her fellow students infer that if she isn't interested in others she would not be interesting herself; they don't see why a concert violinist would have had any experiences worth the attention of a king.

Attitudes toward Nancy, however, were usually negative rather than hostile; our subjects wouldn't send her, and see her as dull and frumpish, but they hold nothing against her personally. Between their attitudes toward Nancy Harris and toward Scott Cowen, next down the list in frequency of choice, there is a real break in continuity. Scott is genuinely disliked. He and Johnny Adams, who is rated as even more unsuitable than Scott for this purpose, arouse in our subjects a wider *range* of response than the others. Scott and Johnny, whom the subjects see as basically similar though they certainly are not so superficially, tend either to be chosen enthusiastically or rejected—more often rejected, especially Johnny.

Scott Cowen

Scott Cowen is supposed to be a genius. When he was twelve years old his parents arranged for him to take a special course in mathematics at the university nearby and he did very well, indeed. Although all the other students in the course were either specially selected senior high school students or college freshmen, Scott came out first in the class. According to the instructor's report, "Mr. Cowen is potentially a mathematician of the first order and with proper training should be able in the future to do work of great significance." At LeMoyen, Scott has continued to do well. His entries in the Senior High School

Division Science Fair won first prize both last year and this. He is a brilliant chess player and managed a draw with the state champion. And he is editor of the LeMoyen *Xantippe*, the school literary magazine. Scott's work at LeMoyen is always original and always competent, although it does tend to be sloppy. He's sloppy also in the way he dresses, and he does manage to argue with some of the teachers. If it weren't for this he would probably be valedictorian of his class. He has the ability to be.

Johnny Adams

Johnny Adams is something of an enigma. It isn't easy to figure out how he managed to make the basketball team. He's not big and he's not fast. It's not clear why he wanted to, either. He doesn't hang around with the fellows on the team. The kids he runs around with are what are called beatniks at LeMoyen, the kind, you know, who usually don't care about things like sports and dances. But when Johnny decided he wanted to make the team, he did. He has drive, and he's smart, too. If he wanted to, he's one fellow who could give Karen Clarke or Scott Cowen a real run for it academically. But most of the time he doesn't feel like it. When he does, though, watch out. It was a big surprise, last year, when he won the veterans' club oratorical contest. He did it against odds, too. No one would ever call him good-looking, he has a sort of squeaky voice, and most of the time he could use a haircut and shave. He's not always an easy guy to be with, either. Still, he took on the best the county had to offer and showed them all how to do it.

Our subjects' antagonism toward Scott and Johnny had four distinct and consistent features: it was moralistic, it was directed against their ability to function effectively in solitude without caring much about group support, it made emphatic use of external characteristics, and it was explicitly and implacably anti-intellectual. Neither Scott nor Johnny would make a good impression on the King and they might offend him disastrously. Habitually sloppy and unshaven boys could not be considered, and did not deserve to be considered, for the honor of being allowed to represent the school. Subjects who did include one of them in the delegation usually argued that such bright boys would have sense enough to shave and dress neatly on such an occasion. Hardly anyone argued that their appearance would be less important to the King than the other features that might make them interesting—Scott's intellectual breadth and Johnny's peculiar intensity and fitful brilliance. In fact, our subjects refused to give these boys credit for breadth; they were not "well rounded." Scott was rejected as "only good at one thing," though his card describes him as editor of the school literary magazine, chess champion, and an advanced scholar in mathematics. To most students in our sample a taste for intellectual activity for its own sake is exotic and suspect, whatever form it takes.

Like Nancy Harris, Scott and Johnny are rejected because they direct their energy and devotion into their own specialized interests. But, since Scott and Johnny are described as having more conventional capacities that they neglect as well as special competences that they develop, our subjects object to them on ethical grounds as well. They are erratic and untrustworthy; they only do what *they* feel like doing; they don't work up to capacity—in short, they are self-indulgent underachievers. Johnny's card says, "If he wanted to, he's one fellow who could give Karen Clarke or Scott Cowen a real run for it academically. But most of the time he doesn't feel like it." Scott's card says, ". . . he does manage to argue with some of his teachers. If it weren't for this he would probably be valedictorian of his class. He has the ability to be." These traits could, of course, be seen as signs of a personal autonomy and self-direction; Johnny and Scott invest their resources only in activities that are important to them. But our subjects see them as self-centered and self-indulgent —autistic rather than autonomous.

Both boys were seen essentially as cranks; Johnny's exceptional ability and success at basketball were discounted because his motives for playing seemed too queer and personal. Scott and Johnny were perceived as security risks, unstable, and unpredictable. Our subjects' distrust of them sharply contrasts with their willingness to take a chance on the "crazy" Bernstein sisters. It seemed far more likely to them that Johnny would appear before the King unkempt and unshaven, cracking insults in jive-talk, than that the Bernstein sisters would indulge their penchant for "pulling gags on people." High school students very readily perceive that the apparent spontaneity of people like the Bernstein sisters masks a cool awareness of what is expected of them and a willingness to deliver it, while boys like Johnny really are responding to their own internal, if often conflicting, cues and neglecting external demands. This is valid enough; but our subjects lacked any corresponding awareness that the inner self could be a source of stability. Self-directed people seem to them on the verge of chaos or revolt.

Eric Pratt

Everybody at LeMoyen knows Eric Pratt. He's cool. He has a great line and really knows how to make the girls happy. He's always lots of fun, anywhere, anytime. He's up on the latest record, in with the newest fad, and on to the easiest way to do the hard things. Eric's sharp, he sure is, you should see the way he dresses. Man, you should see. If you had money like Eric has you could pay for the clothes, but I'll bet you wouldn't get it right, most likely you wouldn't. It's something you've got to know how to do, and Eric does. He's got style in everything he does. Don't get the idea that this kid's just popular with the gang, though. He's more than that. The teachers think he's great, too, especially the women teachers. He knows how to talk to them, and make them love him, and make them do anything he wants them to do.

Still less popular than Scott and Johnny, however, was Eric Pratt, whom more than half the subjects named as the very worst person to send. It is true that three people named him as the best choice, which is better than poor Nancy Harris did; these three were very poor, low-status youngsters who took Eric's magnificence at face value and accepted him as rich, smooth, creamy, and delicious. But most lower-status subjects found Eric as distasteful as their middle-class peers did. "He's just a brownie!" one dignified lower-status Puerto Rican respondent asserted. Actually, Eric is not so much a brownie as an example of bad research technique; this is the only card among the nine that the subjects criticized as overdrawn and a caricature, written by somebody who thought he knew how "teen-agers" talk but didn't. The description of Eric is, in fact, so repulsive that its value to the study is reduced, except that his widespread rejection does suggest that the research-subjects were paying attention and were of sound mind.

After I had discussed with each subject his reasons for selecting the cards he had chosen, I asked him how he would have filled out a blank card so as to describe a person who would have been better to send than any of these nine. None of the 246 gave me any vivid and original suggestion. Most said that the nine cards covered very well the actual range of high school "types" they were familiar with. But there was often complaint that all the cards described people that were too special in some way or another. The King was not being given enough of a chance to meet average students; and only average students were truly representative.

I also added to the protocol a final question as to whether the subject would himself enjoy taking part in such a mission. Rather to my astonishment, most—especially girls— thought they would enjoy it and would handle it pretty well. A distinct minority of relatively nonverbal boys, however, thought themselves unsuitable, criticizing their own limitations quite as sharply as they had those of Scott Cowen or Johnny Adams. And a considerable number of subjects thought of the visit as also an educational experience; they thought, that is, that the students to be sent should be selected partly on the basis of whether *they*, as well as the King, would get anything out of it and learn something from it.

What was chiefly lacking was any confidence that the King could accept conflict or unusual behavior or appearance, or that he might enjoy a good argument. Our subjects took no risks that the spirited young people he would meet might be too spirited; and they were expressly skeptical about the possibility of any real communication between the King and his delegation; this was a ritual, public occasion. The main thing was to see that it went off smoothly, and that the people who took part in it knew their social roles and were competent to discharge them. Real encounter was not to be risked.

Miss H. illustrates these attitudes with particular clarity:

I. For the King's visit, the student that you selected as best was Elfrieda Eubanks. Would you explain your reasons for choosing her?

H. The, uh, the principle is, well, the problem of the school is to pick the pupil that was most likely to be the most like the American students—typical rather. And I think this girl is most, would be the best choice, because she seems to be connected with all the girls' athletic associations; the Chamber of Commerce awarded her the all-around girl. She seems to be sort of a model, and he would get a good impression, I think. She's very popular, and she seems to have no problems, so I think that she would be the best one to go.

I. Then, I take it that you would want the school represented by a person who is not typical so much as—

H. Um, well, she's, she is in everything, but I think she's typical as she's in things most girls would be interested in. She's not totally interested in the academic side of the school. She's in other activities also.

I. So that you're picking her as a rather well-rounded person?

H. Yeah.

I. Would her race affect your choice one way or another? (*Miss H. shakes her head rather blankly*) No. Then, as the worst student, I believe you picked Eric Pratt?

H. I don't think he would be a good choice at all. It said that he's really sharp and I, I don't think a king would be very impressed with this. I think he'd just not be a good choice at all, because he isn't typical of the school, because all the students aren't like this. They aren't like Elfrieda, either, but she's more typical of what most of the students are like. I don't think Eric is at all.

I. She's at least more like what they'd want to be like.

H. Yes (*Laughs*), I hope so.

I. Then quite desirable, after Elfrieda, at least, the Bernstein sisters.

H. I think they'd be a good choice because they showed the other side of the school. I mean, they're not always interested in the educational side of it. But—they are—but, um, they're also interested in outside activities, such as the school paper and cheerleading and most of the things that other girls would be interested in and, I think, again they're well rounded, as the first girl was.

I. Then card 6 [Karen Clarke], favorable.

H. I think she would show that even though her father is a teacher, that it had—it would show the fairness of the school, that it wouldn't show favoritism to anyone, that would be related to the faculty or anyone. Not so much that she's very intelligent, but also that she tries, even though her father is a teacher, she, that has no bearing on it, that he makes her get good marks, or likes her to get good marks, but still she does it on her own. And that'd be a good thing for the school.

I. I don't as yet quite see how that concerns the King.

H. Well, it sort of has to do with the school. What he would think of the school from the way this girl acts in school, I think . . .

I. You mean, if I understand you then, that it would be useful to the King's conception of American education to see that a girl whose father was on the faculty . . . still does make it on her own. This shows something of our policy in action?

H. Umn-hunh.

I. And then the two that you, uh, thought less appropriate, Scott Cowen, whom you would not send.

H. I don't think he would be anywhere near typical, because it says he's supposedly a genius, and he doesn't seem to be interested in too much other than academic subjects and the literary magazine, and he just seems to live in his own little world and he doesn't try to do anything else but what has to do with subjects in school. I don't think he's at all well rounded. He might be very intelligent, but I don't think he'd be a good representative of the school.

I. Yes, just of himself?

H. Yeah.

I. And finally, Johnny Adams, whom you would not send?

H. Johnny Adams seems to be sort of mixed-up. He doesn't have too much of an interest in anything. He has the ability to be almost anything he wants to, but it says unless he wants to, he won't; and I don't think he'd be a good representative because I think he's sort of *weird* (*Laughs*). He doesn't get good marks unless he feels like it; it's sort of an on-and-off proposition, and I don't think he'd be good at all for the representative.

I. (*Perhaps redundantly*) You're assuming, then, that a representative should be typical?

H. Yes, I—from what I read, it said they wanted someone that would show the good points of the school. Um, I don't think he would.

I have begun this discussion of our students' interviews with the fourth rather than the first episode they considered because the subjects' responses to "The King's Visit" show their prevailing patterns of values more vividly than their responses to the earlier episodes. The nature of the card-choices for this episode requires them to make judgments about what is valuable in an entire human being—or at least in a rather stereotypical description of one—which tends to reveal their set of values as a whole. In responding to "The King's Visit," most of our subjects showed very clearly: (1) their dependence on external judgment as more important than self-approval and internal coherence—the importance of "making a good impression"; (2) their suspicion of specialized personal competence unless directed and controlled by the school or the group for social purposes—their distrust of autonomy; (3) their skepticism that the King's visit could have any purpose other than good public relations, despite the King's statements that he wanted to meet *spirited* young people. Accustomed as they doubtless were to the unrealistic conventions of test-construction, our students were not willing to suspend disbelief enough to give the hypothetical King the chance he had sought for a real encounter. They chose to include in his delegation the most externally oriented people they could find. This outwardness served two functions. They wanted to send students who could handle the King and please him. They also wanted the students to be experts on the high school situation itself, and their idea of an expert was someone with a *wide* knowledge of it, who was "well rounded" and could tell the King about high school life from a variety of socially acceptable vantage points. They rejected as unsuitable the student whose experience of the school would run deeper, through continuous experience of it as the situation he must deal with in order to live his own life on his own terms.

With this as the basis for understanding our subjects' general attitude, I wish to turn to their responses to other episodes, which call forth more specific aspects of their view of life. The very first episode—"The Clarke-Barto Incident" —was deliberately designed to be as simple as possible and still raise important value issues. Since the card-sort method itself is strange to most students, we wanted to give them a chance to apply it for the first time to a story that was too brief and simple in itself to add to their possible difficulties. "The Clarke-Barto Incident" was written early in the design of our study; LeMoyen High School did not yet have a name, nor were we yet aware that Mr. Clarke was destined to be Karen's father. The episode reads simply:

Suppose that your school is strict in enforcing the rule against students smoking in washrooms. The following incident takes place:

Mr. Arthur Clarke, a social-studies teacher at your school, is taking his mid-morning coffee break. On entering a men's washroom he discovers Johnny Barto, a junior, and a somewhat notorious character around the school, smoking. Mr. Clarke knows that Johnny should be in class this hour and furthermore, that he is a troublemaker, is having difficulty with his courses, is on probation, and that he is old enough to quit school. While Mr. Clarke and Johnny are approximately the same size, Johnny is not very strong. His whole attitude, though, is one of arrogance, as if to say, "Show me, buddy."

For this episode, the subjects are directed to treat the nine cards as offering possible courses of action that Mr. Clarke might have taken, and to sort them, just as they were later to do for "The King's Visit," until they had them arranged in order from the one best action through the two next-best, down to the one worst. Their choices, again in descending order of popularity, are presented in Table II.

TABLE II

Student selections of courses of action for
"The Clarke-Barto Incident"

$N = 247$

CARD	Best	Good	PILE Neutral	Poor	Worst
School psychologist	116	75	48	7	1
Calls parents	54	127	62	3	1
Send to principal	38	110	82	17	0
Student court	25	112	96	11	3
They fight	4	33	110	90	10
Writing on blackboard	2	10	147	81	7
Example before own class	5	14	104	83	41
Beats Johnny coolly	1	4	49	115	78
Walks out	2	9	43	87	106
Pure chance	27	55	83	55	27

By far the favorite choice of our subjects as the best thing to do about Johnny is given on a card that reads:

> At the faculty meeting that afternoon, Mr. Clarke discusses the "Johnny Barto problem" with the school psychologist, and the school psychologist agrees to set up a counseling program designed to get at Johnny's "anti-social" behavior and straighten him out. The psychologist then calls Johnny in for counseling.

The next most popular card gets fewer than half as many first-place choices. Only about 3 percent of our subjects thought this was a bad thing to do and only one thought it the worst possible thing. Our subjects explained their choice on humane and defensible grounds. This was a *constructive* suggestion, not merely a punitive one. Having the school psychologist call Johnny in would show him that he had not gotten by with anything, but it would also show that people were trying to *help* him. This card recommends treating Johnny and his behavior as a problem—straightening Johnny out, like making a good impression on the King, is an effect to be achieved by using the school's resources efficiently.

But the school psychologist is not supposed to work *with* Johnny; he is expected to work *on* him. He is supposed to tinker with him and straighten him out. Subjects who selected this as the best course of action could seldom say what they expected the psychologist to do, other than "talk to Johnny and straighten him out"—they certainly didn't expect him to *listen* to Johnny. When asked whether they saw any reason to think Johnny was seriously disturbed emotionally, our subjects either said that they did not, or simply said that the story said he was because it defined him as a troublemaker, and troublemakers usually had emotional problems. The psychotherapist has become a familiar folk-myth at all social levels, but he is a myth without a mystery.

Our subjects had no idea what changes in personality psychotherapy is intended to foster; they are interested in results, not in processes. They assume that the result they should seek is to "straighten Johnny out" and get him over being a troublemaker, though the directions tell them only to "Select the cards which, you feel, represent the *best* actions that could have been taken under the circumstances at that time," leaving them free to define as best whatever outcome they choose. They choose, then, to define Johnny's behavior as a technical problem, to be referred to the right expert for solution.

It is consistent enough, then, that the worst card, by an equal plurality, recommends ignoring the problem altogether:

> Mr. Clarke acts as if he hadn't noticed Johnny and leaves the washroom as soon as possible.

Only two subjects, both boys—one in Milgrim and the other in the private co-educational boarding school in our sample—thought this was the best thing to do; and they, though very different persons, played virtually identical roles in their schools—that of the creative, dissident intellectual who could not quite be dismissed as a troublemaker but who was widely feared and detested by the staff. Yet, there is a good deal to be said for this course of action, even on purely empirical grounds, as more likely to lead to an improvement in Johnny than any of the other choices offered. Erik Erikson[1] has repeatedly made the point that many youths fall into patterns of serious and protracted delinquency precisely because they *were* unfortunate enough to be caught and so confirmed in their delinquent identity while other possibilities were closed off to them by their

[1] See "Ego-Identity and the Psychosocial Moratorium," in *New Perspectives for Research in Juvenile Delinquency*, H. C. Witmer and R. Kosinsky, eds. (Washington: U.S. Children's Bureau Publication #356, 1956) pp. 1–23.

record; they preferred to be something bad rather than nothing and nobody. But few of our subjects would take a chance on Johnny. They believe that the enforcement of regulations, rather than any internal tendency toward stability or homeostasis, is what keeps society from breaking down into disorder. A more sophisticated view of the function of law would place less faith in its effectiveness as a deterrent and more in its usefulness in setting up categories under which society can subsume and isolate those whom it defines as miscreant. But our subjects see it rather as an indispensable technique for controlling behavior. Neglect law enforcement and the social structure decays. If Mr. Clarke walked out of the washroom without doing anything to Johnny, he would be derelict in his duty, and would be encouraging infraction and·contumacy. Regulations must be enforced—preferably not harshly; the point is not to punish Johnny but to show him that he has gotten by with nothing. But he must not be ignored.

As a more positive aspect of their conservatism, our subjects show a strong, if simplified, sense that due process inheres in a proper respect for social roles. The next three cards that are generally favorably regarded read:

Mr. Clarke calls Johnny's parents, describes the incident to them, informs them of the seriousness of the offense, and suggests that they take appropriate measures to get Johnny in line. He also warns them that if they do not succeed, it will reflect against Johnny.

Mr. Clarke takes Johnny to the principal's office and turns him over to the person on duty there for punishment. He also requests of the office that it notify him as to the nature and severity of the punishment to be administered to Johnny.

Mr. Clarke reports Johnny to the Student Court at their meeting that evening. At the time he calls on the officers of the Court to remember their responsibility for the maintenance of order in the school, warns them not to be swayed by sentiment, and then requests that suitable punishment be administered.

All three of these cards were usually chosen for about the same reason, and with the same awareness of their limitations. Each of them constituted a referral of the "Johnny Barto problem" to a proper authority; none of these proposals is out of line. Even those subjects who recommended them doubted if they would work; if Johnny's parents hadn't straightened him out in sixteen years or more, they weren't very likely to succeed in doing so now. But it was their responsibility, as running the school was the principal's; and these people should be informed. Most of our subjects were unfamiliar with student courts, which are not common in Eastern high schools, but those who recommended bringing Johnny before such a court usually did so on the sensible and humane grounds that its members would be more likely to understand Johnny's position than an administrative official would, and could communicate with him better. A number of students who favored the use of the court, however, did justify their choice on punitive grounds; Johnny would be more humiliated by being brought up before his peers than by anything that adults—whom he had clearly written off and defied—could do to him. These subjects saw the court itself as a punitive instrument—the act of exposure before it, rather than its sentence, constituted the punishment.

The remaining four cards all describe courses of action that the students tended generally to disfavor. But two of these are seen as much worse than the other two. Our subjects tended to treat as trivial, though unwise, the suggestions that:

Mr. Clarke orders Johnny to put the cigarette out and return to class. Johnny responds by taking a swing at Clarke. Clarke, angry himself now, knocks Johnny down. Afterward, he helps Johnny to his feet, apologizes for his anger, but warns Johnny he will report him if he catches him smoking illegally again.

Mr. Clarke has Johnny report for after-school detention, at which time he (Clarke) has Johnny write the following statement on the blackboard 500 times: "I, Johnny Barto, am sorry and will never smoke in school again."

Actually, these two cards evoked quite different patterns of responses from our subjects, as a glance at Table II will show. The "blackboard" card is treated more uniformly than any other card in the series. Over half the subjects simply leave it in the middle, and fewer than 4 percent pick it either best or worse. Most of those who commented on it simply saw it as a childish punishment that might work in grammar school but that Johnny would either resent or, more probably, laugh off. Rather more of our subjects, though probably not significantly so, thought that it would be still worse for Mr. Clarke to lose his temper and get into a fight with Johnny. But a strong minority felt that this would be one of the better—rarely the best—things that could happen. Mr. Clarke's action would at least be emotionally authentic, would show Johnny that he cared, and, best of all, when it was over it would be over, and far preferable to making a federal case out of smoking in the "bathroom." These subjects made the card appear, on the average, more popular, despite the general tone of disapproval that it usually aroused—and not on wholly humane grounds. The reasons most frequently given for rejecting this card were cautiously bureaucratic rather than indignantly humane. If Mr. Clarke lost his temper and hit Johnny, he himself would be out of line; Johnny could get him into trouble, take him to court, get him fired. Teachers are supposed to control themselves, and if Mr. Clarke didn't, nobody in school would have any respect for him; he would be coming down to Johnny's level—particularly if he apologized afterward. The line of reasoning that led students to reject this card was thus very similar to that which led them to see "Mr. Clarke . . . leaves the washroom" as the worst card. Teachers must stay in role and behave responsibly. What they object to here is Mr. Clarke's misconduct, not the indignity offered Johnny.

But while few of our subjects expressed any respect for Johnny, they usually took his feelings very much into account as factors that would affect his behavior. In their responses to the next two unpopular cards:

> Mr. Clarke orders Johnny to report to his (Clarke's) class-room the next period. At that time, Clarke describes the incident to the class, and then orders Johnny to apologize to the students for having brought the good name of the school into disrepute. After the apology, Mr. Clarke asks the class members to suggest appropriate punishment for Johnny. This is all presented as a kind of object lesson in social studies.

and the more sharply disapproved:

> To teach Johnny a lesson Mr. Clarke strikes him several times. This he does coolly and with emotional restraint. After finishing, he gives Johnny a lecture, telling him what happens to young men like him when they don't mend their ways.

our subjects repeatedly stress the same two points: Johnny would be bitterly resentful and humiliated, and *this would make him behave worse than ever*; and, again, *Mr. Clarke is out of line.* Teachers have no right to punish students personally; what Mr. Clarke should do is report Johnny to the proper authority.

A plurality of our subjects regarded the proposal that Mr. Clarke make an example of Johnny as trivial and either left the card in the middle or explained their rejection of it by saying that Johnny would probably have friends in the class who would help him make a joke of the whole thing. Others, more seriously opposed, stressed that he would resent being humiliated before his friends. Nearly everyone, with reference to the "beating" card, derided the idea of Mr. Clarke giving Johnny a lecture, and again warned that Johnny could probably have Mr. Clarke fired if he hit him. But underlying these responses was the same empiricism that the youngsters later displayed in discussing "The King's Visit." When they rejected a card it was because they thought the action described on it *would not work*, and would make Johnny more of a troublemaker. When they approved a card, it was because they thought the action described on it would help solve "the Johnny Barto problem." They also often raised legalistic or procedural issues, but never purely ethical or moral ones. It would have been possible, for example, for a subject to have sorted the cards, from best to worst, as follows:

> Mr. Clarke walks out
>
> They get into fight
> Send to principal
>
> Report to student court
> Calls parents
> Write on blackboard
>
> Beats Johnny coolly
> School psychologist
>
> Class example

and then to have justified this choice on a civil-liberties basis: Johnny should not have been prejudged as a troublemaker; since he has been, Mr. Clarke should not do anything to add to his "record," although he might understandably blow his stack at Johnny's effrontery without doing too much harm. If he does turn Johnny in, however, he should be very careful to go through channels so that such rights as Johnny has will be protected; cruel or unusual punishments are out, and so is the use of a clinical pretext to invade Johnny's privacy. Only one subject out of the 240 approximated this point of view in any way—the aforesaid difficult and creative boy in the private co-educational school.

Instead, most of our subjects begin by assuming that what they are called upon to do is assist in straightening Johnny out, and they are willing to try anything that will work as long as it is done in an orderly way. Extravagant or humiliating procedures are rejected primarily because they aren't likely to work, not because they are wrong. But if our subjects express little empathy or respect for Johnny as a person, they also rarely express open hostility. They accept the implication that Johnny is a threat—part of the "hoody element"—but they react to threats by redefining them as problems rather than by getting angry themselves.

Our subjects were reluctant to discuss even the possibility that a social institution—or a teacher—might be hostile or destructive in its purpose. Their approach to the "Clarke-Barto Incident" starts with the assumption that the school and Mr. Clarke are essentially benign. The purpose of the school psychologist is to help the school help Johnny; and whatever the school is trying to do to him is, by definition, helpful. Part of its job is to straighten Johnny out. The questions that arise then merely concern the relative effectiveness of various techniques—what will "make an impression" on

Johnny. But this assumption that the school is a benign and valid source of norms and ends does not and cannot square consistently with the students' day-to-day experience of such a place as Milgrim, or Hartsburgh—or any of the schools in our sample except possibly the gentle and balmy Havencrest, a Southern public school we shall shortly consider. Their optimism tends to keep them from being classed as "trouble-makers" themselves, or, if they have been, from struggling against the definition. But in essence it must tend to alienate them from a realistic perception of their world. It is many steps, no doubt, from assuming that the school psychologist *must* be helpful to Johnny to assuming that what the State and Defense departments give the Laotians and Vietnamese is, by definition, aid. But perhaps *il n'y a que le premier pas qui coûte*.

An unusually perceptive subject, whose mother is a guidance counselor in a junior high school, illustrates nearly all these attitudes in discussing his card-choices; then rather uncertainly transcends them in his free comments on the episode.

I. Starting with the Clarke-Barto incident, Mr. R., your selection for the most favorable card, the one you thought was best in this, was card number 8. Could you give us your reasons for choosing that card?

R. Well, I think that in referring to the psychologist, Mr. Clarke is, is doing more to get to the root of the problem than in any of the other reasons, and in this way, he has, he has obviously some sort of psychological prob-lem—he resented authority, I mean, he was rebellious against authority. Maybe this is why he smoked in the bathroom, as a manifestation of his rebellion, and then in just going to the school principal and telling the school principal who will punish this kid he wasn't really—he just—he was just sort of scratching the surface of the problem. He wasn't helping anything. This, this would, in fact, he'd probably engender more rebellion on the part of the student.

I. So that your main point is that this card at least provides a program for dealing with a situation that isn't purely punitive?

R. Right. I think, I think it was in combination of the other cards. You should—I don't think any, any teacher can just go, I mean, doing this, he's ignoring the rules of the schools, which is . . . he has a duty to report this kid, and whether this duty is right or not, whether it's morally right or whatever it is, he still had that duty, so I think what he actually should have done is gone to the school principal and asked him if he could go to the psychologist. That's what I would have done.

I. That, I think, is consistent, then, with your choice of number 9 [Clarke walks out] as the worst card.

R. Well, this is, this is terrible, I thought. He doesn't help the kid at all. The kid—first of all, he's shrugging the duty that he has. First, he has a duty to the school, and second, he's shrugging the duty he has to the kid. He's not helping the kid any by doing that.

I. Yes. I wonder how, generally, uh, you would apply your—what seems to be your first principle involved in this, that is, that flagrant violation of rules is an expression of, in effect, a personality disorder.

R. Well, I don't think it's a personality disorder. I just think it's an attempt on the part of the adolescent to, to establish himself as it were, to say, autonomous?

I. Yes.

R. I think that's what it is then: an attempt to establish himself as a personality. I mean, he doesn't realize that there are some things he can, he can—that he can refute his—as part of society, which he actually thinks are wrong. But then he just goes around re—in, uh, he says then, this is bad, and this is bad, and this is no good, and then let's get together 'cause that guy's a bum, or something like that. It's not a personality disorder, I wouldn't say. Just—just immaturity.

I. Then, what would you expect the psychologist to be able to do?

R. I think the psychologist would be able to talk to the kid and show him that, that this society is just for his benefit, that it's not trying to impose restrictions on him just for the purpose of imposing restrictions; that, that people live in society because it's, it's the best method so far founded. If people thought they could follow their own rules, then we'd all live as hermits, there wouldn't be any need for government . . . so government exists for our benefit. It's, it's not so that it can, it can make prisoners out of us—make us slaves to the State. In fact, actually, I think in a good democratic society, I think the government should be more of a slave to the people. After all, the government is the people.

I. In your experience?

R. Pardon?

I. In your experience?

R. From what, from what I've read, from what, from what I know. From what I think is right.

I. Does it work out that way in your life?

R. Well, I mean, you get good breaks, bad breaks. Well, I mean, things like that happen. Not everything works in your favor. What works against you is working for a whole majority of people, but what seems—when you say "this is against me, this is no good" but there must be, must be a vast number of people who are benefiting by the same thing that's hurting you. Not all the time, but I think that's probably generally true.

I. Then your next favorable card [send to principal], you were inclined to accept.

R. Well, I chose this because I, I relied on the principal's good judgment in handling—in handling Mr., uh, Johnny Barto's problem. I don't think that, that the principal should just, just punish this boy severely, but I rely on the principal's good judgment to, uh, to see that this boy had something wrong with him, and so I couldn't say I'd, I'd end it right there.

I. And card 6 [call parents]?

R. Yeah. That's good, too. He should call the parents, but from what I gather of the situation, probably the parents don't have that much of an interest in their son or else he wouldn't be like this anyway—or maybe I'm wrong. I shouldn't say that.

I. Why?

R. Well, may, maybe the parents do. Maybe the kid has, has all semblances of being a normal child at home; but when he gets outside, he might turn into something else. But I really couldn't say . . . the kid's on probation and she must know about that. She, too, she might, she might love her son so much that she, um, she might not be able to see, see that actually he's the one making all the trouble.

I. Are you sure he is?

R. Yes. (*Pause*) Um, sometimes, I'd say sometimes a teacher can get on your back, but I don't think so. I think this kid, this kid provoked his own trouble. And I feel sorry for him. I don't think he realizes what he is doing. I don't, I don't think he realizes why he's wrong, and that's the pathetic thing about it. He needs someone to show him why he's wrong.

I. Then, in addition to card 9 that we've discussed, you reject card number one [they fight].

R. First of all, why would—the teacher shouldn't hit—a teacher shouldn't hit a student. And if he does hit a student, I don't see why he should apologize for his anger, even though, even though the kid hit him first. I mean, this might be a rationalization—this might be typical of, uh—rationalization or tit-for-tat. I don't know, but that's what I'd say. I'd say he shouldn't apologize to the kid. If he uses as, as a, as a punitive measure, then he should just accept it. He shouldn't have to apologize to the kid, and then he shouldn't warn him that he will report him again if he catches him smoking. He should report him right then. The kid'll think he'll get away with it. He'll think, "Well, this guy's on my side. He apologized to me, and he says, 'Well, I give you a break this time.' "

I. So it's the apology, even more than hitting him, that you disapprove of in this case.

R. Yes. I don't think hitting him's so bad, if the child . . . what's he gonna do, if he—if someone hits you, you hit him back. Actually, I don't know if it was necessary to hit this kid. He probably is pretty weak anyway. That's what it seemed to me . . . I think Clarke's anger is excusable: that he shouldn't apologize for it.

I. Then . . . card 2 [hits him coolly]?

R. Well, this isn't, I mean, this, this—Mr. Clarke's handling of this problem isn't in accord with the rules of the school. And actually, I think if this kid got it, got it . . . Maybe if Mr. Clarke had left him off the kid wouldn't be such a wise guy. He'd realize that, that, that he's smaller than the rest—that he's not the center of his own little universe. He'd realize that there are other people around him. But I don't think this giving him a lecture, "telling him what happens to young men who don't mend their ways," the kid might think he, the kid might think he, he might even think he's special, that he warrants such a lecture, I don't know. He might—probably still be resentful.

I. One thing you would want to make clear to Johnny Barto is that he is not special?

R. He's—he is special. He's special in the sense that he's an individual, and that, that he should be treated with decency. But he's not special in the respect that he can go break all the rules. 'Cause obeying the rules is just obeying the will of other people.

I. Anything else you would care to add with reference to this episode? Anything we've left out?

R. I don't know. This, this smoking in the bathroom, being, being disrespectful to authorities, is typical of adolescents, I think. I think most kids outgrow it. I know, I wouldn't look at that kid and say that kid's going to grow up to be a criminal. I think, I think the kid gets to a certain age—I don't know, even kids in this school, even kids who've been wise guys. They get to a certain age, and they don't want to bother with that any more. They realize how stupid it is . . . I don't know how it comes about, but you, you notice these kids, they say, "I'm going to straighten out; I mean, there's no sense fooling around any more." Or, "Why should I give this teacher a hard time? He never did anything to me. Go home and study or join the basketball team and be just like everyone else." I think most of the kids straighten out. I think, I think it's the kids who—kids who the teachers sort of—like some teachers say, "this kid's a troublemaker," and you always treat him like that. Whatever he does, they'll say, they'll say, "Sit up straight! Do this, do that!" I know I was once, I remember, in the ninth grade, and there was this boy in my class, and he was, you know, he wasn't a troublemaker at all, and he had a, he sort of—sometime he had a funny smirk on his face and the teacher said to him, she said, "Listen," she said, "you better wipe that smuck off your face, because that's just the sort of smuck that everyone's gonna think you're a troublemaker, and they'll give you a hard time for it." And, I mean, that was, was farthest from the kid's ideas, but still, I think, I think the teacher should try to understand that these kids have their problems, too. I think if the teachers were more trained in the, uh, the problems of the adolescent, then that things would be a lot better off. They could take a kid aside and talk to him, like a father would talk to a son, and show him, you know, the right way, instead of just, just giving him detention or doing this or that to him.

I. You think you could train teachers to do that?

R. I don't—sure, I think—it's part of—they go to college; I think you could, you could give them a course or two in the adolescent and you don't have to say to them, "Listen, take these kids aside and speak to them." But, if you, if you give them a course in how to understand the problems of these kids, then, then they probably will try to help them once they know.

I. When you meet a teacher, as one occasionally does, who has the power or skill and so on, to help kids and to have some understanding of what their position is, do you think that this is generally a result of training, primarily?

R. Couldn't say. (*Pause*) Wouldn't know.

The tyranny of the majority, it appears, holds no terrors for R. But underlying his essential decency is a naïveté more irresponsible than ignorance. Bright as he is, R. neither knows nor cares how people grow or how social policy is made. He is no phony; he has real feelings, he cares. R. is not regarded as conformist, and certainly does not regard himself as such; on the contrary, he was consistently one of the most incisive and least suggestible subjects included in the study. He knows the meaning of autonomy when he uses the word; his *clichés* are not applied to himself, but to the world he lives in.

They suffice, however, to keep his intelligence and decency from getting him into serious trouble. R.'s way of side-stepping—by recommending that Johnny should be referred to the school psychologist—the issue raised by the real hostilities he so poignantly describes in the last, long, quoted paragraph of his interview, precisely illustrates our subjects' mastery of this evasive action. Young R.'s statement epitomizes Americanism at its best and worst: our genuine wish to be helpful and benign and our need, in any case, to seem so to ourselves; our legalism and our conception of law as establishing procedures rather than guaranteeing rights; our willingness to give and take that leads us to equate maturity with acceptance of the status quo.

Our subjects' common pattern of response to "The Clarke-Barto Incident" which R. illustrates at the highest conventional level raises some serious questions about the vulnerability of civil liberty to clinical attack. Our subjects object to informal and unauthorized intervention in their affairs *only* if it is manifestly punitive. They lay themselves open to it willingly if the intervention is presented as a psychological service. Despite their empiricism, they are more concerned with the manifest intent of the intervention than with its actual consequences. More than twice as many of our subjects think the best course of action would be to send Barto to the school psychologist to be counseled than think it would be best to report the incident to his parents. More than three times as many pick the psychologist first than select the school principal. Yet, unless one accepts disobedience of regulations and poor relations with authority as *prima facie* evidence of mental illness, there is nothing whatever in "The Clarke-Barto Incident" to suggest that Johnny requires specialized psychological service; and the students who would send him to be counseled themselves say that they don't see anything deeply wrong with him. They cannot then rationally expect what the school psychologist does to be more effective than the formal authority of the parents or the principal.

What they seem to be looking for, however, is not—despite their empiricism—a clinical procedure that they trust because they understand how it works and what it does do and doesn't do. They want an administrative category elastic enough to contain "troublemakers" and tough enough to retain them. Such categories *must* be benign rather than punitive for two reasons. And in our culture, categories of action that are at once benign and impersonal are clinical or social services.

The more obvious, but less important, of the two reasons is that overt hostility makes our subjects feel guilty and threatened. Unless they feel that what they recommend is "for Johnny's own good," they are uneasy about recommending it. In this, they resemble Sir Charles Snow's British civil servants and academicians who ritually observe after any decision that is really fatal to the career of a colleague, "After all, it's in the man's own best interests." But fundamentally, I suspect, they choose the clinical approach precisely because there is less that "troublemakers" can do to resist it; it gets through the obsolescent network of civil liberties that they might still invoke to defend themselves against punishment frankly presented as such. In most schools, Johnny really could take action against Mr. Clarke for striking him, as our subjects point out, and whatever the principal might do would be limited to a single reprisal for a particular offense. But the school psychologist is not so limited in his undertaking to "straighten Johnny out." Once Johnny becomes a case, he himself can no longer limit the flow of help directed toward him, except by leaving school.

This, of course, is, in juvenile form, the same issue that the psychiatrist Thomas Szasz has presented in *Law, Liberty and Psychiatry*[2] with reference to the effect on the liberties of adults of the application of *ad hoc* clinical categories to judgments of their behavior, and of the broadening of the clinical bases for evading criminal responsibility beyond the limits of the old McNaughten rules. Szasz has been widely

[2] New York: The Macmillan Company, 1963.

criticized for opposing the generous provision of mental health services by community agencies, and hailed by patently reactionary social groups for advocating tougher and more realistic treatment of offenders as criminals rather than coddling them as patients. But Szasz' point is actually quite different; he maintains, in part, that patients in public mental hospitals are treated more repressively even than criminals, and have even fewer rights and no reliable prospects of release; and that many of the social and clinical services, ostensibly devoted to helping the emotionally disturbed, function more as administrative adjuncts to the removal and isolation of individuals who are potentially or actually disturbing to others than as service agencies for emotionally disturbed people who want help. While the supporting ideology of mental hospitals and mental health agencies, as of school psychologists, is benign, what actually happens to their clients is less affected by that ideology than by the needs of competing bureaucratic structures to justify themselves, maintain and expand their activities, and prevent patients from causing difficulties to, or threatening the status of, their usually poorly paid and overloaded personnel.

From this point of view, a society that strongly prefers to treat miscreants as psychological cases rather than as offenders entitled to the safeguards and limitations of criminal process is indeed but weakly attached to civil liberty. Our subjects' most common responses to "The Clarke-Barto Incident" suggest that the social attitudes that alarm Dr. Szasz become acceptable to contemporary Americans quite early in their lives and have their institutional roots in familiar school practice. This is as serious an issue, in my judgment, as can arise in connection with public education. In this research, with Johnny Barto's continued help, we explored it a great deal further.

To do so, we made use of the final episode in our series of six, entitled "Alan Slade and His Friends," among whom Johnny Barto figures prominently. By this time our subjects were adept at handling the card-sort procedure and were able to deal with more complicated episodes. "Alan Slade and His Friends" is very complicated, ambiguous, and replete with subtle cues; as one of our subjects noted, it is a complete soap opera in itself. It reads:

Early in his senior year, Alan Slade, a short, well-proportioned boy who is captain of the tennis team at LeMoyen High School, and has been an honor student through his whole high school career, began to run into trouble. His grades have fallen off sharply, though they are leveling off at a point well above passing. He has been seen around town in one or two taverns that have records of violating the law against selling liquor to minors, and which the principal of the school has been trying unsuccessfully to have permanently closed. He was picked up a few weeks ago for drunken driving, but the lab test showed an alcohol content just below that necessary to establish intoxication. His father, a lawyer with a reputation for sharp legal technique, was quick to point this out and prevented the boy from being formally charged. But he also forbade him the use of either of the Slade cars for an indefinite period, until "he got himself straightened out." Not being able to drive now, Alan seems to spend most of his time hanging around the house or a candy store near the school that few students patronize, not doing much of anything. His tennis game is shot, and so are LeMoyen's chances for the year.

Nobody seems to know just how Alan's trouble started, though Monica St. Loup, another senior who is a cheerleader and president of the girls' Pan-Hellenic council, has hinted to several of her intimate friends that she does know, although she would rather not talk about it. She did, however, overcome her aversion to doing so long enough to go to Mr. Blakely, the dean of boys, and plead for help for Alan before anyone else had even noticed that there was anything wrong with him. Despite his encouragements —"The kids all know my door is always open," Mr. Blakely has often said—not many LeMoyen students feel free to go to the dean unless sent for. But the dean of boys is also, *ex officio*, in charge of student activities at LeMoyen. Mr. Blakely's admiration for Monica St. Loup is well known in the school. "Monica is about as close to an All-American girl as you can get," Mr. Blakely once observed. "Pretty as a picture; smart, too; any group she's in seems always to have a lot of fun. But her mother doesn't have to worry about her a bit; Monica can be trusted. She knows just how far she can go and not lose her self-respect. If this school had more like her, my job would be easy."

It was to Mr. Blakely, then, that Monica turned, not on her own behalf, but on that of Alan Slade. The discussion was, of course, confidential, but immediately afterward Mr. Blakely sent, separately, for Johnny Barto, a junior with a bad reputation in school as a troublemaker, and for Alan. Mr. Blakely took no formal action, but when Johnny left school that day, he never came back. Some of the kids say he has left town; he has certainly not been seen around school. To Alan, Mr. Blakely spoke gently but firmly, if somewhat ambiguously. "I'm here to help you, son," he said. "I think you know that. This kind of situation isn't a disciplinary matter; intelligent people don't think of it that way any more, really. But you do need professional help. During the year, you'll be applying for college; then there's the army to think of; these people count on us to be honest with them about the emotional adjustment of our students. You have such a good record here, Alan, and I'm going to see to it that you don't spoil it. I don't even want you to worry about it, son; normal growth is our business."

Mr. Blakely's tone became less warm, however, when Alan insisted, and continued to insist more and more anxiously, that he did not understand what Mr. Blakely was talking about. "It would be better, son," said Mr. Blakely, "if you could trust me. It would be better if you could trust *yourself*; the only way out is to face up to this like the man we hope you will become. The first step is to be absolutely honest; and that is what you'll have to do. I'll tell you what we'll do. I'm going to set up an appointment for you with Dr. Bruch [the visiting school psychiatrist for the LeMoyen district] when he comes next month. I'm not a psychiatrist, and I don't pretend to be. But I am Dean of Boys, here; and I am responsible for your wellbeing and for that of the other boys you are in contact with here. Until we get this report—and I'm afraid Dr. Bruch is a pretty busy man—I'll do what I can for you. Meanwhile, don't worry."

This was three months ago. Whether or not Alan took Mr. Blakely's advice not to worry, he is, as has been stated, in trouble now. Dr. Bruch's report, when received, recommended regular psychotherapy; but the school has no program for providing this. Mr. and Mrs. Slade, when Mr. Blakely told them of Dr. Bruch's recommendation, were unco-operative and ungrateful. "I'm afraid you interpret your responsibility and your mandate both too broadly and too loosely," Mr. Slade replied. "I'm not certain that I know what you are talking about any better than Alan does, but if I do I can well understand your vagueness, since you are quite right in supposing that a more forthright statement would be libelous." "If we *should* think— as we do not—that our son needed psychiatric help," Mrs. Slade added, "we would send him to our own analyst. Dr. Liebig has kept our marriage going for twenty years, which is a tribute to his competence if not to his judgment. We know that Alan has been miserable at school this year and we have been worried sick about him, but we didn't know what was wrong and he doesn't seem to be able to tell us. Now that you've told us what you've put him through, we can begin to understand it. All we ask of you is that you attend to his education, which seemed to be going pretty well, by your own account, until you brought all this up."

Here, however, Mr. Blakely was adamant. His responsibility, he said, extended to all aspects of the welfare of LeMoyen boys while they were in school. Mr. and Mrs. Slade could ignore Dr. Bruch's recommendation if they chose, but if they did he would insist that Alan report to him for a weekly conference, at which "I'll try to help him as much as he will let me." Otherwise, he would be forced to recommend to the principal that young Slade be suspended from school, "without prejudice, for reasons of health." So far, there have been six of these conferences. During them, after polite greetings, Alan sits silently, while Mr. Blakely waits patiently "for you to get tired, Alan, of your resistance."

No one at LeMoyen supposes that Monica St. Loup asked Mr. Blakely to help Johnny Barto also. Nor did she. Monica's usually inexhaustible good will never extended to young Barto, except for a brief period early last year when Monica did try to take an interest in him. "He could amount to something, you know," she said to one of her sorority sisters who had warned her against getting "mixed up" with Johnny. "He's bright, even if he is a couple of years older than the other boys in his class. That's just his background. And he's attractive, in a kind of feline way, like a tiger. He could learn, if he had somebody to take him in hand. Don't worry about me. It's Alan you ought to be worrying about. He's such a sweet boy, and so shy; I really wish I knew how to help him. I've tried, but I can't seem to reach him, somehow. I'm sure he hasn't any idea what he's getting into."

But Monica had no more success with Johnny than with Alan. The two boys were discussing her, rather casually, late one night during a camping trip, which they often took together. "You watch out for her, Shrimpboat," Johnny told Alan. "She isn't what she thinks she is. Oh, she's all for good, clean fun, and no passes accepted. But just fail to make them when she expects them, and see what happens. I know."

Monica was not the only one who disapproved of the friendship between the two boys. Mrs. Slade had also complained about it to her husband, but he had disagreed with her. "I can't go along with that, dear," he said. "If you'll remember, Johnny's grandfather just about got my career started for me; though if Johnny knows it, he never said anything to Alan. There was always a streak of the gentleman in those Bartos. Oh, they have no talent for legitimacy, and the whole line has just gone to hell since repeal; it was probably a blessing the old man got bumped off when he did. There was nothing any lawyer could have done for Johnny's father, and I'm glad he didn't come to me. But there's plenty of people jumped all over the boy since he's been down, and you know, I don't think we'd like to join them. Alan can take care of himself as well as I could at his age, and he'll have to, won't he, against people more dangerous than Johnny Barto?"

The card-statements for "Alan Slade" are of a different kind from those the subjects sorted in responding to "The King's Visit" or "The Clarke-Barto Incident." They are less discrete; they are not descriptions of individuals or simple statements of alternative actions. They are complex, morally evaluative comments on the story, which the subjects were simply directed to sort from *best* to *worst* comment. Two earlier episodes, not yet discussed, had similar card-choices, so that this detail, too, was familiar to the subjects by the time they reached "Alan Slade."

Their choices, again in descending order of popularity, are presented in Table III.

TABLE III

Student selections for
"Alan Slade and His Friends"

N = 245

			PILE		
CARD	Best	Good	Neutral	Poor	Worst
Co-operate with school	106	88	42	6	3
Self-pity	29	119	65	27	5
Right track	41	94	61	41	8
Neurotic parents	11	49	114	49	22
Parents care for him	21	40	98	67	19
Democratic and tolerant	8	39	130	48	20
Middle-class prejudice	9	34	110	73	19
Invasion of privacy	20	19	64	87	55
Young punks	0	8	51	92	94
Pure chance	27	55	81	55	27

The most popular card reads:

The attitude of Alan's parents illustrates how necessary it is that parents co-operate with the school, if as much as possible is to be done for students when they need help. In a world as interdependent as ours, the individual must co-operate with the legitimate institutions of society if progress is to be made.

This card, the choice of Karen Clarke for "The King's Visit," and the school psychologist card for "Clarke-Barto" are the three most favorably regarded cards in the entire set of fifty-four for all six episodes.[3]

---

[3] This is calculated as a weighted mean, which is also used in ranking the cards for presentation in the tables. Selection of the card as best is assigned a rating of 4; as worst, —4. Rating the card as one of two next best counts as 2.5; two next worst as —2.5. Leaving the card in the middle counts 0. On this basis, Karen Clarke's average placement is 2.57; the school psychologist, 2.55; "co-operate with school," 2.52.

Parents must co-operate with the system; this most of our subjects regard as incontestable. The reader may recall that, in responding to "Clarke-Barto," these subjects rated "informing parents" well ahead of turning Johnny over to the principal, though both were considered less promising than the intervention of the school psychologist. But this was a matter of trying to enlist Johnny's parents on the side of the system and getting them to "help straighten Johnny out." The elder Slades, however, are depicted as willing to oppose Mr. Blakely on sight in what they regard as the defense of their son, whereas Alan's position is not made clear; the story leaves him caught helplessly between Mr. Blakely's aggressive philopaedia and his parents' effort to repel this attack on their family's privacy. Most of our subjects find the Slades objectionable, and I cannot say how much of their insistence that parents must subordinate themselves to school policy reflects their uneasiness about these particular parents. But the cards they choose state a general principle that they enthusiastically endorse, and state it unambiguously. Most of our subjects expect their parents to sustain authority and help them get back in line if they should wander; excessive support for individualism would embarrass rather than sustain them.

Alan, of course, does make one thing clear—he does not want to talk to Mr. Blakely, either. But as our subjects interpret the story, Alan has been certified by experts—Mr. Blakely and Dr. Bruch—as emotionally disturbed; he is drinking and carrying on—"stuff like that"—and this discredits him as a witness in his own behalf by reducing anything he might say to a symptom before he says it. Alan, whether he wants to be or not, is seen as a patient in the original sense of the word; he should be passive, and allow himself to be acted upon by the appropriate social agencies. The second most popular card reads:

Bad off as he seems to be, the root of Alan's trouble is probably basically self-pity. Certainly, he is lucky at least to have both a friend and a counselor so devoted to helping him. If he won't let them, he can't expect things to get much better.

Again, however, as in responding to "Clarke-Barto," it is the *helpfulness* imputed to Mr. Blakely that legitimates his action. The most strongly rejected card in the series reads:

> The worst thing that can be said about Mr. Blakely's policy in this case is that it is too soft and compromising. Knowing what he evidently does—or he wouldn't have dared to go this far—he ought to have kicked both these young punks out of town rather than just one. Of course, under the circumstances, he has to watch his step legally.

This card, with an average rating of -2.4, is one of the four most unpopular cards in the entire set of fifty-four, along with "Clarke walks out" for "Clarke-Barto" (-2.6), Eric Pratt for "The King's Visit" (-2.5), and "Beats Johnny coolly" for "Clarke-Barto" (-2.4). Our subjects rejected this card on a wide variety of grounds: that the story did not say that Mr. Blakely had run Johnny out of town, only that he had disappeared the next day; that school officials had no authority to run anybody out of town; that Mr. Blakely was doing all he could to help Alan, and, indeed, was open to some criticism for not trying equally resolutely to help Johnny. The reason he didn't was probably just that he had given up; Johnny had been a troublemaker so long that there was nothing more to be done for him except let him go.

Our subjects' interpretation of Mr. Blakely's purpose as benign makes it possible for them to reject the next most unpopular card:

Mr. Blakely's action is both unprofessional and a gross invasion of privacy. He is allowing himself to be influenced by one student against another, has used his office to break up a private friendship between two students, and has done grave injury to both. To call this "helping" is either hypocrisy or lunacy.

The issues raised by our subjects' handling of this card are perhaps the most significant of the entire study. The very consistent majority position was that the card was a misstatement. Mr. Blakely was not invading privacy; he was just trying to do his job as dean of boys by helping Alan, and neither Alan nor his parents would co-operate with him. It was they who were clearly in the wrong in the matter. Most of our subjects accepted Mr. Blakely's helpfulness as existing *ex officio*. Once they accepted it, they did not review their judgment of his policy in the light of its actual consequences, *except in terms of success or failure*. Thus, in their interviews, our subjects would quite often temper their selection of "must co-operate" as best card with the observation that Mr. Blakely didn't seem to be very competent at his job, having made such a mess of this case. But his failure was at worst a technical failure; it did not lead them either to question his sincerity or—more relevantly—to question whether such interference as his must not be in some respects *inherently* hostile, regardless of the intruder's intentions.

Our adolescent subjects' most common responses to "Alan Slade" provide a perfect scale model of the attitudes on which our government depends to legitimate much of its foreign policy. Our major commitments to oppose Communism have for many years been presented and financed as appropriations for foreign aid to states we presume to be threatened by it. This requires, of course, that the state which receives the "aid" be governed by officials who are willing to "co-operate" by accepting such aid and agreeing that the presence of American equipment and the activities of American military and intelligence personnel is in fact beneficial to the welfare of their people. We are disposed to regard as hostile those neutralist governments that tell us firmly to keep out and permit them to manage their own affairs; we assume that they have some inherent obligation to co-operate with the "Free World." We either do not perceive, or avoid mentioning, that the political leaders who refuse to regard our intervention as a form of aid and reject it may simply have been wise in their judgment. We resent such recalcitrance, and do not, I believe, really respect the sovereign right of neutralist or Communist governments to be on their own side rather than ours. But we resent even more fiercely any suggestion that our own policies are aggressive.

Our young subjects' emphatic rejection of the "young punks" card seems to serve the same psychological function as "middle-of-the-road" Americans' rejection of extreme Rightist attacks on the U.N., or paranoid suggestions that we start preventive wars while the balance of overkill is on our side. By refusing any part of the gloating hostility implied in this card, they make Mr. Blakely's policy and their support of it seem reasonable, simply because it is orderly and not emotionally extreme. But in order to express their need to be co-operative rationally, they would have to understand clearly what Mr. Blakely is trying to get done, and, therefore, what is supposed to be wrong with Alan.

On this point the story is deliberately ambiguous, and many of the subjects complain that the story does not really tell them what is wrong with Alan. This is fair enough; the point is that even though they complain that they don't know what is wrong, they still insist that "The attitude of

Alan's parents illustrates how necessary it is that parents co-operate with the school, if as much as possible is to be done for students when they need help." The irresponsible philanthropy of this point of view is, however, reduced by the comments of a reassuring minority of subjects who endorse this card. These explain that the Slades, like all of us, have an obligation to listen to official advice before deciding whether to act on it; they are perfectly free to ignore Mr. Blakely's advice, but they ought not to put him down before they have heard him out. In principle, this position is unexceptionable; as applied to the story of Alan Slade and his friends, such good-humored tolerance overlooks the distinction between official advice and the advice of officials, and dismisses the fact that in the story Mr. Blakely does not leave the Slades free to consider his advice and decide for themselves, but threatens to suspend Alan unless they follow it.

A part of our subjects' willingness to have Alan interfered with results from their mechanistic conception of the function of psychotherapy: if what a therapist does is talk to you and straighten you out, the question of invasion of privacy is not very deeply involved. Our subjects, when they attempted to explain the series of events, usually kept issues superficial and external by altering the time-sequence in the narrative. This states that Monica St. Loup went to Mr. Blakely to "plead for help for Alan before anyone else had even noticed there was anything wrong with him"; and also quotes Mrs. Slade as telling Mr. Blakely, "All we ask of you is that you attend to his education, which seemed to be going pretty well, by your own account, until you brought all this up." To a careful reader, these quoted comments would seem to establish that Alan's decline and fall occurred after, rather than before, Mr. Blakely's intervention and Johnny's departure. But the most frequent explanation attempted by our subjects was that Mr. Blakely had called Alan in because his grades were slipping, and they supposed that what Monica had told Mr. Blakely was that she had seen Alan drinking around town *with Johnny Barto*, the troublemaker, though the story does not imply that the two boys went to taverns together. Our subjects were inclined, on the whole, to accept this as friendly interest on Monica's part, though many more were suspicious of her role in the episode than of Mr. Blakely's. Monica may have meant well, but she should have minded her own business; when she didn't, though, and brought Alan's problem to Mr. Blakely's attention, it was his duty to call Alan in. Mr. Blakely, however, is well regarded for his palship with Monica; few suggest that he ought not to listen to her tales though more are skeptical of her motives for bearing them.

A small sophisticated minority of students gave deeper interpretations of what had happened. Several working-class boys thought that Johnny had brought his friend Alan low by cutting him out with Monica and making out with her, but that Monica had then got Johnny run out of town by denouncing him to the dean. The handsome, successful, tough, and sensitive captain of the Havencrest football team, who will appear later in this account in a brief but striking role, swung straight into the heart of the matter by smilingly observing, in a Southern drawl, that "this seemed like kind of a Dorian Gray situation." A bright and articulate student leader from the parochial day school sample offered no interpretation, but angrily denounced Alan as sick, and his parents for acting like members of "that Front organization, the American Civil Liberties Union!" Subjects with greater insight by no means consistently expressed greater compassion or respect for Alan.

Besides the Havencrest captain, only two or three other

subjects ventured to suggest that Alan might be responding with grief and terror to the destruction of his friendship and his friend. It is, of course, probable to a degree that more students thought of this than mentioned it. But if so, their demeanor suggested that their reticence was not due to personal reluctance to discuss a homophilic relationship. It seemed due rather to a culturally induced inability even to imagine that grief for Johnny could have laid Alan so low and that dumb hatred might lie at the root of his refusal to talk to Mr. Blakely. Passion lies beyond the grasp of most of our subjects, as we shall see in considering their responses to episode five, "Miss Post's English Assignment." Our subjects did "Miss Post" and "Alan Slade" at the same session— their last; and ordinarily discussed "Miss Post" first. In it, they rate, from best to worst, a series of nine poems dealing with different aspects of love, as appropriate for submission to a wise, tolerant, elderly, and highly esteemed English teacher who had assigned them to bring to class several lines of poetry which best expressed what love meant to them. We will discuss our subjects' specific responses to "Miss Post" later; it is worth noting here, however, that although they considered "Alan Slade" just after they had considered "Miss Post's English Assignment," it occurred to only about 1 per cent of our subjects that the story of "Alan Slade and His Friends" might involve love in any way.

Our subjects' limited view of the scope and function of human passion leads them to take a dim, though not a strong, view of the elder Slades. In writing the narrative I tried to portray them as warmly concerned about Alan and willing to defend him and respect both his feelings and his privacy, and as both scornful of Mr. Blakely and terrified of what he was doing to their son. Our respondents did not see them in this way. Two cards that praise the Slades:

The most remarkable factor in the situation is the Slades' wonderfully democratic and tolerant attitude. Despite their apparent wealth and success, they recognize that a boy with Johnny's background should be encouraged to make something of himself, and, despite their misgivings, permit their son to befriend him closely. This is the kind of thing that America means.

and

The most hopeful factor in the situation, as far as Alan is concerned, is that his parents basically respect and care for him so much, and can still say no when they have to, both to him and to the school authorities. Nobody is proof against fools, busybodies, or a woman scorned; but with this kind of home life to draw on, Alan will probably come through, scars and all.

The first of these cards is, on balance, slightly less popular than the second, and far less divisive; our subjects tended to leave it in the middle or reject it mildly as blah, while they divided more sharply in their response to the idea that Alan's parents' behavior showed deep affection for him. Modally, they disagreed. Alan's parents, they said, couldn't really love him; if they did, they'd let somebody help him, wouldn't they? They were afraid, though, that if it got around that their son had to see a psychiatrist it would reflect on them. They didn't take much interest in their son, personally; if they had, they wouldn't have let him get mixed up with a troublemaker just because Mr. Slade had been mixed up with Johnny's grandfather before Alan was born. Our subjects used the idea that American society is classless—which they seemed to hold—in a curiously illiberal way. They didn't see Johnny's background as an inequity that placed him at a disadvantage which the Slades should be commended for ignoring. Instead, they treat the equality of all Americans as a metaphysical *donnée*, like original sin, which Johnny had squandered by becoming a "troublemaker" when he could have been as good as anybody else. In official relationships, Johnny should have been treated like everybody else—Mr. Blakely should have tried to help him, too, if he was going to try to help Alan. The fact that he didn't probably meant either that he thought Johnny was too far gone to be redeemed or that he wasn't quite competent to go about it. But this, too, had nothing to do with class. The third most unpopular card in the series reads:

> At the heart of Mr. Blakely's attitude is essentially middle-class prejudice. If Johnny Barto were Alan's social equal, their friendship would appear perfectly natural to him.

Though a minority of comparatively lower-status students selected this as one of the better cards, our subjects were preponderantly against it. There was no reason to think Mr. Blakely prejudiced—he was just doing his job. The friendship wasn't natural, because boys with a good record like Alan don't and shouldn't go around with troublemakers. If the Slades had really cared about their son they would have stopped it before he got involved with the "hoody element."

Our subjects particularly objected to the statement on the "parents basically care" card that "With this kind of home life to draw on, Alan will probably come through, scars and all." What especially put them off was Mrs. Slade's comment in the narrative that " 'Dr. Liebig has kept our marriage going for twenty years . . .' " I had included this to prevent our subjects from attributing the Slades' rejection of Blakely's demands to hostility to psychoanalysis itself, intending to show that they took it as a matter of course when it suited their freely chosen purposes. This didn't work; our subjects used the statement against the Slades as evidence of mental ill-health, while continuing to attribute their resistance to Blakely to their fear of being stigmatized for having a son who needed psychiatric care.

So, again—as on "Clarke-Barto"—our subjects' conceptions of and attitudes toward psychotherapeutic intervention tell us a great deal about what, if anything, human dignity means to them. Superficially, they are glib about it. The card that states:

> Neurotic parents rear neurotic children, this is the iron law of psychoanalysis. The older Slades' hostility to getting any psychiatric help for their son is but an extension of their guilt for the entire situation.

they treat more nearly neutrally than any other card that deals with the episode. A plurality leave it in the middle, exactly as many regard it as fairly good as regard it as fairly bad, but twice as many call it the worst card as call it the best. Their criticisms of it are sound; our subjects know, and state, that there isn't any iron law of psychoanalysis, and that, in principle, it is absurd to state as a general truth that "neurotic parents rear neurotic children." But they still attribute the Slades' resistance to fear of being blamed for Alan's condition, and they still blame his condition themselves on the fact that his parents were so sick that they have gone to Dr. Liebig for twenty years.

Part of the trouble is that virtually none of our subjects have any sense of irony, especially when they are taking what they think of as a test. They take Mrs. Slade's comment as a datum, without considering that she made it in her husband's presence while the two of them were fighting a hard, joint battle to get Mr. Blakely off Alan's back. But, more important, what keeps them from applying what they have learned about psychotherapy from its ubiquity in popular culture is their disrespect for human personality itself. They still think of it as something that is judged to be out of order if it gets away from the norm, and that therapists tinker with; if the therapist hasn't got it fixed after twenty years, it must have been an utter wreck to begin with. One of the most popular cards—second in rank on number of choices as best of all—for this episode, reads:

> Mr. Blakely seems to be on the right track, but the school's resources do not extend far enough to back him up. When the school psychiatrist recommends that a student be given psychiatric help, the school should require that he accept it and, if necessary, provide the funds for facilities to make it possible.

On the face of it, the popularity of this card seems further *prima facie* evidence of our subjects' contempt for privacy and willingness to invade it. This interpretation, though, would overstress the point. Subjects who put this card among the better choices did not justify their choice in the interview by taking out more aggressively after Alan. Again, they were trying to be helpful; the point they were trying to make was that they approved of Mr. Blakely's helpfulness and wanted him provided with every resource, both in the form of facilities and of authority. Similarly, the subjects who rejected this card were not usually defending Alan's privacy; they were opposing socialized medicine.

What is most threatening in our subjects' endorsement of this card is not, therefore, so much their approval of what it recommends as their gullibility in believing it to be possible. There is, after all, one iron law of psychoanalysis: the patient has to want it. Whether one has much or little respect for privacy and regard for freedom, it is absurd to suggest that *anybody* be required to accept psychiatric help. The most any school can do, like the sergeant in the old story, is make a student wish he had. And what keeps our students from perceiving this is not ignorance—they aren't ignorant about psychotherapy. It is, essentially, their mechanistic view of themselves and of other human beings, as objects that can be adjusted to do what a situation requires of them, within certain mental and physical limits.

Up to this point, my observations about the subjects' responses to the episode of "Alan Slade and His Friends" have described an essentially modal position. But, as Table III shows, there is considerable variation among our subjects in response to this episode; more than in their responses to "The King's Visit" and much more than in their responses to "Clarke-Barto." And our subjects varied more in their response to the "invasion of privacy" card than they did to any other card relating to any of these three episodes. Twenty subjects rated this generally unpopular card as the best in the lot; their reasoning was not, of course, identical, but it did in general represent the defense of civil liberty and dignity whose absence I have hitherto deplored. There is such a minority among our subjects. They are to be found in several of the schools in our sample, and none is enthusiastic about the school he is in. But some are notably successful, making their way into honor societies and positions of informal student leadership—though not into the power structure of official student government; some are self-consciously bright and defiant, and alienate themselves from their peers rather more than their pride and autonomy would necessarily require. Some of the most moving are very simple, academically mediocre youngsters who appear to have enjoyed few advantages save possibly that of delivery by an unusually perceptive and responsible stork. Since my two earlier long quotations from interviews have been chosen to illustrate the more conventional position on the episodes concerned, and since I recall very vividly my mounting ennui on hearing it repeated substantially unchanged from interview to interview—I shall present, instead, as an illustration of our subjects' responses to Alan Slade, one of these minority documents. In this discussion of "Alan Slade," the student respondent is a fifteen-year-old working-class girl of Italian extraction and unassuming demeanor, whose name has—if read as an English word—a slightly pejorative connotation. The principal and assistant principal of the school, themselves also Italian, used the English pronunciation in referring to her.

I. Your selection of the best card is Number 7 [invasion of privacy].

MISS A. Mr. Blakely's interference in this matter is very much an interference in Alan's private life. What Monica told him in his office—well, I don't think he should take it too seriously. I mean, she might have lied or maybe exaggerated something, so I don't think he, he ought to take anything upon himself to frighten Johnny, or call Alan into his office. They . . .

I. This just isn't called for.

A. That's right.

I. And, uh, very much in line with that, but going considerably beyond it, is card 9 [parents care for him].

A. Well, I—his parents, I think, have the right to say no; it seems that Alan got worse when Mr. Blakely talked to him, so I think it's their privilege to say no. But about their home life, I don't think it's that good since a counselor has to keep them together. This might be the trouble, too, that Alan is going off. I think it's mostly because of Monica.

I. Yes, and, in any case as, as the parents, they have the right to judge the degree of co-operation required of them.

A. Right, right.

I. And card 8 [democratic and tolerant].

A. Well, it said in the story that Johnny has been picked on since he came out because of his grandfather and his father, so I think that it, uh, the Slades are very nice in, John—respecting Johnny's background and letting Alan stay with him.

I. Yes. From the basis of the comments between the two elder Slades themselves toward the end of it and their responses, what would you say from that, the quality of the home life probably is?

A. I think it's very nice. I mean it, in the paragraph about them being in the office, gave me the impression that the home life wasn't too good, but later on, when I read it, it sounded like it was better, it was very good, at the end of the paragraph.

I. Then the worst card, card 5 [young punks].

A. I don't think he should have kicked anyone out of school. I think he should have kept them both in school. If he was going to, if he was gonna keep Alan in school, I think he should have took, kept Johnny in school, even though Johnny does have a worse reputation than Alan. I think Johnny didn't do anything that bad. I mean, he might have a bad reputation but that's about all. I mean, it sounds like Mr. Blakely scared Johnny by telling him to keep away from Alan, so Johnny just left.

I. Yes. And this was out of line for him?

A. Yes, very much so.

I. And card 1 [self-pity].

A. I don't think it's self-pity, actually, I think, Monica and Johnny got too friendly. Then when Johnny told Alan, I don't think Alan liked it very much, 'cause he could have liked Monica, so I think that's what happened, and I just think, I think, Alan hates Monica now.

I. Yes, and that in it—

A. . . . and, and he doesn't, he doesn't want anything,

he doesn't want to have anything to do with her or the counselor or Mr. Blakely shouldn't—he broke Alan and Johnny up.

I. Yes. And finally, card 6 [right track].

A. I don't think a student should be required to take psychi—psychiatric care at all. I think it should be all up to them, well, or up to his parents.

I. Is it possible, even, to require any—is it possible to give psychiatric help to a person who doesn't want it?

A. No, I don't think so.

I. I never heard of a psychiatrist who thought so, either. (*Laughs*) Are there any other issues in this that you . . .

A. Well, I don't think of any of the suggestions on the cards are very good. I mean, I just picked the best out of all of them.

I. Yes. What would be better, do you think?

A. I, I just think that Monica and Alan should have a talk out—just by themselves.

I. Yes. It's a good idea.

A. And that's all. I, I think if they talked it out, and maybe even Johnny, too—I mean, they could get, I think, Alan'd do much better.

I. And that would be the way to get the root of what was going on?

A. Yes.

None of our subjects manifested great anxiety in dealing with the story of "Alan Slade and His Friends." They showed much more in response to the far less controversial but more personal episode, "Miss Post's English Assignment," which they handled at the same session as "Alan Slade." The story follows:

Miss Elsie Post is, by consensus, the finest teacher Le Moyen has and probably ever has had. Her subject is English, and her skill lies in drawing the best out of even the most reluctant student. Under her guidance young people develop a real respect for literature, no matter what their background, and for many of them her class is the first time in their lives in which they have attempted seriously to express their thoughts with style and distinction. Miss Post is often gay and sometimes even frivolous while teaching, but underneath there is a resolute spirit. She is stern and surprisingly demanding in her assignments. "You know, she expects the impossible," is an often-heard student comment the first day of class. Yet, when the year is over, many own up that she'd gotten that impossible. "It makes you feel proud to do well for Miss Post," is the way Ronnie Jackson said it to Scott Cowen one day, while they were working at putting *Xantippe* together for publication. "Yeah," answered Scott. "I never thought I'd go for poetry and all that stuff, but after you've heard about it from her, and then read some of it, well, it's great, it's something she does that makes it real."

Miss Post is just as demanding of herself as she is of her students. She spends hours each day correcting class themes and homework assignments. And she has a reputation for uncovering each and every error the thoughtless, ignorant, or deceitful student has let slip into his work, this despite her advanced age and notably weak eyesight. Her comments on the papers are in themselves something of a form of art, always precise and to the point, and yet affectionate, amusing, interesting, and, where necessary, devastating. As the students at LeMoyen soon discover, Miss Post is not an easy person to fool.

Miss Post has taught at LeMoyen for many, many years. A number of the parents of the present student body had her as a teacher when they attended LeMoyen, and they always seem to remember her much as she is today. However, Eric Pratt, exercising a scientific bent he generally kept well under wraps, found her picture in the 1934 annual, and announced—much to his surprise, he claimed

—that she had once been a most attractive young lady. After Eric's discovery had gained currency throughout the school, rumors of a tragic love were rife around LeMoyen, but nothing was ever proven. Whatever her private life though, Miss Post must always have been a very good teacher. For, only last summer, while attending a summer basketball clinic at a famous Eastern university, Mr. Regan met an eminent scientist who, on hearing of LeMoyen, asked about Miss Elsie Post, his once-upon-a-time teacher. The scientist then went on to say that she was the finest teacher he had ever had, bar none, and this despite his many years of education in college and graduate school.

*   *   *

Assume that you are a student in Miss Post's class. Today she told her class that each member was to bring to class tomorrow several lines of poetry which he felt best expressed what *love* means to him. She indicated that the students would be expected to read and discuss their selections in class the next day. Assume further that it is evening, and you have come up with nine possible selections. The nine cards you have been given for Test V are the nine selections we will assume you have found.

From this point, the directions are similar to those for all the other episodes; our subjects sorted cards, each of which bore the text of one of the poems, ranking them according to their suitability for "Miss Post's English Assignment."

"Miss Post" is the only one of the six episodes that any considerable number of our subjects said they disliked dealing with. A large proportion complained that they did not like poetry or understand it, and did not feel qualified to judge it. I observed no sex difference in this; the girls seemed as uncomfortable with poetry as the boys, even though most of our selections are not so much poetry as verse. They seemed more afraid of poetry than actually incapable of understanding it. They were, in any case, occasionally poetic in their ordinary speech, though they did not know it; while those who were most outraged at the idea of poetry tended rather consistently to select as best the most sentimental and poorly constructed poems of the nine—their wretched taste was grounded in a refined and reliable poetic sensitivity.

A more subtle and perhaps even more important issue is raised by the fact that many of the students complained that the story itself was irrelevant and wasted their time, since all they actually had to do after reading it was to sort the poems according to their power to express what love meant to each of them. But this is not quite the case. The account of Miss Post is intended to establish her firmly as a competent teacher and critic, and a worldly and sympathetic woman capable of accepting the ambiguities of love. We intended to imply that she would appreciate good poetry more than nice poetry, and that the student would please her best by selecting the more penetrating and better constructed among the nine available—providing his own view of love also permitted him to accept such a statement. The poems included in the nine are all portions of standard works of variable quality, selected so as to express views of love as commanding or abasing, as affection between specific individuals or as more abstract devotion to nature or the nation; as a sentimental aspect of a world of sweetness or as an experience with tragic and ironic overtones as well. "Miss Post," then, was designed to convey to our subjects that they might expect an empathic response from a teacher capable of respecting strong erotic feeling, if they had such feeling and attached importance to it themselves. "Miss Post's English Assignment," in short, was an invitation to communicate authentically in a poetic mode with a mature, experienced adult who was a teacher—the sort of teacher reborn in the nostalgia of successful middle-aged writers.

Except for Adam Holmes, one of the two boys I have described as "creative, dissident intellectuals" who responded to "Clarke-Barto" by preferring that Mr. Clarke walk out of the washroom and leave Johnny alone, all of our subjects either ignored or explicitly rejected this opportunity. They did not refer to Miss Post in discussing their reasons for picking the cards they chose for the assignment, except to complain that her character and personality were irrelevant or, more rarely, to assert that they were not "brownies" who would try to butter-up a teacher by pandering to her tastes. Only Adam Holmes referred to Miss Post as another human being whose personal qualities, if respectfully used, might contribute to her students' growth and enrich their lives.

The rest, then, chose to limit the task to that of arranging the poems in the order they found best expressed their own view of love, rejecting at the outset the premise that this view might well be shared with their imaginary English teacher. On this basis, our subjects sorted the poems as shown in Table IV (see page 118).

Of these nine, our subjects' favorite poem is a portion of Scott's *Lay of the Last Minstrel*:

> True love's the gift which God has given
> To man alone beneath the heaven;
> It is not fantasy's hot fire,
> Whose wishes, soon as granted, fly;
> It liveth not in fierce desire,
> With dead desire it doth not die;
> It is the secret sympathy,
> The silver link, the silken tie,
> Which heart to heart and mind to mind
> In body and in soul can bind.

TABLE IV

Student selections of poems for
"Miss Post's English Assignment"

N = 245

| | | PILE | | | |
FIRST LINE	Best	Good	Neutral	Poor	Worst
True love's the gift which God has given	77	77	76	12	3
He prayeth best, who loveth best	49	77	89	23	7
No man is an island	37	100	65	31	12
There is pleasure in the pathless woods	19	69	87	61	9
Yet in herself she dwelleth not	23	39	122	49	12
Breathes there the man, with soul so dead	9	50	83	81	22
Ah, love, let us be true	12	35	67	88	43
When our two souls stand up erect and strong	12	21	94	74	44
No thorns go as deep as a rose's	7	22	52	71	93
Pure chance	27	55	81	55	27

Our subjects used this poem to emphasize that love, to them, meant something more than lust, though including it. The reference to God made the poem especially appealing; the youngsters used it to defend themselves against the popular conviction that "teen-agers" are wanton and sexually irresponsible. But God, in any case, enjoys an extremely favorable public image among American adolescents. His appearance in the stanza from the *Ancient Mariner*:

> He prayeth best, who loveth best
> All things both great and small;
> For the dear God who loveth us,
> He made and loveth all.

seems to be enough to commend it to the students as a love poem. God, after all, is love, if we are to believe St. John; and our subjects do not question his word for it. They like to identify Him as the source and origin of love.

Their third choice:

> No man is an island,
> No man stands alone,
> Each man's joy is joy to me,
> Each man's joy is his own.
> We need one another
> So I will defend
> Each man as my brother,
> Each man as my friend.

is enough, along with their first two choices, to establish the nature of the major deficiency in their conception of love: it is almost completely sentimental. Love is protective and yummy. Related to this deficiency, undoubtedly, is their execrable poetic taste. Ignorance assists them; several subjects confidently, gratuitously, and, of course, erroneously identified this poem as the work of John Donne. This sentimentality and their distaste for irony combine to make them reject most strongly Swinburne's lines from "Dolores":

> No thorns go as deep as a rose's,
> And love is more cruel than lust,
> Time turns the old days to derision,
> Our loves into corpses or wives;
> And marriage and death and division
> Make barren our lives.

They see this as a poem *against* love; it says that love hurts people; while everybody knows that it is better to have loved and lost than never to have loved at all.

There is no significant difference in the rank our subjects, taken as a whole, assign to the next two less popular poetic selections given them for consideration. Both selections receive essentially the same number of placements for best card and also for worst card, though the "Dover Beach" stanza is left in the middle as trivial far less often than the couplet of Elizabeth Browning. Both selections are decidedly disliked.

> Ah, love, let us be true
> To one another! for the world, which seems
> To lie before us like a land of dreams,
> So various, so beautiful, so new,
> Hath really neither joy, nor love, nor light,
> Nor certitude, nor peace, nor help for pain;
> And we are here as on a darkling plain
> Swept with confused alarms of struggle and flight,
> Where ignorant armies clash by night.

and

> When our two souls stand up erect and strong
> Face to face, silent, drawing nigh and nigher.

"Dover Beach" asserts that the world is barren and treacherous, though it may be made endurable through personal devotion and fidelity. Our subjects' responses to "Alan Slade and His Friends" suggest that this possibility would not give them much hope; fidelity and personal devotion are not what they value. They find "Dover Beach" far too uncheerful; life can and is expected to be beautiful. This expectation does not give them robust confidence; they pursue it, rather, with a grim determination to think positively. The Browning couplet usually aroused blank, hostile incomprehension: it didn't really say anything, it was too short, it didn't even mention love. Our subjects did not even find it allusive; our boys seldom hope, and our girls seldom expect, that the expression of love will be erect and strong.

Love should be friendly; all the world loves a lover. It is personal, even though not passionate. Our subjects mildly rejected the stanza from *The Lay of the Last Minstrel*—"Breathes there the man, with soul so dead"—because patriotism, though estimable, is not what they mean by love. Yet, many rather liked Byron's observation that:

> There is a pleasure in the pathless woods,
> There is a rapture on the lonely shore,
> There is a society, where none intrudes,
> By the deep sea and music in its roar;
> I love not man the less, but nature more.

The mildness of this poem, and its freedom from hostility, made it appeal to many subjects as an amiable protest against the conditions of their life; many Milgrim students, certainly, had reason to sigh for the possible pleasures of the pathless woods. Though fewer subjects assigned it first place, this poem did slightly better on average than James Russell Lowell's extremely sentimental "My Love":

> Yet in herself she dwelleth not,
> Although no home were half so fair;
> No simplest duty is forgot,
> Life hath no dim and lowly spot
> That doth not in her sunshine share.
>
> She doeth little kindnesses,
> Which most leave undone, or despise;
> For naught that sets one heart at ease,
> And giveth happiness or peace,
> Is low-esteemed in her eyes.
>
> She hath no scorn of common things,
> And, though she seems of other birth,
> Round us her heart intwines and clings,
> And patiently she folds her wings
> To tread the humble path of earth.

Lowell's "Love," hopefully, is not theirs; such love as this sounds picky and compulsive; it reminds our subjects of motherhood and they find it rather irritating. The poem is too fussy; too cheerless and dutiful; our subjects may see love as a fountain-confection, but they expect it to play and not just dribble.

For most of our subjects, the reading of poetry is a solemn, even ceremonial act. It tends, therefore, to evoke their most cherished clichés. Occasionally, however, and especially in youngsters saddened or depressed by the conditions of their actual lives, "Miss Post's English Assignment" provided an opportunity for self-expression. Such youngsters were seldom more able than their conventionally happy peers to give a valid response to the poetry itself. But it provided them with an occasion to waive the optimism their culture usually demanded of them, and an opportunity to send to know for whom the curfew tolls the knell of parting.

I have chosen one of these rather unusual, moving subjects as an example of the range of possible response to "Miss Post." Mr. D., a small, very quiet, wiry, blond tenth-grader in Parma High School—like his classmate Miss A., of Italian extraction—a shy fifteen-year-old with a miraculous medal around his neck.

I. Your favorite poem was number 9 ["Dover Beach"].

D. Well, sir, if the countries would get together instead of always fighting it would be a much better world.

I. Mm.

D. Here, always, everybody's arguing over something. If they could only live together and work together they could do so much more. Instead of keeping secrets from each other. But there'd still be somebody who'd want to get ahead. They'd do it anyway. So I mean it's, this won't happen for a long time.

I. So this picture is a pretty . . .

D. It's pretty accurate.

I. Yeah. And card number 6 [*Ancient Mariner*]?

D. God does love everybody. That's the way He wants it. It should be that way; but not everybody loves God, really.

I. I see.

D. I mean, not everybody believes in Him. Not many people follow Him any more. Religion is just something to go to church and that's all that people do now. Some people don't even go to church.

I. And card 8 ["pathless woods"]?

D. Nature is much easier to love than man. 'Cause man, it's hard to get along with . . . but nature is, is usually, it's, it's easier to get along with. It's beautiful; can't, in a way, deceive you, or really fight against you.

I. Not as dangerous?

D. No, not half as dangerous—some animals might destroy things; but look at what man destroys. Nature is much easier to love than man.

I. Hmmh. And your least favorite card is card 4 ["No thorns"].

D. Well, this says you should—you shouldn't even get married because, when your husband or wife dies, it's worse. It is bad; but, you, still—you live. When you are living, it's good that way.

I. Yes—

D. But it's not cruel, like it says.

I. Then, card number 1 [Lowell].

D. (*Long pause*) It says "life hath no dim and lowly spot"; but it's—there's so much poverty in the world. And so many people are suppressed, and—well, it's less in the United States. We probably don't see too much of it; but, from the history books and everything that we read, it's really terrible in many places.

I. Hmmh. So—I don't quite see how that connects with rejecting this card?

D. So she—she has no dim and lowly spot?

I. Oh, I see; you're saying there are plenty of dim and lowly spots.

D. She has no scorn of common things?

I. How is that different from what you are saying? [This is dull-witted; I realized a moment later that Mr. D. was again saying that there was plenty of scorn where he lived.]

  (*Long pause, followed by raucous buzzer.*)

I. You really have to go now, don't you?

D. I can wait a few minutes.

I. OK—And finally, this one you didn't like, card 7 ["native land"]?

D. It's very easy to love your native land if it's doing you good and when it's free of poverty and . . . it's bringing you poverty you really can't love it. So it depends on which country you're . . .

I. This, then, sort of underestimates the difficulties that are really there.

D. Yes.

By this time, one of the teachers to be interviewed had arrived, seated himself at a desk a few yards away, and was busy shuffling papers and addressing genial remarks—"nice and cool in here!"—to me, apparently not noticing the presence of the microphone, the tape recorder, or Mr. D. The boy excused himself, but asked if he might return to the interview room at the end of the school day to talk about something that was worrying him. This is what it turned out to be:

Mr. D., like several of the boys in the study, was a member of the Parma High wrestling team. Wrestling is an important sport in this county, and the wrestlers put all they can into it. D. is not a first-string wrestler, but his best friend is the varsity wrestler in D.'s weight class, and was also, as D. knew, being interviewed in the study. Like D., this boy, Mr. Q., was small, wiry, and Italian; but unlike him, Q. was tough-minded, realistic, and quite capable of turning his hostilities where they would do the most good. Wrestling was his glory; the team needed him, and he knew it.

But Q. was quitting the team, and D. wanted to talk to me about what was at issue: did Q. have any right to quit. The wrestling coach at Parma, eager to use his sport to build character and discipline, expected his boys to be like men. One inflexible rule by which he ran his team was that a youngster who qualified in a particular weight class must wrestle in that weight class; it was his. He could not be challenged by a boy who had wrestled in a smaller class, and he could not himself wrestle in a heavier class if he gained weight. It was up to each boy to have the guts and self-control to stay in his class.

These are excellent rules for adult wrestlers, but they are a little hard to follow during the adolescent growth-spurt. Q. was just beginning his, and like the other smaller lads on the team, had been trying to live on black coffee and vitamin pills in order to stay within his weight class. But he couldn't do it; his nerves were shot; and he had decided to pack it in. I knew Q., and knew what sort of boy he was; did I understand that he wasn't a bad sport?

Adolescence is not an emotionally flat experience. Like the surface of the earth, its scale is distorted by the conventions necessary to depict it. Starvation in Asia and the Fall from Grace make the desperation of a "teen-ager" starving himself to make a team seem petty.

Since "Miss Post's English Assignment" dealt specifically with love poems, it may astonish some that the subjects were not drawn by it into discussions of sexuality and sexual behavior. But none was. In my experience, adolescents rarely discuss sex with adults unless the adults insist on it. Even though sexuality is central to adolescence, it would have demeaned my subjects if I had tried to engage them in a discussion of it. For the first time in the high school experience of many of them, they were being seriously consulted. Sex, to American adolescents, is seldom a serious topic; it is either clinical or comical. They would not have been shocked at all if somebody doing research on adolescence had turned out to be another Kinsey-type shrinker, avid to count their orgasms and stuff like that. But they would not— and quite rightly—have mistaken such a preoccupation for an interest in *them*. Conversely, I was interested in them only as *functional* human beings: that is to say, as they saw themselves, on their own terms. Only a masseur or a physician can learn more that is relevant about another person by seeing him naked; others learn more by watching people be themselves in role and in action—and this requires clothes. To intrude on the privacy of the young teaches their elders nothing useful about them, though it doubtless reconfirms what the young suspect the basis of their elders' interest to be.

I have deferred until now discussing our subjects' responses to two of the six episodes that were actually presented to them fairly early in the series. At their first session, they were given "Clarke-Barto" and "The LeMoyen Basketball Team"; this story of the team marks, then, their first encounter with LeMoyen High School in which it is identified by that name. At the second, they were given "The LeMoyen Dance" and the episode with which I began the discussion, "The King's Visit." I have discussed these episodes and the subjects' responses to them in an order different from that in which they dealt with them so as to improve the clarity of my presentation; the patterns of response to both the "Team" and "Dance" episodes are less evocative and more ambiguous than to the four already discussed; and it would, I believe, have been very difficult for the reader to see just what we were getting at if I had discussed these episodes early on.

In part, this ambiguity is due to methodological defects in the study; while in part it is in itself a legitimate and important research finding. The reader may already have noticed that the choices with which our subjects dealt in responding to "Clarke-Barto," "The King's Visit," and "Miss Post" differ in one important respect from those pertaining to "Alan Slade." The former three episodes all call on the subjects to rate a series of actions, persons, or poems, each of which was discrete and distinct from all the others. These were separate alternatives; the card-statements in each case lent themselves to the kind of intellectual approach to which our subjects were accustomed and predisposed. They could consider each card-statement as presenting a possible solution to a problem they were called upon to solve, and could make a comparative judgment about the effectiveness of the proposed solution. By simply assuming that they were to select the treatment that would most effectively bring Johnny back in line and the delegate who would make the best impression on the King, they could handle these episodes entirely as technical problems, avoiding moral confrontation with the issues involved; while for "Miss Post's English Assignment" the situation was, in fact, presented as a problem. By treating these episodes as if they had been asked simply, "What would work here?" our subjects could give responses that made perfectly good sense; and this is what they usually did.

The cards for "Alan Slade," however, are quite different.

They present a variety of different moral judgments, not a set of possible courses of action. A particular individual, whatever his point of view on the issues raised by this episode, could produce an intelligible pattern of response only by adhering to that point of view as he sorted the cards and expressing it through his choices and subsequent comments. This was quite easy for our subjects, because "Alan Slade" does call into play a system of moral attitudes that most of them possess. For the most part, they do firmly and sincerely believe that people should co-operate with their immediate social order, and that people who don't are troublemakers who come to a deservedly bad end. They are genuinely suspicious of, and hostile to, people who insist on their own privacy and dignity against group demands. They are convinced that strong feelings and loyalties are hazardous, and that it is not merely unwise but *wrong* to allow such commitments to jeopardize one's future chances. These are all moral principles; in fact, they are just the moral principles that good empiricists need.

The cards for "The LeMoyen Basketball Team," like those for "Alan Slade," are morally evaluative comments that cannot be ranked as alternative courses of action. They can be used to make an intelligible statement only if the subject sorts them according to a coherent pattern of values. Our subjects do this, but the patterns they most commonly produce are less striking than those that emerge in response to "Alan Slade," because they express familiar elements of conventional American ideology. In responding to this episode, our subjects display not only a reassuring confidence in, and allegiance to, democratic values; but a rather astonishing—in view of their commitment to co-operation at any cost—defense of individual competence as the basis on which status and recognition should be allotted. The fact that this episode deals with sports and membership on a team, which is a relatively clear and decent area of adolescent life, probably encouraged our subjects to express moral attitudes that many of them would have regarded as square if applied to a more "realistic" situation.

This is the story of "The LeMoyen Basketball Team":

At LeMoyen High School, about a fifth of the students are Negro; the rest include young people of Irish, Italian, and Eastern European descent—the latter, chiefly of the Jewish faith—as well as some students from families that migrated from Northern Europe several generations back and think of themselves as just Americans. Because of the way the neighborhood served by LeMoyen High School has developed, the Negro students come from homes in which the father, on the average, earns more money and has had more years of education than the fathers of the average white students at LeMoyen, who are mostly from working-class families.

For the past two years, LeMoyen has had the best basketball team anywhere around and has won the regional championship. The seventeen-man squad has ten Negroes on it and five boys from Irish families. Three of the four regular starters on the highly successful team are Negro players, while the fourth is a white student named Johnny Adams. The coach, Mr. Regan, who also teaches shop, passes the fifth starting position around among the Irish lads on his bench. There has never been a Jewish boy on the basketball team at LeMoyen. Mr. Regan says the Jewish boys are "fine students, but too short to make good ball players."

This year, there transferred into LeMoyen, as a junior, a boy from an Irish background whose father was recently sent to the community as a director of plant operations from the oil refinery that is by far the biggest in-

dustry in town. The only LeMoyen student this boy,
Kevin McGuire, knew before he came to town was Grant
Eubanks, the captain of the basketball team and the son
of a Negro physician who is the chief heart specialist at
the local Veterans' Hospital. The two met at a camp in
France where students from other countries go to spend
the summer and work with French people and get to
know them. McGuire, who as a sophomore was already
a basketball star at his old high school, was drawn to
Eubanks by the game; during the summer, they taught
about 50 kids of various nationalities, who had never seen
a game, to play fairly good basketball. Eubanks has told
Mr. Regan that the six-foot-five McGuire is without a
doubt the best basketball player ever to come anywhere
near LeMoyen, and that they must get him on the team.
At this moment, McGuire is driving over to the gym to
try out for the team, and Mr. Regan is trying to decide
what to do next.

The subjects' choices are presented below in Table V.

TABLE V

Student selections of card for
"The LeMoyen Basketball Team"

N = 247

CARD	Best	Good	Neutral	Poor	Worst
			PILE		
unmixed delight	53	128	51	11	4
the only important thing	91	69	35	36	16
official school organization	34	81	100	25	7
irrelevant racial issues	27	69	115	31	5
take a good, hard look	22	53	115	49	8
sounds like just what he needs	15	67	104	40	21
certainly on the spot	1	7	128	71	40
not really in best interests	2	12	48	115	70
too risky	2	8	45	116	76
Pure chance	27	55	83	55	27

The two most popular cards, by a wide margin, read:

> If Mr. Regan is the kind of coach who puts competence above race or religion, he and the LeMoyen team will surely welcome young McGuire with unmixed delight.

and

> The only important thing for Mr. Regan to consider is whether McGuire is as good a player as Eubanks thinks he is. This is what should determine whether a boy gets on the team; the rest of the story is irrelevant.

The first of these two cards is, on balance, somewhat the more popular by our criterion;[4] many fewer subjects choose it as the very best; but only a fourth as many choose it as the very worst, and less than a third as many include it anywhere among the poorer cards, while slightly more rank it among the better ones. "The only important thing" in fact, aroused a more varied response from our subjects than any other card of the fifty-four.[5]

These two cards, in different words, affirm a basic moral postulate of American society. But the phrasing of the first of these makes it inapplicable to the episode, and its popularity with our subjects suggests that their adherence to it has a somewhat wooden ideological character. The conflict suggested in the episode has its origins in socio-economic, not in racial or religious, differences. In the narrative, the Negro players have subordinated the Irish minority through a combination of superior competence and superior status. But Grant Eubanks, the upper-middle-class Negro captain, is Kevin McGuire's sponsor and friend as well as his social

---

[4] The mean pile placement for "unmixed delight" is 2.0; for "the only important thing" it is 1.6.

[5] In the sense that its distribution has the highest standard deviation of any card.

equal and athletic peer. The difficulty presented by Eubanks'
sponsorship of McGuire is that if McGuire is granted the
place on the team to which his competence gives him a
claim, he will displace the other, poorer Irish boys from
the starting line-up altogether.

To choose "unmixed delight" as the best card in this context is therefore either to ignore what the story is really
about or to assert an egalitarian cliché about race and religion in order to avoid confronting the actual social conflict
inherent in the situation. This seems naïve, considering the
exquisite sensitivity of high school youth, and even grade
school children, to status factors, which August B. Hollingshead in *Elmtown's Youth*,[6] and Bernice Neugarten in W.
Lloyd Warner's *Democracy in Jonesville*[7] establish, should
ordinary experience provide insufficient proof. Yet our
subjects were not simply naïve; if pressed in the interview,
they identified the issue the story raised but dismissed it as
not likely to be important to the members of a basketball
team: as long as McGuire was a good guy and didn't act
stuck-up or claim special privileges, the poor Irish boys
wouldn't resent him because he was rich, and the team
would certainly want to win too badly to resent him because
he was good.

Basically, this response seems to me both healthy and
sound. Athletic teams are bound together by mutual respect
for competence, which makes them cohesive under strains
that would disrupt purely social groups. For this reason, as
several of our subjects said, the whole episode seemed to be
making a fuss about a situation that could be handled in the
usual course of events; we should have had a card that said,

[6] New York: John Wiley & Sons, 1949.
[7] New York: Harper & Row, 1949.

in effect, "Mr. Regan ought not to make such a fuss about nothing; if McGuire is that good, put him on the team and be done with it." Nevertheless, our subjects' preference for "unmixed delight" still strikes an artificial note. It introduces a highly fashionable but extraneous issue which was avoided by the subjects who preferred the card beginning "The only important thing." For this card asserts a moral proposition that *is* relevant to the narrative; more than a third of our subjects pick it as the best comment. Those who reject it, moreover, did not do so because they placed any consideration above competence in deciding who should play on a team. They were repelled by a quite unintended consequence of the phrasing of the card, which probes a highly sensitive area of American ideology.

Despite the last sentence of the narrative, which states that McGuire is driving over to *try out* for the team, the students who rejected "The only important thing" most often did so because they interpreted the card to mean that McGuire should be admitted to the team without tryout, solely on Eubanks' recommendation. This they felt would be unfair, and while I would agree I still cannot understand even after hearing forty-odd students say this how they could have read this meaning into the card. That they did so suggests a rather widely generalized edginess and hypersensitivity about equality of opportunity.

But if McGuire qualified by passing whatever tests were usual in the situation, there should be no problem. Perhaps not; but people are not really that nice, and I still suspect that most of our subjects know it. It isn't true, as the card states, that ". . . the rest of the story is irrelevant"; only that it ought to be. A more precise appraisal of the situation from the same moral position, though generally favored, was left in the middle as trivial three times as often as "The only important thing," and was picked as either the best or the worst card of all only a third as often:

> This story shows how two boys who share the same skill and enthusiasm in sports and general social background can accept each other as individuals, without getting involved in an irrelevant racial issue. Their problem now is just to finish what they have started; Mr. Regan will be risking upsetting his team by letting McGuire on it; but if he is really a good teacher and a good man he must do it.

Several factors account for this card's comparative lack of appeal: its length, a touch of liberal cant, the students' quite-possibly-justified conviction that there wasn't anything in the whole episode to be this pompous about, and again, the tendency of some to interpret this card as implying that McGuire should be put on the team without even having to demonstrate competence. Nevertheless, it is a more just appraisal of the situation than the two more popular cards previously considered; and our subjects' preference for these still suggests a preference for slogans. A related issue arises in connection with the brief but thoroughly unpopular card:

> There doesn't seem to be much of a moral issue here, but, politically, Mr. Regan is certainly on the spot.

Only one subject thought this was the best card and forty thought it was the worst; but the fact that a majority of the subjects left it in the middle—more frequently than any other card of the nine—keeps it from falling lower than sixth place. The popular reasoning about this card asserts that the very opposite is true: Mr. Regan is *morally* obligated to see that McGuire gets his chance to show how good he is, but there is no political issue facing him. A coach, if he knows his business, should rise above political pressures and ignore or resist them if they impinge on his job. He has no business trying to run his ball team according to a quota system.

This tells us very little more than we knew about our subjects' prevailing values, but it tells us a great deal about their conception of politics. Quite uniformly, they thought of it in terms of external pressures and manipulation. It never occurred to them—though this is what the card was meant to suggest—that a ball team, like any other organization, has internal politics of its own. Conversely, it does not occur to them either that politics and political accommodation are legitimately concerned with the formation and carrying out of *policy* and are therefore an essential part of the social process; political considerations, by definition, are extraneous, intrusive, and dirty. There is nothing political about Mr. Regan's job, or at least there had better not be. Politics, as they see it, is inherently sneaky and anti-democratic.

Their suspicion—in itself healthy and commendable—of sly, canting, or manipulative *political* approaches to the episode and their rather naïve confidence that the benefits of democracy will naturally follow if equality of opportunity is preserved, togther with their probably justified faith in the power of a team to preserve itself and solve its internal problems by good will and mutual accommodation, combine to lead them almost universally to reject the following cards:

It is too risky to take McGuire on the team, especially if he is as good as Eubanks says he is. Coming from a rich home, and as Eubanks' friend, it would be the last straw for the poor Irish boys. You can't really expect them to take a thing like that. A team may like to have stars, but it needs its back bench, too.

and

> Mr. Regan might find it very helpful if it were pointed out to him that letting young McGuire join the team would not really be in the best interests of either the boy or the school. Having the richest boy in school as a star athlete as well would be very likely to lead the basketball team to think of itself as a group of privileged characters which, under the particular circumstances described, would be most unfortunate.

Our subjects are not hostile to wealth, as long as it acts like a regular guy; they identify with it. And they reject any reasoning that would deny McGuire his chance to qualify. In athletics, at least, they respect excellence; though their responses to "The King's Visit" show that they are quick enough to abandon it when it is displayed in a more critical and less circumscribed context than that of the playing field. McGuire, however, is not seen as dangerous; he is obviously fully socialized already, and he must be given a chance to demonstrate and use his athletic talents; he isn't an odd-ball player like Johnny Adams. Our subjects' solid position on this issue resulted in a rather comical inversion of their response to one card, which they treated in just the opposite way from that which we had—I still think logically—expected. Despite their strong and almost derisive rejection of the two cards just discussed, they rather strongly approved:

> A basketball team is an official school organization, and official school organizations should be representative. It is the responsibility of the principal and the board to see to it that the basketball coach—no matter who he is—runs the

team for the benefit of the whole school and not as his
private club.

while they left in the middle as trivial, though tending
slightly to favor:

> If he doesn't want things to get out of hand, Mr. Regan
> had better take a good, hard look at what basketball is
> being used for at LeMoyen. The business of a high school
> basketball coach isn't to win games but to give every boy
> his fair chance to participate, even if he isn't such an
> expert.

In writing these cards, we had intended them to express
essentially the same egalitarian value position, and to be used
primarily as part of the argument of subjects who thought
it would be wiser to exclude McGuire in a nice way. Again,
on the basis of "The King's Visit," we now know that our
subjects do use just these arguments to justify excluding the
divergently creative from the King's delegation regardless
of—or perhaps in recognition of—their excellence. Indeed,
the only concrete suggestions we got with any frequency
when we asked subjects how they would describe a possible
delegate who would be preferable to any of these on the
nine cards we had given them was that we ought to have
included a thoroughly average student among our selection,
since only such a student could be truly representative.

But our subjects did not respond in this way to "The
LeMoyen Basketball Team." They used "official school organization" as an argument *in favor* of McGuire. The team
should be representative, which meant that, like the King's
delegation, it should make a good impression, which meant
that it should maintain its previous championship caliber
and *win*. Mr. Regan had no right to impair its chances in
order to keep things peaceful and easy to handle by letting

only his favorites on the team. The idea that "the business of a basketball coach isn't to win games . . ." was silly; this is just what his business is, and the only way to do it is to seek out and welcome the best players. Of course the team should be run for the benefit of the whole school, and the kind of team that benefits the whole school is a winning team. There is no obligation to give every boy a chance to *participate;* the obligation is to give him a chance to show what he can do. Participation can be, and is, taken care of in intramurals and stuff like that, where it doesn't matter whether you can play or not.

The card which arouses the most nearly neutral response of the nine is, finally:

> Mr. Regan is being offered another top-flight player who comes sponsored by his captain and has the same national background as the boys on the team who haven't been doing so well. McGuire sounds like just what he needs.

Many of the subjects accepted this comment as just and pertinent, but they were counterbalanced by others who stereotypically rejected any consideration of "national background" as irrelevant, or who thought it inappropriate for the coach to recognize his need for any particular individual.

In summary, our subjects, in their responses to "The Le-Moyen Basketball Team," showed great confidence in, and commitment to, the democratic process, especially as this is concerned with the issue of equality of opportunity. The fact that this is based on a doctrinaire and apolitical idea of how that process works makes it difficult for them to examine it critically or discuss it intelligently. But this does not, I suspect, much hamper them in making the process work. What saves them is, again, their empiricism. They don't really care whether their idea of how a democratic society works makes sense, because to them understanding something means knowing how to handle it; it does not mean being able to relate it to a larger, metaphysical, whole. They responded to the problems implicit in the narrative the way good-humored, moderately intelligent astronauts might to a theoretical physicist who was making rather a nuisance of himself: when something goes wrong, this is what you do; it can get pretty rough but all our systems are go. If turbulence due to intergroup hostilities fails to dissipate itself automatically, the coach has to get rid of it by manual control. Presumably, he knows how to do it; he'd better, he's the coach.

Their conception of social decision-making as apolitical and of politics as essentially an intrusive and inequitable use of external pressure to gain a special privilege is, however, reactionary by its very nature. For only those who are trying to change something are seen as political; the establishment, whether in the team or the nation, is only trying to gets its job done. Politics, then, is not an expression of citizenship but a vicious alternative to it. Social conflict is not seen as a contest among policies but as either a struggle among special interest groups or an effort to impose political doctrine on guys who are just trying to get along, as the ball team is. From this point of view, the NAACP is political and CORE is more so, but landlords and employers who oppose them are not; they are just trying to maintain standards, hold the line on property values, and make a living. Since we fear ideologues as the worst kind of troublemakers, our political principles—even consciously held democratic ones that the culture nominally endorses and supports—detach themselves from their social context and float around weightlessly.

Democratic values, however, like all values that have

commended themselves to viable societies over extended periods, have a validity that cannot be wholly vitiated by ideological misuse. However dangerous or absurd they may become when extended to social contexts beyond their range, the basic values of any culture must under some circumstances express real experiences and feelings that its members actually have had and may still have. Democracy probably has most meaning under circumstances virtually antithetical to those that prevail in a mass society. The natural substrate of democracy is a small society of genuine peers who share common purposes and a common level of competence related to them. Athletic teams, particularly in small, intense sports like basketball, provide situations in which mutual respect among individuals and a high level of empathy are essential gut-and-bone experiences, which is why the claim that athletics builds character retains a certain plausibility despite extensive commercialization and the impact of myriads of brutal but homely philosophers who are called Coach only because they could not conceivably be called First Class.

One of our interviews at Havencrest, in the South, illustrates this almost miraculous rebirth of mutual response and support as two of our subjects discuss "The LeMoyen Basketball Team" in the light of their highly relevant personal experiences. The subject who had just completed the card-sort is Tom Tanner, the captain of the Havencrest football team who referred to Dorian Gray in connection with the "Alan Slade" episode. This is his first interview; he is joined in it by Ken Slocum, a teammate who plays in the Havencrest line and who was waiting for his second interview, having already done "The LeMoyen Basketball Team" a day or so earlier. This is not our usual procedure even for a joint interview—ordinarily both subjects would be dealing with the same episodes—but the warm, casual atmosphere of Havencrest and the friendship and ease of communication that the two boys already enjoyed made it possible. Their mounting and expressive exuberance cannot, unfortunately, be transcribed.

I. The best card, you thought, was card number 2 ["take a good, hard look"].

TANNER: Yes. Well, I chose this card because it's, it's, well it's like what I've always been taught.

I. Umnh.

T. You play ball for everybody to participate.

I. Umnh?

T. But it's not, it's not what I play under. We play to win.

I. Yes.

T. But this is what I think, if I were the coach, this is what I would, my policy would be.

I. Well, that means, then, that with reference to this situation, that you probably wouldn't let McGuire on the team?

T. Oh, I'd let him on.

I. Yes?

T. Not letting him on or off, if he wanted to join the team, I'd join, I'd leave him join.

I. Umnh!

T. But I'd let him join. That's all there is to it.

I. Why do you think, if you were coach, you would do this instead of playing to win?

T. Well, because, participating in sports, I know that, I know what sports can do for you.

I. Umnhnh.

T. And even if you're not the best, if you get in there and play, it, it helps you out in life, then.

I. How is that?

T. Well, it, say in football, let's say, now, if you get

cross with an opponent he knocks your, knocks your block off. You have respect for him.

I. Umhnh!

T. And if you're not chicken, you go knock his block off.

I. Umnhn?

T. And, now, that's parallel to, in business, competition, and . . .

I. Is it really?

T. Yes.

I. Umnhnh.

SLOCUM (*Intervening for first time*): Well, if you're in business, or something like this, you have a rivalry, or rivals, and they come up with something, or they do something that you didn't think of, then you just work a little harder to try to improve yours, or come out with something better than them.

T. In sports you haven't got that endurance. Endurance carries you through your business life and . . .

S. I, myself, do think that participation with other people, I mean of other, in this case, other nationalities or people from nationalities, and other people, other races of life, they help. I believe it's . . .

I. Umnhnh.

S. We don't have this problem here yet, so—

T. This next game we're going to play with a different race of boys. None of us feel any prejudice towards the team, or towards the boys; just, it's the game, you know.[8]

---

[8] The card-sort data bear Tanner out to the point of at least suggesting that subjects in the two Southern schools are no more prejudiced than working-class Americans generally. Expressly prejudiced comments were hardly ever made in any of the schools. Havencrest subjects did, however, rate "The only important thing" lower than the subjects from any other school by a wide margin, tending to treat the card as only mildly good— they gave it a mean pile-placement of 0.28, compared to an average of 1.55. Their comments in the interviews, like Tanner's, explain their choice by emphasizing that *teamwork*—not whiteness—is also an important qualification for team membership.

T. It's a residue, also; yes.

I. Yes. Why do you enjoy it?

T. Why?

I. Yes.

T. Because it's fun. I enjoy it because it's—I get satisfaction from playing football and basketball.

I. What's the nature of the satisfaction?

T. Uh.

I. Go ahead.

T. Uh.

S. In football, I like, I don't like the hard work we have to go into; I mean, I guess nobody does, but I mean you enjoy the sport and, some boys, they go out for the glory of it.

I. Umnh.

S. There's little glory in the line, what we play, but the backs are what get all that love, you know.

I. Umnh.

S. But it makes me feel good to know that I've done something to participate for the school, and for myself. I, I just, it just makes me feel good to know I made a tackle or I knocked somebody on his, uh, rear end, to . . .

I. The word you were groping for is ass, isn't it?

S. Yes. (*Laughter*) But I mean, in the sense that I played the game for several years, three years now—It's just, I know it to do. Eleven boys together and work as a team. That's . . .

T. That's the joy.

S. That's the joy, right there. To know that you've got eleven boys working together.

T. Umnhnh!

S. For the school, for the spirit, for the coaches, for, for a lot of things. There's eleven of them working together.

I. Umnh.

S. And then you've got boys on the bench there, out there, they're rooting for you and if, if anything happens, any of them, they'd go in there and they'd do their best just to keep the eleven, that one eleven, strong and going.

T. It's, it's like a, like a unit, like an army unit. And it's war out there, and that's the enemy.

I. Umnhn.

T. And if you defeat the enemy, you're victorious, you're, it's, it's, it's glory, you know.

I. Umnhn.

T. And, and defeat, you know that everybody tried, or they looked like they tried. (*Laughter*)

S. We, we've had a pretty rough season this year, the first half, and we've lost four of our ball games and we've got boys on the squad, the eleven, the original eleven that are out there ninety percent of the time that we play. They feel the bitter defeat. So does the people. So does the school, and the other ball players.

I. Umnhn.

T. They're not in there all the time.

I. Umnhn.

T. And it kind of builds your morale and, you know, you kind of feel that they, you did the victory together.

I. Yeh.

T. And it's teamwork, I mean you work, everybody works hard and tries to do his job for, to work together in one group. To work together.

I. Now, that doesn't sound like something to be endured.

T. No. You got me all wrong in that. Like you said, that endurance is a residue.

I. Yeh, that it, it takes endurance to go through this and get the opportunity to have these joys?

T. Ummnh.

I. —and these satisfactions. But it's the endurance that you say is valuable in later life. What about the physical joy and the warlike spirit and whatever the—aren't those of any value in later life?

T. Well, I guess so. I mean—

I. You're less certain of that, though, life being what it is, as you see it.

T. It's not a whoop and holler. But you know what whoop and holler is like, so—

I. Having once tasted it.

T. More joy. More richness of life.

S. Now, we're through the next card! (*Laughter*)

. . . . .

I. Then the worst card was card 4.

T. Well, the first part, there doesn't seem to be much moral issue here, that's, that's absolutely wrong.

I. Yeh. There is distinctly a moral issue.

T. That's the worst one, I thought.

I. Can you state the moral issue?

T. Well, in the previous card you mentioned him not being able to join the team?

I. Umhm.

T. So, the boy came out, and the coach told him he can't join the team. Now that's, that's morally wrong.

I. Umhm. Then, card 3?

T. Well, this unmixed delight.

I. Yeh.

T. That's . . .

I. Exceeds all reality.

T. That's right. (*Laughter*) Exceeds the truth, I do believe.

In the next chapter, we shall observe the social ceremonies attendant upon Havencrest's next football game, the Homecoming Game, which broke their four-game losing streak. Tom Tanner plays a small but spectacular role in these ceremonies, and the reader may wish to recall the feelings he expressed about the game in this long interview excerpt when the half-time ceremonies at Havencrest are described.

The last episode to be discussed, "The LeMoyen Dance,"

was less successful by far than "The LeMoyen Basketball Team" in providing us with any reasonable consistent picture of prevailing student values and attitudes. Like the "Team" episode, the "Dance" is intended to force our subjects to choose between high quality and maximum spread of opportunity; and again the rich—this time the clearly undeserving rich—are pitted against the poor. But our subjects do not feel as strongly that dances should be within everybody's financial reach as they do that a basketball team should be open to any boy who can prove himself good enough to play on it—and perhaps the prevailing popular image of an affluent society has convinced even the poor that financial barriers are generally unimportant, except to them. Nor does the episode refer to race or religion; it provides no easy cues to elicit popular democratic slogans.

THE LEMOYEN DANCE

The Student Council at LeMoyen High School is planning the annual Spring Dance. This event is held in the high school auditorium, and about one fourth of the cost of it is covered by a subsidy from the school. The rest of the money must be raised by selling "bids" (or admission tickets) and refreshments. The dance has been held every year for the past six years and has become more and more popular each year. It is open to any LeMoyen student. Bids are generally $1.50 per couple, or $1 stag. Refreshments have consisted of hot dogs, hamburgers, and pizza slices at 35¢ each, and soft drinks at a quarter. The music for the dance is recorded. Last year, a large proportion of the junior and senior classes attended the dance—over three hundred couples and about seventy-five stags. Except for an occasional girl dated by an older boy, freshmen and sophomores rarely attend.

However, last year's dance was marred by the obstreperous behavior of several stags who appeared to have drunk their fill, and whom the teachers designated to act as chaperons were unable to keep at bay. Afterward, a rumor went around the school that these boys had been "troublemakers" from the school's vocational track, though vocational students have generally supported the Spring Dance enthusiastically. "They get *so* much out of it," Miss Leigh, the speech and drama teacher who has served as chaperon since the first dance was held, had earlier observed. "It's the one big event of the year for them." And, in fact, the only students who were actually identified as contributing to the disorder that broke out on the floor were seniors, now in college, who, the dean of boys reported sadly to Miss Leigh afterward, "come from some of the finest homes in the city— I never thought I would have to call them into the office." "I'm sorry, sir," one of these boys told the dean; "we didn't particularly want to spoil anybody's good time, but the whole thing was so jammed you couldn't move, and it has gotten so *corny* it didn't even seem real. I mean, like we go to dances all the time, and, *you* know."

Though the dean accepted this explanation and let the boys off with a reprimand, pointing out to them that their conduct had shown them to be deficient in just the qualities of leadership he had counted on them to have, the Student Council is anxious to avoid any repetition of the disaster this year. Accordingly, one faction of the students on the Council has proposed a radical revision of the plans. These suggest that the price of the bids be raised to $7.50, a couple or stag, and that the cost of the refreshments be included. For this money, they calculated that they could provide a tempting cold buffet, or *smörgåsbord*, and that they could also hire a small orchestra that the school jazz club has said is the coolest in town. Although the Student

Council has final responsibility for planning the dance, it has held a survey of school opinion to guide it in reaching a decision. The survey indicates:

1. A majority of the entire student body oppose the new, more expensive plan.
2. A small majority of the students who attended last year's dance, however, favor the new plan.
3. Enough students indicated that they would still attend if the price of bids was raised to $7.50, with supper included, to give a predicted attendance of about a hundred couples. This is enough, by a wide margin, to pay for the dance.

Our subjects' choices among the card-statements provided are set forth in Table VI.

TABLE VI

Student selections of cards for
"The LeMoyen Dance"

$N = 246$

CARD	Best	Good	PILE Neutral	Poor	Worst
corny and crowded	45	69	91	40	1
brawl or a rat-race	39	75	87	33	12
such an undemocratic plan	47	63	82	45	9
exclusive social affair	29	67	99	43	8
cheap, comonplace, institutionalized	37	57	97	43	12
if he had cracked down	11	44	105	68	18
there is nothing undemocratic	11	60	70	71	34
does not know how to act at a dance	21	41	64	79	41
suspend the dance	6	16	43	70	111
Pure chance	27	55	82	55	27

Even before reading the card-texts, it is evident that "The LeMoyen Dance" is technically less discriminating than any of the other episodes. There are no statistically significant differences among the cards that the subjects tended more to favor than to reject; and they left all nine cards in the middle as trivial more often than they placed them in any other pile. There is no strongly favored card, and the five mildly favored cards do not consistently favor or oppose the new plan. The three mildly rejected cards are almost as indecisively placed. Only the least-favored card elicited from our subjects strong, consistent treatment—rejection. It reads:

> Unfortunately, the Student Council is not the proper body to get to the root of a problem like this. Youngsters have to learn—sometimes the hard way—to bear the responsibility for their own misconduct. The school authorities should suspend the dance for a year, to teach the students that the privilege of holding it depends on their power to discipline their own conduct. This is a far more important question than what kind of dance they have.

In view of what most of the schools our subjects attended were really like, they had ample reason to reject this card strongly on purely rational grounds. In every school of our nine there was, indeed, at least one major administrative official who would have responded to the situation in the narrative just as this card suggests, and the subjects were quite right to be defensive about so probable a violation of their autonomy. Their arguments against this card were generally sound and reasonable: they pointed out that this policy would punish everybody except the offenders and would destroy any possibility of the students learning by experience how to conduct their affairs more competently. There seemed, moreover, to be an increment of hostility, similar to though much less intense than that aroused by the "young punks" card on "Alan Slade" attributable to the punitiveness with which the card was phrased.

It would be possible to note a number of other popular responses to portions of cards that shed light on our subjects' values, pointing out particular phrases, for example, that even those who favored a particular card protested against. It would seem a bit overconscientious, however, to scan "The LeMoyen Dance" like the curate's egg, looking for parts that were excellent. For the most part, it didn't work. The subjects found it realistic enough and seemed interested in the story, but here their empiricism defeated our research intentions completely. They accepted the situation briskly as a problem in keeping an orderly dance and chose the cards that promised best results as they saw it, without consistent regard to whether they favored the old plan or the new or whether the costs of the dance would rise— though most amended their choices of the more exclusive cards by suggesting modification that they thought would limit the increase.

In view of this, I shall not reproduce the card texts here for detailed exegesis as I have done in discussing the other five episodes. They are available to the interested reader in the Appendix. But no amount of fancy handling can extract more meaning from data than is in them; and my recollections of the interviews themselves bear out the evidence of the figures that "The LeMoyen Dance" yielded us a rather barren harvest. Instead of belaboring it, I shall conclude this chapter on specific research findings by considering the question I have most frequently been asked by persons with whom I have discussed preliminary findings, on the supposition that readers are equally likely to have been troubled by it.

That question is, "Were the subjects telling you what they really felt, or what they thought you wanted to hear?" This question is probably more frequently raised than any other by critics of research based on questionnaire or interview techniques, and it is, of course, a serious one. In the present context, however, it seems rather circular. If our subjects' desire to give me what I wanted led them to pretend to be more conventional than they think they really are, who are they kidding, anyway? If they only said— almost to a man or woman—that they thought it important to make a good impression on the King, in order to make a good impression on me, I am prepared to tolerate the deception as within the limits of experimental error. It is true that there were several subjects, like Adam Holmes, whom I liked and trusted immediately for their veiled autonomy and warmth and who diverged more from the norms for the entire group of subjects in their treatment of each successive episode. The articulate, expressive soccer player at Parma who was one of these and who strode over to the Intercom during his final interview to ask the office to send down two beers probably would not have done so at the first interview; at any rate, he didn't. But such joyful creatures, who really were giving me what I wanted, whether they meant to or not, were not very common.

My impression was that there was, indeed, an underlying bias that originated in our subjects' responses to the interview situation and to me, but that it was not the result of their trying to please me. I do think, though, that most of them were trying to give me their best, most adult judgment, and were therefore less spontaneous, more conventional, and perhaps less sensible than they might otherwise have been. They were trying too hard to earn their consultation fee, which was generous in comparison to the prevailing rates of pay for adolescents, and this often seemed to make them too judicious, too "mature."

Many of our subjects seemed to be responding to the experience of being respectfully interviewed by becoming a little bigger than life-size, and betrayed a certain confusion between maturity and gentility. This is a true source of bias; but I think that whatever our procedure may have contributed to these 250 adolescents' sense of their own dignity is worth what it may have cost in precision of estimate. Even in a scientific investigation, the values of science are not the *only* consideration. A more neutrally toned experience might have given us more precise—though more superficial—estimates of our subjects' values. It would not have done as much to show them that they were valuable themselves.

Our subjects' ego-enhancement must be suspected of having tinged the data on which the inferences and interpretations in this chapter were based. This difficulty can hardly occur in the chapters to follow. *Caveat lector*; the second half of this work is not based on the data systematically collected in our research at all. Where convenient, I shall illustrate my premises concretely with observations made in the course of this study, and I shall draw in some detail upon the published findings of other investigators. But the point of view and the conclusions presented are personal, though I trust not illogical. Not a single statement to follow in this book claims the authority of empirical scientific observation. Most are based on evidence, and that evidence is generally cited except where I have judged it to be sufficiently established to be part of the public domain. But they are made, like the observations of John Lennon, in the author's own right.

4

The

FRAGMENTATION

of

EXPERIENCE

By almost any standard, Havencrest High School is the most pleasant school included in our study. It—and it alone—was free of most of the abuses affecting the social climate of Milgrim and Hartsburgh. It has no corridor passes; in fact, it has no corridors. Havencrest is located in an area whose climate is highly suited to elderly people and space research and development. The high school building is semitropical in architecture: sprawling at ground level, its rooms open into sheltered outdoor walkways. All the washroom doors are marked either "Ladies" or "Gentlemen," and there are tablecloths on the tables in the faculty dining room. Smoking is forbidden, and there are dress regulations, but nobody bothers about them much. There is no atmosphere of tension.

Havencrest is superior academically. It has become nationally celebrated for a curricular plan that permits an
unusual degree of flexibility; and that also permits students
of similar ability to be grouped in classes on a basis less
invidious and stultifying than IQ, by placing together students of comparable ability in each subject without regard
to grade level. The library would be adequate for the first
two years of a small college. Its open stacks are located in a
large, handsomely appointed room in the front of which
are many individuals carrels for private study, which any
student may freely use. The collections, though limited, are
notably adult; Edmund Wilson's *Patriotic Gore* is there
along with de Tocqueville; the major journals of opinion
are to be found alongside regional church publications.
There is a librarian, but most of the services students need
are provided by the Research Co-ordinator—who, at the
time of the study, was a recent college graduate from
Michigan with the build and manner of a bright and imper-
turbably good-natured javelinist. The greater part of his
work is routine assistance to students doing fairly conventional assignments, but the most capable students at Havencrest are on special tutorial programs of independent study
which require him to draw on a wide range and depth of
knowledge.

Clearly, Havencrest High School represents and transmits
a conception of education that stems from the best liberal
tradition. It represents other things as well, however. At the
time of the study, Havencrest was still segregated. Despite
the Supreme Court decision, the school day is always opened
with a brief Christian worship service. The atmosphere of
the school is highly competitive; the students are always
being tested for something. Havencrest High, in any case,
must come to terms with its community and continue to

obtain its support; it must transmit the values of the community as well as—or, indeed, far better than—the ways of the mind.

The town of Havencrest is not much shaded by the groves of academe. Situated on an inlet among palms and pines, Havencrest could be lovely. In fact, it is hideous. Directly across the street from Havencrest High is an enormous shopping center, and directly across from *it* is another, even more atrocious. The town itself, which has about ten thousand inhabitants, is completely gutted. Day and night, trucks roar along a major highway that cuts through what used to be the center of town, but which is now a strip of mostly third-rate motels. The better-equipped and gaudier motels are across the lagoon on the ocean front. On the bridge leading there, elderly people stand side by side, fishing. They seldom catch anything, and they do not look as if life had led them to expect to.

Until a mammoth air force base and space installation were established in the vicinity, Havencrest was a poor community, in a marginal agricultural area. Even now, it is not particularly prosperous, although thoroughly federally impacted. Policy is not made in Havencrest; the people who have moved in are workmen and technicians, and there is not much loose money around. These people have no roots in the community, which has become quite flavorless; it has no regional character. The elderly, who find it a cheap place to retire, do expect to stay, but have no interest in education. Salaries in the school district are low. Havencrest High has a superior staff, but this is due to the principal's skill in making it an exciting place to work and in getting supplementary foundation support to eke out the meager salaries. The soil of Havencrest is sand, and Havencrest High is built squarely upon it.

To the extent that Havencrest is a community, Havencrest High has two ties to it that work. First is the town's widespread commitment to education as the way to get ahead in the world and make a place for oneself. To Havencrest, the technical skills required in missilecraft are a living reminder that education is still the highroad to opportunity. If and when the populace perceive that education also provides the basis for radical criticism and rejection of the way of life that culminates in missilecraft, they will probably be disturbed. Second, the school holds the kinds of athletic events that Havencrest enjoys. There is, generally, a lot to be said for this. High school athletics require real skill and competence; at their best they are beautiful to watch. Football and basketball provide almost the only occasion in American life when adults can empathize with and take pride in the qualities of youth with a minimum of guilt or envy. If this opportunity is frequently exploited to serve viciously competitive ends, it is also frequently the occasion for a real appreciation and affection for the young, in response to what they are actually like.

Athletic events, therefore, could serve as a real force for integration—though another term might be more happily received—in Havencrest. For the teams, they do. Vigor, joy, and a sense of erotic prowess as well as prestige may be the lot of the high school athlete, even in an age that de-emphasizes him as a meathead and tries to sell an image of a National Merit Scholarship winner in his place. But athletic events, too, are subject to the same pressures as other school activities, and express community values more often than they transcend them.

This becomes apparent in the way that even so good a school as Havencrest uses its major athletic events. High schools are well aware of the appeal sports have for the populace, and cancel classes in order to prepare their students for a demonstration of school spirit in carefully organized pep rallies before the game. While this helps to insure that the show will be impressive, it also greatly impairs the value of the game to the students themselves; what they might otherwise have felt as a personal expression is engineered into public relations. The show, in short, is partly phony.

The half-time celebration at the Havencrest Homecoming Game in 1963 is a case in point. The ceremonies opened with the playing of the National Anthem, followed by the administration to the standing spectators of the Pledge of Allegiance with which the school day normally begins, while the cheerleaders—mostly very young girls dressed in slinky gold blouses and shorts—held their batons out rigidly in various directions. This was followed immediately by a procession of comic floats pulled around the running track by automobiles. These had been judged at the pep rally earlier in the day. The Havencrest team are called Bulldogs, their opponents at Homecoming were called Terriers, and those who designed the floats had attempted to dramatize the theme implicit in these totems.

First prize was for a large papier-mâché bulldog, dressed as a pugilist with a big H on his jacket, which revolved slowly as it was towed along. The second-prize winner was more elaborate. The float consisted of a large box on wheels labeled "Terrorizing Machine," with an open platform projecting from its curtained back end. On this platform two boys stood: one in the guise of an arrogant, gesticulating player for the Terriers; the other in a white jacket, with clipboard and stethoscope. The "doctor" ceremoniously ushered his "patient" from the opposing team into the box. There was a flash of light and a puff of smoke, and a third boy who had been concealed in it stumbled out scorched and dispirited, to represent the Terrier after he had been terrorized. This was repeated as the float moved around the track.

The remaining floats were less imaginatively conceived. When they had passed, Homecoming got down to solemn business: the presentation of the Homecoming Queen who had been elected that noon at the pep rally. A throne was set up on the fifty-yard line, while the band disbanded and re-formed behind it as a small, and bad, orchestra. As it played with exaggeratedly slow tempo pop tunes of yester-year, a procession began marching across the field toward the throne. It consisted of young couples; the boys mostly in summer dinner jackets with a sprinkling of dark suits; the girls all in elaborate formals. Each girl had been nomi-nated as a candidate for Queen by the organization of which her escort was president. At the throne, the elected Queen was identified as an attractive French exchange student who seemed to be enjoying her role, though she could hardly have felt as much at home as a Homecoming Queen should.

The captain of the football team then advanced upon her, covered with mud and sweat and bearing a bouquet of roses, which he presented to her. This boy, as we have seen, is a serious and perceptive athlete possessed of a solid, colloquial, penetrating wit. The world at the moment must have seemed a bit odd to him.

After Tom Tanner had played his role, a young man in a white dinner jacket drove a black 1964 Pontiac convertible, which had been loaned for the occasion by the Havencrest dealership, slowly across the field to the throne. The Queen entered the car, sat on the folded canvas of the top, and was driven around the track, bowing and saluting to the spec-tators. Meanwhile, a warm drizzle began, and the campus leaders in their finery slunk off to shelter. Play was resumed, and the game was good, but they were not there to see it when Havencrest broke its four-game losing streak in the next half.

What is wrong with this? In most respects the Haven-crest Homecoming is an example of our Free Enterprise System at its most effective. The over-all purpose is set by responsible school authorities in response to their perception of the interests and values of the community. Within the structure they set up, the youngsters are given a place in which to act out their competing interests, however dis-cordant these may be, so long as what they express is not disturbing to the spectators. Themselves exploited for public-relations purposes, the students are encouraged to exploit the occasion in order to advance their own special though minor claims to status and recognition.

Fair enough, but the result is that the occasion no longer makes sense. At a football game, the football team has a right to be central. If the enthusiasm and school spirit cen-tered on their games were genuine, the issue would not even arise. Activities unrelated to the football match itself would just not take place; if the school tried to introduce them they would arouse derision or apathy, like a hymn singer at a jazz festival. If the student leaders cared about the match as their swooning at pep rallies would suggest, they would not attend it on a cloudy night in clothes that would compel them to leave in case of rain. But the Homecoming Game at Havencrest, though a serious occasion, is not serious about football. It is serious about enlisting widespread public inter-est, about demonstrating to the public that Havencrest High, despite its academic emphasis, teaches youngsters to respect the importance of automobiles and formal dress, and is sup-porting the values these represent. The football team also has its chance, but at the half it must yield for, and take part in, the commercial.

The Homecoming Game then becomes, in its own way, the equivalent of the shopping centers that surround Havencrest High. Its parts are unrelated to one another, and do not serve their own functions well, either; the restaurants are not only ugly in their setting, they are bad restaurants that clearly establish that their managers, though careworn, care very little about good food; the stores sell *Kitsch*. Each shoddy enterprise cramps its neighbors and breaks into their opportunity to develop even a modest personal style. Whether the shopping center itself makes money is a secret between the bank and the real estate developer. But the enterprise keeps going, and customers seldom look for anything that cannot be found there. The community, by and large, is proud of it.

Against this electicism, Havencrest's academic excellence does not avail. Every book in the library and every course in the curriculum is organized into a more consistent pattern than the Homecoming Game, and suggests that experience might be so organized as to be true to its own pathos. But the students as I observed them seemed to be immune to the suggestion; they used these courses and their readings for essentially the same sort of display that they put on at half time. In fact, they become little shopping centers themselves, and regard one another as both customers and merchandise.

That this is literally rather than just metaphorically true was illustrated by another public occasion at Havencrest, of a far more solemn character than the Homecoming Game, which took place about a week after it. In the high school there is a student committee, appointed by the administration from among its more trusted students, whose job it is to meet with, and counsel, students who are known to be about to drop out, or—if they can be induced to return for a conference—who have recently done so. The local PTA arranged a meeting at the school to discuss "The High School Dropout" at which the members of this committee were to report on their activities. Following their report, the manager of the local branch of the largest chain department store in Havencrest was to speak on the fate of the dropout in the business world.

From the beginning, the tone of the meeting was evangelical. The chairman, a professional man who was currently president of the PTA, spoke effusively of the wonderful work the student committee was doing to save its errant peers. The committee responded by explaining its task and describing its procedure. Its task, as the members saw it, was to retain the potential dropout: to induce him to remain or return. At no point in their counseling session did they even consider discussing openly with him whether he might have been wise to drop out. Their approach was essentially an act of salesmanship; and in this they were ingenious. They would and did encourage the disaffected youngster to air his grievances; they tried to help him schedule classes with more sympathetic teachers or arrange his schedule so that he could hold a part-time job. But they also tried to seduce him into feeling more at home by self-consciously coming down to his level. The student who chaired the committee described, to indulgent laughter from the school administration, how they would win the dropout's confidence by offering him a forbidden cigarette, explaining conspiratorially that it would probably be all right as long as nobody found out. In this way, they showed him that the school was really on his side.

The climax of their presentation was a little talk by a student who was a redeemed dropout from the previous year and who now sat on the committee to which he owed his redemption. This unusually intelligent and sensitive boy performed a real *tour de force* of self-abasement, and seemed to enjoy every syllable of it. He described how his initial feeling of freedom quickly gave way to idleness and despair. Just as he had been told, he could not get a decent job; he had nothing to do; he no longer saw his friends. Thanks to the committee, he had been given another chance, and he was grateful for the opportunity to save other youths from straying down the path that had tempted him. His comments were received by the audience with little murmurs of sympathy and welcome.

The chain-store manager who followed him supported him completely. His firm no longer hired dropouts; they didn't get along well; they couldn't make it. It wasn't that they couldn't do the jobs they were hired for, which were poor and menial in any case, but that they were unambitious and had no future. His firm had no interest in hiring people it could not promote. The audience response suggested that it felt the manager had stated both a sensible economic policy and an unassailable moral position. Yet, it seemed strange to me that, if the manager's chief complaint against the dropouts was that they were unambitious rather than incompetent, he was so reluctant to hire them for dead-end jobs that more ambitious people dislike anyway.

There were several odd things about the conception of "dropout problems" that developed at this meeting. For one thing, nobody in the audience or among the speakers questioned or analyzed the problem itself. Like the students whose responses to the LeMoyen episodes described in the preceding chapter, everybody accepted the problem as given, and set himself empirically to solving it. The problem was that the kids were dropping out; the solution ought to keep them in; the discussion was about how to do it, not about the wisdom of doing it. Furthermore, despite all the fuss about the problem, nobody seemed interested in the dropouts, as people, at all. Nobody listened to *them*, until after they had duly repented. The procedure wasn't set up to make this possible.

Nobody present at this meeeting, in deploring the serious error the dropouts were making, said a single word about education. They spoke only of the trouble the dropouts were going to have getting and keeping jobs, achieving a high standard of living and a satisfactory level of social status. Nobody suggested that they might be missing anything in school that was worth while for its own sake or that might enrich their later life aesthetically or conceptually. No member of the school administration raised this point, although they had made their school nationally—and justly—famous for the superior intellectual opportunities it provided and, especially, for the school's really remarkable resourcefulness in getting a far wider proportion of its academically less-gifted students than usual to enjoy these opportunities. Abstractly stated, this point would undoubtedly have been strongly endorsed by the audience; but at this meeting, the school administration and its clientele were thinking seriously together about the concrete function of education in Havencrest. The idea that it might have any intrinsic value was overlooked.

In adapting its appeal to the community's habit of thinking of education in terms of the economic advantages presumed to stem from it, the school placed itself in a false position. The argument that high school graduation confers great economic benefits is fallacious at several points. It is true that high school dropouts have enormous difficulty finding jobs, and that for this reason they are unwise to leave school. But this does not mean that people who graduate find jobs more easily because high school has prepared them for a wider range of employment in any clearly demonstrable way. It means that our economy has no place to put adolescents except in schools, and that if they challenge this rule by leaving the custody of the school they will quickly find this out.

It is true that high school graduates make much more money over a lifetime than dropouts do. But what does this mean? Dividing the population simply into people who have graduated from high school and people who have not, includes among the graduates everybody who goes on to finish college or to enter professions. But no very large proportion of the youngsters who now drop out could qualify at present for such careers; they could not get into the kinds of colleges that pave the way. Dropping out of school is more a correlate of low status than a cause of it; the youngsters who make it are better able to handle the world of opportunity, have more outside support and connections, and are more familiar with bureaucratic modes—they are better operators. They stay in school, and make more money, *because* they are better operators; poorer operators would not have comparable careers simply as a result of deciding to finish school. And finally, the argument that staying in school makes for easier employment and higher income is flawed even statistically. It depends, for such validity as it possesses, on the fact that many youngsters do drop out. If all remained to compete for jobs or entrance into the kinds of colleges that serve as major gateways for opportunity, the average would fall and the economic advantage of high school education would prove largely illusory. Already, the big gain in average income follows graduation from college, not from high school—though twenty years ago high school would have done it. As college education becomes more nearly universal, with the opening of more and more—but more and more marginal—community colleges and public facilities of all sorts, even college graduation will probably cease to bear any very significant relation to income.

Middle-class parents know this—in fact they know it too well, which is the reason for their status-panic about getting their youngsters into well-connected Ivy League schools. Yet at Havencrest, the PTA meeting was a solemn affirmation and celebration of the premise that the public school is the gateway to economic opportunity. And, in a sense, it is. For what youngsters learn in their public school careers does fit them to take part in the economy on the economy's terms, which, for most of them, are the only terms on which they can survive at all. This learning, however, does not consist primarily in a set of marketable skills, but of attitudes toward the self as it relates to other people and to the student's potential economic function as an adult.

The high school cannot do much to provide most of its students with the skills and technics they will actually use to earn a living, because the jobs that will be available to most of them require only the mastery of certain machines or administrative routines that the school cannot duplicate and that must therefore be learned on the job.[1] Yet a society that ignores every advantage that education may bring except economic advancement and security, and that is notable for its suspicious aversion to public support of any

[1] This statement is valid only as applied to adolescents who fail to master material at high school level. There are, of course, also large numbers of adolescents who have failed to master even the skills taught in elementary school, and their unemployability is indeed substantially the consequence of educational deficiency—but not a deficiency that can be remedied by inducing them to stay in high school.

nonmilitary enterprise, continues to assume the necessity, and the burden, of supporting a huge public school system. Compulsory public education is one of the very few functions of government that are never seriously questioned, though we constantly, and justly, complain of the quality of educational service the schools actually manage to provide. What, then, *do* the schools do for us?

As in the past, the public school holds our society together. It establishes a working consensus on values, tastes, and behavior, among students whose backgrounds and experience might otherwise be so greatly in conflict as to prevent their assimilation into a commonwealth. But the nature of that consensus has changed as immigration has ceased or been closed off and as the society, and especially the economy in which most Americans must find their place, has changed. The school has changed, too, more completely and more rapidly than many of its staff realize, as it should and must in response to fundamental change in other parts of the social fabric.

This change has affected not only the curriculum but what the curriculum is expected to do for the students enrolled in it. The academic curriculum, particularly, has preserved its status at the expense of its authority. What has happened to it is rather like what has happened to royalty in those countries that still maintain it. Royalty still symbolically integrates the whole nation. But it does so by implicitly, and with the best possible humor, renouncing its earlier claims. It does not unify its subjects by imposing its will upon them, but by behaving so unpretentiously that no citizen can feel excluded by incompetence or inferiority. If the King himself has no special qualities and his job requires—indeed permits—no special qualifications, he becomes the most convincing possible demonstration of the equality of man.

The schoolteachers and employers of fifty years ago treated their students and employees more imperiously than their modern counterparts could easily do today; they thought of their subordinates as candidates for a position in a relatively fixed social order whose terms and values both accepted. They had something definite to offer: real membership in a fairly stable social group which did in fact dress and act more or less the way the school required and sometimes, inadvertently, through inexperience, parodied. Not everybody belonged to this group, and the doctrine of equality of opportunity was not then interpreted as a promise that everybody necessarily would. What was promised was that those who sought to become qualified would be admitted if they succeeded in doing so. Even this limited promise was often enough violated, but the fact that it was made on fairly specific grounds meant that those youngsters who accepted the terms of this somewhat-demeaning social contract and repudiated their immigrant or lower-status characteristics felt that they were headed toward something they had come to value, and not just away from their past.

If they made it, the conventions imposed upon them became genuine tastes, expressive of, and congruent with, their new position in life, and they adhered to those tastes with an allegiance that showed that they were accustomed to having strong tastes, even though theirs has changed. This was true because the immigrant family came here from a society in which they had enjoyed full membership, even though they had abandoned it in favor of one that promised greater opportunity. Their status in their old society had almost always been low, and their children were taught in school to despise their former way of life. But it had never-theless *been* a way of life; the immigrant child, in his family, had experienced culture, if only to exclude it from his self-image. To call a child a dago or a Polack, in the archaic terms of yesterday's abuse, was not only to insult him. It was also to confirm that there existed, across the Atlantic, a scorned but independent source of meaning. It had no power to comfort the child who had rejected it, and it earned him the contempt rather than the interest and respect of his peers of British or German descent who had already succeeded in defining their style as American. But an identity is no less an identity for being unwelcome, as the toughness, strength, and inner conviction of many American Negro youths have demonstrated.

Today, as always, the school is the instrument through which society acculturates people into consensus before they become old enough to resist it as effectively as they could later. There is still a dialectic among elements of society that, left to themselves, would prove too discordant to live in peace and harmony and enjoy the benefits of democracy, as the municipal radio station daily reminds us the people of New York do. But the participants in the dialectic relate to each other very differently, and the consensus sought is of a wholly different order.

Instead of the immigrant from another culture, we have the so-called "culturally deprived"; the internal rural-urban migrant; the slum victim, the mass of Negro children who, unlike the politically acute minority among them, have no racially based social consciousness except a massive and justi-fied sense of insult. In contrast to the true immigrant, these have no other culture, hard but sustaining, to fall back on. They are already completely implicated in the dominant American culture that rejects them, and their self-rejection is much more complete. There is no "culture of poverty" in this country because poverty itself is regarded as the ultimate indecency and the poor cannot respect themselves or one another enough to form institutions of their own. Social studies of poverty in this country, whether undertaken from the standpoint of social dynamics or the quite different issue of mental health, generally confirm one another in revealing the poor to be the most alienated element in our population.[2] They have fewest contacts with other people; belong to few formal organizations; develop states of mind and behavior that in middle-class individuals would establish them as full-blown paranoid psychotics but that are hardly unrealistic among people who have so little basis for self-esteem and so much in their lives to justify fearfulness and suspicion.

But there no longer is a smug and secure middle class, capable—however misleadingly—of establishing its own image in the minds of lower-status children as worthy of emulation. We now have a fluctuating corps of administrative officials—properly ashamed to use words like "nigger" but trained to grin when they themselves are called "wasps"— who often feel their existence to be empty and unsatisfactory and who arouse more envy than respect for their lives of ambitious caution. These people are underestimated; they perform useful administrative functions that are essential to a

[2] Some of the many investigations that have dealt with diverse aspects of this issue are Leo Srole, Thomas S. Langner, Stanley T. Michael, Marvin K. Opler, and Thomas A. C. Rennie, *Mental Health in the Metropolis: The Midtown Manhattan Study*, Vol. I. New York: McGraw-Hill, 1962); James V. Mitchell, Jr., "Identification of Items in the California Test of Personality that Differentiate Between Subjects of High and Low Socio-Economic Status at the Fifth and Seventh Grade Levels," *Journal of Educational Research*, December 1957; A. B. Hollingshead and F. C. Redlich, *Social Class and Mental Illness: A Community Study* (New York: John Wiley & Sons, 1958); and Elizabeth Douvan and Joseph Adelson, "The Psychodynamics of Social Mobility in Adolescent Boys," *Journal of Abnormal and Social Psychology*, 56, 1958.

bureaucratized, rationalistic society, and the subtlety and complexity of their work would earn them more respect if it were better understood. But they are hard people to weep for. Heisenberg's principle of indeterminacy now stands as one of the three or four fundamental theoretical corner-stones of our understanding of our physical universe; and we must all now accept that, because the act of observation always interferes to some extent with the system being observed, the more certain we are where anything stands, the less sure we can be where it was going in the first place or what it is going to do next. But Heisenberg meant this general truth to apply primarily to small, sly particles of matter and energy. It still comes as rather an embarrassing shock to find that it applies equally well to the behavior of our neighbors and colleagues, our wife, and even of her husband.

When he is young, nobody really wants to live like this; we learn to, gradually, nevertheless, because we want status, power, money, or a sense of being a part of things and being useful that we cannot get in any other way. Mr. Rabinow, quoted at length in the first chapter of this book, illustrates how painful the process can be even for a young man who is already a long way advanced in it. The public school is still the gateway to opportunity, but the opportunity is intrinsically less attractive to the young than it was, or appeared to be, fifty years ago. There is more of a squeeze on them, and the squeeze is more complicated, than in the past.

Not only is the middle-class life-style too constricting to arouse much enthusiasm even among its own children, much less to win enthusiastic and ambitious converts from below; middle-class roles are declining in scope and availability. Automation, having devastated the blue-collar work force, is rapidly attacking the white-collar. Today's business machines can make anything except basic policy; and middle-range executives do not make basic policy, either; they make decisions on the basis of information supplied them from other sources. This is what the machines do best. It is becoming increasingly unrealistic for the school to demand or promise *anything* in the way of long-range career expectations. The "culturally deprived" child has little or no reason to accept or adapt to the standards of the school, and the people he sees who do don't seem to be getting or expecting much either, beyond the satisfaction of putting them down as a "hoody element."

He has, however, no bearable alternative to the kind of life the school tries to lead him. His immigrant predecessor did; in his time there was still an American working class with a life-style of its own and some prospect of steady employment to sustain it. There was, in short, decent poverty, and, while the poor never have been respected in this country, it was not then technologically feasible to remind them of this continuously. But the "culturally deprived" child cannot be permitted to opt out of the economy at a low level. There is no demand for his service at lower levels, while his service as a consumer is becoming rapidly more indispensable to the economy. As the cold war thaws, the demands he can be induced to make on the economy become the chief bulwark of our corporate elite against becoming poor themselves.

In a profit economy with a high and rising rate of productivity per man-hour, the abdication by any large segment of the population of its duty as a consumer constitutes a national emergency; there is no time to wait for demand to grow out of the consumer's felt need. But this also means that there is no time to wait for the consumer to develop any tastes of his own; in our society, the word "discrimination" has lost all its positive connotations. Moreover, the very idea of taste is distasteful to people who have been kept for a long time in a socially marginal position and have come to resent it; if the television commercials needle viewers constantly into feeling inferior because they cannot afford what is offered, they also tacitly promise that nothing will be offered that takes more than money or credit to comprehend and enjoy. The very vulgarity of the commercial assures the viewer that no qualifications are needed for his part in the proposed transaction, except, of course, financial ones.

Mass societies have special difficulties with taste. Their economy and technology demand consensus. But taste is inherently divisive. It always develops from a particular social situation and expresses a pattern of response appropriate to it but grotesque in the hands of people who have not shared it. People who go native are offensive to the actual natives; the excessive zeal of converts is usually an embarrassment to the church; *Le Bourgeois Gentilhomme* is a farcical character and Von Faninal, in contrast to *Der Rosenkavalier*, a faintly sinister one as well.

But a mass society cannot accommodate the authentic responses of specialized minorities; it keeps going economically by obliterating distinctions and selling fragments of experience out of context: "The mass is all," Ortega wrote

> that sets no value on itself—good or ill—based on specific grounds; but which feels itself "just like everybody" and nevertheless is not concerned about it . . . Thus, in the intellectual life, which of its essence requires and presumes qualification, one can note the progressive triumph of the pseudo-intellectual, unqualified, unqualifiable and by its very mental texture disqualified . . . *The characteristic of the hour is that the commonplace mind, knowing itself to be commonplace, has the assurance to proclaim the rights*

of the commonplace and to impose them wherever it will.
[Italics Ortega's.][3]

In a mass society, a principal function of the media of communication, and especially of the schools, is to forestall the development of real taste, to root out and wither both real elegance and real vulgarity and replace them with the banal, the generalized other. In discussing this process, critics of education—including myself—have generally spoken of it as imposing a middle-class way of life on public school students, whatever their own class-origin might be. This is true, insofar as what the school imposes is the pattern of life and values accepted by its own staff who are mostly lower middle class, and which is generally in practice throughout the country.

But this does not mean that the school imposes middle-class taste. This, in a sense, is what it used to do, when the middle-class was sufficiently self-confident and self-conscious to have taste-patterns of its own. But real middle-class taste—with its emphasis on solid comfort, durability, and the look of being both expensive and paid-for—is as much a specialized-minority taste as any other, and wholly out of place in a mass society. In their effort to serve the cause of uniformity, school personnel have been no more respectful of middle-class tradition than of any other.

What they offer expresses the taste of no class, but a refusal to recognize that human experience varies according to the social and economic situation one lives in. The middle class have, historically, been perceptive and sometimes generous patrons to those artists, like Rembrandt, who seriously and intelligibly interpreted their lives. But the school is training consumers for a mass society that deals in goods and ideas too meaningless to divide the market. The

[3] José Ortega y Gasset, *The Revolt of the Masses* (New York: W. W. Norton & Company, 1932), Chapter I.

people who produce and distribute them are not artists, but, in every sense of the word, designers. They avoid the kind of craftsmanship that might alienate some potential customers while reminding others of the customers' right to have their goods, and their cognitive and emotional equipment, custom-made instead of merely personalized.

In this context, the attitude of the department-store manager who spoke at the conference on school dropouts becomes understandable. He has good reason to avoid hiring people who are not interested in advancement, even though they can do the jobs they were hired for well enough. Such people are likely to be relatively immune to external motivation, and inclined to seek satisfaction from the job itself; and from his point of view, no good can possibly come of this. His low-level jobs really are repetitive, monotonous, and highly rationalized; the people who hold them are likely to become dissatisfied and quit, unless they view the job as a step toward a better one. If they actually *like* the job, they are probably either imposing some personal style on it, expressing an idiosyncrasy of their own in the way they do it that will confuse his system, or they are exaggerating its importance in relation to other things that go on in the mercantile process and thereby making of themselves an irritating and compulsive bottleneck. They are also likely to antagonize their fellow workers by grossly exceeding the informal work-norms that they have established among themselves and thus putting them on the spot. The last thing management needs, at almost any level, is a self-generating enthusiast.[4]

[4] For a remarkable and highly readable illustration of these issues in operation at another time and place, and at a much higher level, see the account of the "Second Interview of George Passant" in Sir Charles Snow's novel *Homecoming* (New York: Charles Scribner's Sons, 1956), Chapter XLIV.

An extremely important social function of the school—and, I believe a major reason for our continued unquestioned support of it—is to protect society from "subjectivity"; from people with an excessively personal style or approach to situations, who threaten or antagonize their co-workers, fellow citizens, and indeed, in extreme cases, society itself. Our comparative neglect of the humanities in the school curriculum is, I should judge, another aspect of this, not passive, but active. The arts and literature are not ignored as useless; they are quarantined as dangerous. We keep the humanities on a low budget, much as we do the federal antidiscrimination agencies—to keep them from getting too dynamic. Yet, we cannot afford to break with the tradition they represent; in a mass society they must be preserved—indeed, pasteurized—to render their vital ferment inactive while preserving as much as possible of their flavor.

The humanities deal directly with disciplined, but subjective, experience and are the most effective individuating agencies known to man. They attest to the validity of unique experience; they destroy isolation and calm fear by putting us in touch with people who have something serious to tell us across whatever barrier. With a strong light, heavy spiked boots, and a copy of *A Passage to India*, we can explore any cave in which it is still possible to breathe. This is a freedom intolerable and disruptive to a mass society. Yet, such a society cannot afford to do Forster in, either. It needs the humanities as symbols of excellence, because it hasn't enough taste of its own to judge for itself, and continually suspects that it is being cheated. Candidates for status in a mass society demand the best, and simultaneously demand assurance that no special qualification is needed in order to enjoy the best. They prize most highly cameras that set themselves automatically so that the photographer need never realize that he does not understand the reciprocal relationship between lens aperture and shutter speed, or wines selected by Amy Vanderbilt that they neither like nor dislike.

The most serious threat to their self-esteem is the possibility of meeting somebody who really *is* qualified and does know how to do something special, thus opening to them limitless vistas of inferiority. Paradoxically, in view of our cultural tradition, the most immediate danger of such an encounter in school occurs outside the academic curriculum altogether; in sports, shop, or even the much ridiculed driver-education courses. A need to belong, or the school's commitment to equal opportunity, is not enough to make the *Antigone* intelligible; you have to understand what a play is and be able to sit still, alone, long enough to read one that was written in an unfamiliar language. But neither are they enough to make the ball go into the basket, or the radio you have tried to build play, or the car stay on the road. Any flunkable subject is to some degree liberalizing, because it teaches students something about their unique qualities. Ultimately, you either know how to do these things, or you learn how, or you realize that you don't know how although some people actually do, and that neither whining nor truculence will eliminate the difference between you. For adolescents, sex, undoubtedly, has a similar educational potential, though instruction is less formal.

But athletics and the vocational curriculum do not, after all, live up to their potentials as threats to mass complacency, because they seldom lead to large-scale success, and students, therefore, do not take their experience of competence in these areas as a serious validation of their personal distinction. Tommy Heinsohn may be one of the best basketball players the Celtics ever had, and Holy Cross before them, but in real life he is an insurance salesman.[5] And no matter how good you are in shop, there is plenty in most high schools to remind you that, if you're in the vocational track, you're already dead.

The liberal-arts curriculum presents more of a problem; and the problem may be stated as: How can liberal education be prevented from creating self-confident, specialized minorities? Those who begin to experience mastery of its language and organization, its subtle power as an instrument of self-revelation, are thereby strengthened—much as earlier immigrant children were, but much more—by contact with a tough and sustaining culture that preserves them from triviality and supports them in their own critical judgment. They are likely to become tougher and more authoritative than a mass society can bear.

This is an old issue in our culture, more familiar when stated with reversed bias, as the problem of keeping intellectually gifted youngsters from thinking that they are better than other people or entitled to special privileges while nevertheless training them to develop their gifts fully and to use them for the benefit of society. In our society, a free style and a sense of personal authority which are derived from one's own qualities, rather than from one's position in an administrative hierarchy, are certainly rare privileges, which are most grudgingly vouchsafed even to men in the highest positions. When a President begins to show signs of this kind of uncommonness, we usually shoot him, though Mr. Roosevelt's assailant fortunately missed. Nevertheless, any society that is to remain viable must somehow preserve

[5] Though in all fairness, I must record that the *Wall Street Journal* (February 18, 1964) featured a front-page story on Tom Gola, paying respectful tribute to his basketball skill and scrutinizing in detail and with approval his family life and investment program.

a capacity for originality and innovation and must therefore encourage, within limits, individuals of special capacity to become aware of what they can do and grant them some access to positions in which they can do it. An open society, in this respect, has a dual problem and is likely to confuse the two issues it must deal with. On the one hand, it must search for talent in its lower reaches and try to prevent its potential Miltons from remaining, mute and inglorious, among the poor. On the other hand, it must make sure that they remain like Milton, safely on the side of Cromwell and unpretentious. There is always danger that they may come to find Charles I more dignified, and Charles II more humane, and this is a danger that liberal education tends to increase.

Bureaucratic societies have many institutionalized ways of minimizing their exposure to special competence, and the high school is surely one of the most effective of these.

High school teaching in our society is defined as a comparatively low-status occupation; about the lowest, indeed, for which so much formal education is required.[6] It has also traditionally served, and still serves, as the first—and often the last—step up from working-class status for moderately intelligent members of recently assimilated ethnic groups. In the suburbs around New York City, for example, a school administrator is likely to seem rather exotic unless he has an Italian surname. High school teachers, like members of any occupational group, vary greatly among themselves in character, competence, and motivation. But any student encounters a great many teachers in the course of four years or

[6] In the most recent status-rating of occupations by the National Opinion Research Center, which correlates almost completely ($r = 0.99$) with the 1947 study on which this comment is based, "instructor in the public schools" rates just below "sociologist" on a very detailed list. Robert W. Hodge, Paul M. Siegel, and Peter H. Rossi, "Occupational Prestige in the United States, 1925–63," *American Journal of Sociology*, November 1964, p. 290.

more, and these differences tend to even out in his experience. If he wants to make a good record in school, he must learn to get along with average teachers. Teachers in most schools form a close-knit, if not especially friendly, social group, gossipy and malicious; the teachers' room is the scene of remarkable feats of character assassination. Every high school student knows that the worst thing that can happen to him is to get a reputation as a "wise guy" or a trouble-maker; and this will happen if he offends as many as two average teachers.

Nobody is as vulnerable to malice as the involuntary client of a petty and resentful bureaucracy that has its own troubles with its superiors while being protected from the complaints of its clientele. "Teen-agers," prisoners, and mental-hospital patients are helpless in the toils of their respective institutions. By definition, they are there for their own good; and the staff has an ideology that is highly effective in reconciling the putative needs of its clients with its own convenience and security. There is no hypocrisy about this. Every social group sincerely believes its own ideology and concludes from it that its incursions operate to benefit others less fortunate. This is what an ideology is for.

Every high school student can therefore be virtually certain that he will experience successive defeat at the hands of teachers with minds of really crushing banality. The paradigm, perhaps, is Charlie Brown impotent before the invincible ignorance of Lucy.

A large proportion of working-class adolescents manage nevertheless to pass through school with their selves pretty well intact, but they have very little subsequent impact on the social structure. Partly this is because they have too little status to make their pattern of life attractive to middle-class people who have never experienced it. But partly it is be-

cause they handle experience too concretely; they are mala-
droit with symbols and therefore fearful of general ideas.
They are solid enough to keep their feet on the ground and
retain much of their self-esteem, but they simply do not
understand what is happening to them in terms of any conception of social dynamics complex and subtle enough to
shed light on their situation and to suggest to them any
alternative to absorption into a mass society.

The real threat to the hegemony of the school comes from
youngsters who have independent access to a cultural tradition that still commands a measure of respect, and who therefore retain both a standard against which to judge the
pattern of values the school conveys and a source of self-
esteem beyond its control. But these, I have already argued,
would also constitute a threat to the mass society if they
were allowed to mature. The function of the school, in
socializing them, then, is to deprive them of access to that
source of self-esteem and to shake their confidence in the
standard from which it is derived. The technique by which
the school does this resembles, conventionally, that used by
victorious armies of occupation to impress on the minds of
defeated civilians that an important change has indeed occurred.

A wisely led army of occupation, if it hopes to make use
of the talents of defeated civilians during the subsequent
period of occupation, does not needlessly abuse or deliberately humiliate them. It simply, and as absent-mindedly as
possible, diverts their treasure to base purposes. Its officers
admire the solid construction of their churches, and billet
soldiers in them, leaving these to make such arrangements
as they find convenient for cooking and other domestic
functions. The victors inform the vanquished that their
household gods are interesting, attractive objects that attest
to a higher level of cultural development than they had

really expected, and carry them off to be displayed, if there is room, in a minor gallery of the National Museum. The losers' crown jewels, though old-fashioned and pretentious in design, are amusing enough to be widely reproduced as ornaments for beach hats. If this seems a far-fetched and unsuitable analogy to apply to what the school does to students with really cultivated minds, consider what a recent book on teaching English in high school advises teachers to do to *Macbeth*:

> Your first difficulty is with the witches. . . . Did Macbeth believe in witches? Of course, and so did Shakespeare, but our students should be taught not to, either here or in *The Rime of the Ancient Mariner*. Your job, as an English teacher, is to remove your students from primitivism, ghosts, witches, and cheap, hand-me-down miracles.
>
> Can you do so without weakening the drama?
>
> First, determine for yourself whether the function of the witches is to suggest or prophesy. Suggestion, if strong enough, molds minds and behavior so that the future becomes predictable; but prediction is not prophecy, any more than suggestibility or gullibility, though they make the future more predictable, are proof of prophecy.
>
> We sometimes see this in parlor tricks, where the magician "forces" us to select a card and then "reads our minds." But, in an even wider area, affecting all society, the advertising campaign in the promotion of new products is the supreme analogue of the witches' role in suggestion rather than in prophecy. We will go into this in greater length in our discussion of the mass media, but here and meanwhile observe how the weird sisters behave like Procter and Gamble after a new soap or toothpaste market.
>
> Procter and Gamble* invested several million dollars in a new toothpaste even before it was officially placed on the

---

* "P and G Plans Multi-Million Dollar Push as Gleem Is Introduced in New York," *Advertising Age*, February 8, 1954, p. 1.

market as a full-scale competitor of its rivals. The sum was expended in laboratory research, in manufacturing plant, in consumer attitude research, in market testing, and in purchase of newspaper, magazine, radio, and television advertising facilities. Executives at Procter and Gamble predicted the sales volume on the basis of this investment. But the prediction depended also on the suggestibility of the consumer and the amount of money required to force gullibility on toothpaste buyers. Adequate investment in suggestion warranted the prediction. And so Gleem toothpaste was successful. But prediction, even with suitable investment, is not infallible, as Ford's experience with the Edsel car shows.

Macbeth, however, *was* suggestible. The weird sisters could thereby predict, but, though prediction looks like prophecy, it isn't. The weird sisters think they are witches, so does Macbeth, and so does Shakespeare. We know they aren't. We don't believe in witches. How then do they prophesy? By gullibility and suggestibility.[7]

The school does not, of course, plan to haze its more sensitive or cultivated students into submission. For the most part, the process requires no planning at all. It is the natural consequence of assigning the liberal-arts curriculum to teachers and administrators who have shared only minimally in the experiences necessary to understand it, and of requiring students, by virtue of their subordinate position, to accept as authoritative what the school makes of it.

The point of this, so far as the more cultivated student is concerned, is not to convince him that such teachers are right. It is to demonstrate to him that it does not matter whether they are or not; that their interpretation goes, no matter how limited or vulgar their treatment of the material

---

[7] Abraham Bernstein, *Teaching English in High School* (New York: Random House, 1961), pp. 216–217.

may be. The basic lesson the school teaches him is that in a mass society it is unwise even to claim authority on the basis of special competence; the more competent the student may be, the more humility is demanded of him.

But the school does not depend on the banality of its teachers as its sole resource in adapting adolescents to the demands of a mass society. They are the spearhead of an enormously effective apparatus for indoctrination with mass attitudes. If the teacher herself is "mass," the apparatus supports her attack closely; if she is herself a person of wit and distinction, it frustrates her very thoroughly. Most of the student peer group is itself already "mass," and eager to put down any response that seems "far out" to them. Our subjects' responses to "The King's Visit" and "Alan Slade and His Friends" show that Scott Cowen, Johnny Adams, and Alan Slade fare no better at the hands of students than of teachers; in fact, a slightly higher proportion of teachers are willing to accept these deviants, at least tentatively, because of their "potential." But the teacher who tries to nurture students who respond very differently from their peers, whether through originality or as a result of a consistently different experience of life, is likely to find her efforts neutralized. The "mass" students respond, not with hostility, but as if they were spectators at a new kind of panel show where, naturally, you have to have all points of view represented.[8] Scott Cowen and Johnny Adams soon learn that even in those instances where the teacher listens to them, nobody else does; the others just sit and congratulate themselves on being

[8] Thus, more than four-fifths of our nearly one-thousand-student pretest sample agreed that: When a class here is discussing a problem, the teachers think the most important thing is to have all possible points of view represented.

In fact, the only item of the 150 in the instrument more generally agreed with is the previously quoted "You have to be concerned about marks here . . ."

liberals who allow people they disagree with to express themselves.

Techniques for democratizing discussion operate as a very effective means of discrediting competence. "That's a very interesting point, John; now I wonder what the other members of the class think about it?" This, depending on the intonation, can be a great deal more than a stimulus to more widespread discussion. It is a way of informing John that what the others think about it is going to be more decisive in judging the value of his statement than the quality of his thought or theirs; if he can't get group acceptance, at least for purposes of argument, he is lost. It is a reminder to him that he is not to dominate the discussion regardless of his level of competence: "We all know how interested you are in the French Revolution, John, but don't you think it's time that Paul had a chance?"

So Danton died; yet it is true that Paul has an important task to perform. Whether he knows anything about the French Revolution or not, he can still help teach John the importance of being simple, of talking so that other people can understand him and not feel that he is way above their heads, of having no more ideas than can be packed into a brief, punchy statement. Paul breaks the flow of John's analysis, and keeps him from taking himself too seriously. If it hadn't been Paul, it might have been a fire drill, or an announcement over the ubiquitous public-address system, to assert the principle that civic virtue and public policy take precedence over private meanings and the affairs of the mind.

Don't the school and society know that what John is doing is important? Of course they do; that is why they interrupt him. The teacher does not want to stop John or totally arrest his development. But a central part of her job is to engrave on his mind that his development must take place on society's terms rather than on his. This is true of all formal schooling; for no society maintains such costly and unproductive enterprises except to gain its own ends. But it makes a difference what those ends are.

In our society, a basic clause in the social contract provides that authority based on superior competence or insight must defer to more popularly acceptable social formulations than it can in good conscience support. In this way, we protect ourselves from the arrogance and possible tyranny of an elite. The risk of being tyrannized by an arrogant elite while crossing our great cultural plains has certainly been reduced to manageable proportions; it is about as great as that of being charged by a maddened buffalo. There are rational historical causes for the precautions we have built into our culture against both misadventures. But it is necessary to examine the current costs as well. We may not be able to live without an elite as well as we can without buffalo.

The major cost is that John's experience of life is broken up before his eyes, and handed back to him with instructions that he use the pieces as tools with which to do the job he is hired for. He is not even permitted to try to fit them together on his own; this is not what they are for, and it would be antisocial for him to try. The school is not there to help John find himself or be himself; its purpose is to help youngsters "make something *out* of themselves." Some useful thing.

In this respect, the school is still the instrument of the Protestant ethic, which judged a man by his empirical effectiveness in hewing out a place in the world and controlling his environment—clearly an immensely profitable, if seldom quite satisfactory, undertaking. To carry through an industrial revolution, clear continents, and enlighten or exterminate the indigenous savages you had to use yourself as a thing. But the things have been quietly catching up. They are now in a position to demonstrate, conclusively, that things make better things than people do. Most of us will, I am sure, agree that here in America things have never looked brighter. It's the people who give cause for concern.

5

The

NATURE

of the

ANIMUS

There are three quite different groups of people who have great difficulty in school, and very much the same sort of difficulty. We are most familiar with the plight of the unambitious, or ineffectually ambitious, poor. But all children who are aristocratic in the demands they make either on others or on themselves fare as badly or worse. They constitute, to be sure, a small and dwindling proportion of affluent Americans, in comparison to the large majority who protect themselves by adopting a bland and shifty folksiness. But nobody has more trouble in public school than the few who do not. Since Andrew Jackson's day, we have given ever-shortening shrift to people who demanded a measure of privilege in response to their superiority, especially if they really were superior, and especially if the privilege they demanded adhered to the original meaning of the word: a peculiar, private right to personal respect and inviolacy.

The third group of people who fare badly in school are the divergent. We sometimes speak of these as creative, or nonconformist; but these terms are imprecise and misleading. It is usually too early to tell whether youngsters who show in school an unusual degree of originality, spontaneous feeling, and a highly idiosyncratic, personal response to the people and events in their lives will survive to create anything; though if they don't, no one else will. And conformity, like adjustment, is a concept that has been so beaten out of shape by vulgar abuse as to be useless. Self-conscious nonconformity, for the time, has become quite fashionable, and schools rather encourage its more conventional manifestations as evidence that they favor creativity. They cannot, however, favor genuine diversity of response among students without jeopardizing the underlying institutional assumptions and arrangements on which a mass society depends; and they do not favor it. Even when a school attempts to dispel apathy and conventionality among its students by facilitating independent study on individual topics of interest to them, it is likely to undercut its own efforts through its commitment to egalitarianism. For example, one very superior New England high school recently obtained a large foundation grant to set up a program whereby one hundred students could pursue their entire high school program under five excellent teachers who were both enthusiastic and intelligently self-critical, organizing their work as a protracted investigation of serious issues identified by the students themselves. But since this project was called an "experiment," the school decided that they would have to approach it in a scientific spirit. They thereupon excluded all voluntary participation, all honors students, and all "exceptional" or "handicapped" students, and began seeking a way to recruit participants by some purely random process.

Nearly everything that has been written about how school experience differs for different groups of youngsters contrasts the treatment and fate in school of rich youth and poor, bright and dull, examining school practice as it responds to variations among its clientele in family income, measured IQ, and the subtler social concomitants of these two highly correlated factors. This kind of analysis has yielded and continues to yield much valuable insight into how the school functions in society. But it also obscures some important relationships. All cartographic conventions make it easier for the mapmaker to emphasize the features that are important for his purposes and tend to conceal others that from a different point of view become equally or more salient.

Discrimination against lower-status pupils in the schools is so pervasive and important that it cannot be said to have been exaggerated despite the continued emphasis it has received during the twenty years since the classic study *Who Shall Be Educated?*[1] was published. Seventeen years later, Patricia Sexton, in *Education and Income*,[2] established that income and educational opportunity were as closely related in a Midwestern metropolis as they had been, twenty years earlier, in the small town Warner and his colleagues had described. It is an incontrovertible fact that, in the public schools, nearly every benefit a child might receive is positively correlated to family income. The more a child's parents earn, the more years of schooling he will, on the average, complete, and the better his grades will be. The richer child in a large city will probably attend a newer

[1] W. Lloyd Warner, Robert J. Havighurst, and Martin B. Loeb (New York: Harper & Row, 1944).
[2] New York: The Viking Press, 1961.

school with better facilities and better-qualified teachers. Wherever he goes to school, he will occupy more honorific positions of leadership in school activities; his IQ score will generally be higher,[3] and the school will consider him more intelligent than poorer children, even though the latter may demonstrate very superior acumen in their informal out-of-school life that middle-class adults ignore or deplore.

The children of the poor may, in fact, tend to be more stupid than those of the rich, whether congenitally or because they have been so damaged and stunted by early experience as to be less able to profit by education by the time they begin school. It is certainly true that poor children make lower IQ scores even when tested in the early elementary years, though in school they deteriorate further. It is also true that poor children show more signs of severe emotional disturbance and generally bad mental health than middle-class children, as is likewise true of their elders. They are frequently irritable and depressed, they have a low opinion of themselves that they tend to take out on other people, have few friendships or memberships in social groups beyond their family, and are often highly suspicious of strangers.[4]

But the fact that poor children rate lower on IQ tests than richer children almost certainly tells us more about the tests than it does about the children. We must grant, I think, that

[3] Cf. W. W. Charters, Jr., "Social Class and Intelligence," in *Readings in the Social Psychology of Education*, W. W. Charters, Jr., and N. L. Gage, eds. (Boston: Allyn and Bacon, 1963), pp. 3–21, for an excellent recent discussion and summary of research on this topic. Cf. particularly Ernest A. Haggard, "Social Status and Intelligence: An Experimental Study of Certain Cultural Determinants of Measured Intelligence," *Genetic Psychology Monographs*, 49, 1954.

[4] James V. Mitchell, Jr., "Identification of Items in the California Test of Personality that Differentiate Between Subjects of High and Low Socio-Economic Status at the Fifth and Seventh Grade Levels," *Journal of Educational Research*, December 1957.

such tests are a valid means of detecting certain rather artificial cognitive skills that tend to develop early and to remain
stable, and that attract schoolteachers much as feminine musk
attracted Don Giovanni, leading them to keep, as he did,
extensive numerical records. We must also grant that middle-
class children who were as touchy and unstable or as apathetic as many lower-status children often are would probably be on the verge of paranoid schizophrenia. The actual
conditions of lower-class life, however, are grimmer than
most middle-class paranoiacs could imagine in their most
detailed fantasies of persecution; and lower-class children
who could accept the sugary gentility of the classroom as
the way life is would be seriously delusional. They are,
indeed, sometimes misled because they do not understand
the rhetoric of middle-class hostility; it may take them some
months to learn what teachers mean when they say things
like, "Johnny dear, I'm afraid we'll have to let you stay after
school today." But the fact that lower-status children are
realistic in their defensiveness and direct in their expression
of it does not prevent the school from judging this disruptive
and as evidence of a defect in character, though the child's
low status may keep the teacher from seeing his behavior
as pathological: "Those children are all like that; you have
to remember they haven't had many advantages."

In short, the massive evidence that poor children fare
worse in school than richer ones does not show that they
are less capable in any fundamental sense. But—and here I
differ very markedly from the usual interpretation of the
evidence by scholars, from Warner through A. B. Hollingshead[5] to Sexton, who have studied it—neither would I call
it evidence of a bias on the part of the school. Bias is not

[5] *Elmtown's Youth: The Impact of Social Class on Adolescents* (New
York: John Wiley & Sons, 1949), another undoubted classic.

quite the right word; it suggests that the school misperceives the people whom it mistreats; that it is misled by errors of measurement built into its tests and methods of observation. But the attitude of the school toward lower-status children who do not wish to better themselves or do not know how to go about trying is not to be accounted for by any error of estimate. One might as well say that dogs are biased against cats.

This, on the contrary, is genuine hostility to these children and their cognitive style, often expressed as contempt, solidly based upon fear. But I would stress that the school does not respond in this way to poverty itself; it has, indeed, been the friend and mentor of many generations of poor children, asking only that they be properly ashamed of their poverty and their foreignness and properly anxious to get on in the world. The historic function of the American public school, and especially of the high school, has been to serve as a social and economic ladder—though today's school personnel, referring to a more passive clientele, sometimes think of it as an escalator. The school has taught millions of poor children whose parents were often new to America the vocational skills, the speech and manners, and the attitudes that would help them to find a place and advance themselves in the American social order. There is nothing in the history of the public school of which its personnel are prouder.

But the school's commitment to assist the children of the poor to better themselves implies no corresponding respect for them in their present condition. Between the traditions and staff of the public school, on the one hand, and the "culturally deprived" among its clientele, on the other, there is real conflict and often enmity. It is frustrating to deal with these children who ignore, reject, or misinterpret the school's efforts to transform them, who find its offerings meaningless, and are unmoved or annoyed by the arguments it offers on its own behalf; who cheerfully shrug off its pretensions as they use it as a place to eat lunch and meet their friends, just as if they were human already.

This conflict cannot be understood simply in economic terms. No class conflict ever can; the difficulties always go deeper, and arise because social-class differences show themselves in conflicting views of what the world is like and of what in the world is good or evil. Nor can the conflicts fairly be ascribed to the unwillingness of the school to change its ways of dealing with youngsters whom it regards as "culturally deprived." It will not, or cannot, change its values; but it is eager to change its techniques. The professional literature of education is burgeoning with reports of new procedures for adapting instruction to the limited though colorful and expressive vocabulary of lower-status children; to their shorter attention span and higher perceptual threshold, their need for continued reassurance that they are not incompetent in the classroom, and their lower level of motivation toward conventional school activities.[6] Judged on its own terms, much of this material is of high quality; the proposals made are imaginative, flexible, and realistic in the sense that the lower-status student is often perceived very accurately as a target for new instructional approaches.

Nevertheless, I find them rather offensive. Their sophistication is essentially that of the research division of a competent advertising agency, which becomes more effective in selling the client's product as it becomes more astute at picturing in detail what the customers are really like, and more willing to adapt its appeals to their actual motives and

[6] For example, Frank Riessman, *The Culturally Deprived Child* (New York: Harper & Row, 1962); or *Education in Depressed Areas*, A. Harry Passow, Ed. (New York: Bureau of Publications, Teachers College, Columbia University, 1963).

life-styles. What the agency does not do is question the value of the product to the client or the legitimacy of exploiting his motives. The school is eagerly experimenting with new ways of reaching its captive audience and enlisting its active participation; and in this it is likely to succeed. But the conflict lies deeper. The most effective merchandising techniques violate individual privacy and dignity more thoroughly than those that are less "scientific," while the conflict of interest between the salesman and the consumer continues unresolved. The newer approaches are better, in short, only if the "culturally deprived" will in fact be better off for accepting the school's values and promises of a better future, and only if the school can in fact deliver on them.

But there can be no doubt of the schools' determination to be helpful. The prevailing ideology of professional education has been favorably disposed, though patronizing, toward the children of the poor for more than thirty years. Since the great depression of the thirties forced thoughtful observers of the American social order to take account of its potentiality for misery and to explore the possibilities of using the State to foster at least a minimal level of social welfare, required education courses have systematically indoctrinated teacher-candidates with a special sense of obligation toward the "disadvantaged," the "underprivileged," and, more recently, the "culturally deprived," especially if they were also "nonwhite," "nonacademic," or "retarded." None of these groups were customarily viewed as having positive value or strength in their own right, but as mutilated versions of normal middle-class youth. As such, however, they were vouchsafed heartfelt sympathy. Nearly all education students, in my experience, latch on early to the concept that the schools, being middle class, give lower-class youngsters a hard time, and they nearly always—while they are still in college—support what they conceive to be the cause of the "underprivileged."

Despite the conclusive evidence from Sexton, Warner, Hollingshead, and many other able students who have reached similar conclusions that the poor fare consistently worse in school than those who are richer, I believe there is more actual hostility toward rich youngsters, except for those who garb themselves in almost masochistic humility. The techniques of these sociologists were not, for several reasons, designed to detect hostility toward the more affluent. American sociologists themselves share the egalitarian ethos, despise privilege, and are inclined to dismiss whatever unpleasantness the rich may encounter as a small but satisfying contribution to the redress of a more democratic social balance. Youth of higher status, moreover, are better able to defend themselves by a range of skills, from verbal facility to external community pressure: the fact that schools often yield to this is adduced as further evidence of bias in favor of the upper-middle- or upper-class student; but it is also evidence that the school is at odds with them. Parents of higher-status children, by definition, are in a better position to demand what they want of the school; if they get it, this, too, goes into the record as a bias of the school in their favor, but what their sons or daughters actually experience is not likely to feel like favor. Richer parents can, and do, take their children out of public school and place them in a private school—though, in my observation, the experience is unlikely to be very different—if they find the public school unbearable, whereas poorer children must either bear the situation or drop out of it. The fact that many *do* drop out, while nearly all youngsters who regard themselves and are accepted by the high school as college material complete the course, is again taken as evidence of a social-class bias in education. But youngsters who attend private secondary schools are not counted as dropouts, though they, too, are rejecting the education to which they are entitled as citizens. And they include a large proportion of upper-middle- and upper-class youth, especially in the East—where public education has never been held as sacred as in the Middle West and West—and in large urban areas.

It certainly cannot be denied that higher-status children get a disproportionate share of what there is to be had in school; this, after all, is an essential part of what status means. If it is also all that bias means, then the schools are biased in their favor. But the youngster himself is likely to feel as much beset by niggling hostility as any lower-status student. A boy who had been brought up to expect life to have a certain style, some space and leisure would certainly dislike Milgrim, and if he showed these tastes publicly he would be as much loathed as any lower-class "trouble-maker." The shop teacher, to be sure, would never drag him through the corridor bodily to the principal's office to be disciplined, as happened to at least one working-class miscreant during my visit there; he would probably never meet the shop teacher at all. He would, however, be subject to other, subtler harassments: lugubrious reminders that the school was disappointed that a boy of whom it had a right to expect so much should get out of line and fail to measure up; the special sneer that traffic policemen and "attendance teachers" reserve for boys who drive Jaguars; the special attention school counselors devote to those they define as "underachievers."

One of the principal social functions of the American public school is to teach youth from wealthy homes that they are *not* aristocrats, and that aristocracy will not be tolerated in our society. These youngsters learn to cringe under the barrage of sarcasm directed against "heavier tax-payers' scions" as it was once put by an irate correspondent of mine[7] who had been aroused by an article I had written on education.

To paraphrase Oscar Wilde in *The Importance of Being Ernest,* it is evident that many schoolteachers find that it is more than their duty to discredit the pretensions of the rich: it is their pleasure. They find it, however, rather nerve-racking as a daily task, and occasionally dangerous. These children talk back, and talk out of school.

Howard Becker, in a classic series of papers on the career-patterns of teachers in the Chicago public schools, makes it clear that the teachers in his sample come to prefer even the slum school, though they perceive it as a source of physical danger, to the school in which they must deal with upper-status children on their own home ground. These teachers preferred, and sought assignment to, schools with a pre-dominantly working-class clientele, where the children are docile, well-disciplined, and not threateningly smart in any sense of the word.

Beginning teachers usually fear assignment to the slum school as worst of all, but are placed there nevertheless, as beginners in all hierarchical systems are generally placed at the bottom. Once there, the teacher is likely to press for transfer to a working-class school. But if she cannot get it, she develops hegemony throughout the years in the slum school by making use of her superior social status and her growing familiarity with the informal social system of the school. As Becker puts it:

> These very adjustments cause her, at the same time, to fear a move to any new school, which would necessitate a rebuilding of these relationships and a complete reorganization of her work techniques and routine. The move to

[7] *Commentary*, November 1962, p. 43.

a school in a "better" neighborhood is particularly feared, desirable as it seems in the abstract, because the teacher used to the relative freedom of the "slum" school is not sure whether the advantages to be gained in such a move would not be outweighed by the constraints imposed by "interfering" parents and "spoiled" children and by the difficulties to be encountered in integrating into a new school structure.[8]

The teachers' fear in these and similar situations is that intrusion by the parents, even on legitimate grounds, will damage their authority position and make them subject to forms of control that are, for them, illegitimate—control by outsiders. This fear is greatest with high-class groups, who are considered quick to complain and challenge the school's authority. Such parents are regarded as organized and militant and, consequently, dangerous. In the lower-class school, on the other hand:

> We don't have any PTA at all. You see, most of the parents work; in most families it's both parents who work. So that there can't be much of a PTA.

These parents are not likely to interfere.

To illustrate this point, one teacher told a story of one of her pupils stabbing another with a scissors, and contrasted the reaction of the lower-class mother with that to be expected from the parents of higher status whose children she now taught:

> I sure expected the Momma to show up, but she never showed. I guess the Negroes are so used to being squelched that they just take it as a matter of course, you know, and never complain about anything. Momma never showed up at all. You take a neighborhood like the one I'm teaching in now, why, my God, they'd be suing the Board of Education and me, and there'd be a court trial and everything.

[8] Howard S. Becker, "The Career of the Chicago Public Schoolteacher," *American Journal of Sociology*, March 1952, p. 475.

It is because of dangers like this that movement to a school in such a neighborhood, desirable as it might be for other reasons, is feared.[9]

If this teacher is still at her desk, she may have noticed that the status, and the social behavior, of Chicago Negroes have changed in the fifteen years since she made the statement quoted. But this is beside the point, which is that the teachers in Becker's sample, though scornful of their slum charges, preferred them to children of greater gentility whose self-confidence and realistic sense of status made them hard to control or dominate. This does not establish that these teachers disliked high-status characteristics as such, though they certainly did not find them attractive; their reactions could simply have been a response to a threat to their authority. Becker, however, suggests that it was not simply this:

> Children of the upper group are felt hard to handle in some respects, and are often termed "spoiled," "overindulged," or "neurotic"; they do not play the role of the child in the submissive manner teachers consider appropriate. One interviewee, speaking of this group, said:
>
> > I think most teachers prefer not to teach in that type of school. The children are more pampered and, as we say, more inclined to run the school for themselves. The parents are very much at fault. The children are not used to taking orders at home and naturally they won't take them at school either.[10]

In this excerpt, authority is still the focus of the teachers' attention. But more is expressed than a fear of being worsted in a power struggle. There is also a note of moral judgment

[9] Howard S. Becker, "The Teacher in the Authority System of the Public School," *Journal of Educational Sociology*, November, 1953, pp. 128–141.

[10] Howard S. Becker, "Social Class Variations in the Teacher-Pupil Relationship," *Journal of Educational Sociology*, April, 1952, pp. 451–465.

and irritation, not directed just at the threat of disorder, but at the "pampered" children's inclination to run things for themselves; submissiveness is seen as a virtue as well as a convenience. This note of whining complaint and the values it expresses *are* anti-aristocratic; and Becker develops this point more specifically a bit further on in this article:

> Children from the "better" neighborhoods are considered deficient in the important moral traits of politeness and respect for elders:

> > Here the children come from wealthy homes. That's not so good either. They're not used to doing work at home. They have maids and servants of all kinds and they're used to having things done for them, instead of doing it themselves . . . Well, it's pretty difficult to deal with children like that.

> Further, they are regarded as likely to transgress what the teachers define as moral boundaries in the matter of smoking and drinking; it is particularly shocking that such "nice" children should have such vices.

• • • • •

> It is worth noting that the behavior of the "better" children, even when morally unacceptable, is less distressing to the teacher [than that of the slum children], who feels that, in this case, she can produce a reasonable explanation for the behavior. An example of such an explanation is the following:

> > I mean, they're spoiled, you know. A great many of them are only children. Naturally, they're used to having their own way, and they don't like to be told what to do. Well, if a child is in a room that I'm teaching he's going to be told what to do, that's all there is to it. Or if they're not spoiled that way, they're the second child and they never got the affection the first one did, not that their mother didn't love them, but

they didn't get as much affection, so they're not so easy to handle either.[11]

The note of compassion in this excerpt, though doubtless quite genuine, tends to conceal the ruthlessness with which clichés derived from popular versions of psychoanalytic thought are used to justify intervention in the affairs of youngsters with too much social skill to jeopardize themselves by overt breaches of school regulations, but who nevertheless behave in ways offensive to the school. Whether or not such youngsters are, in particular cases, neurotic, the invention of the "behavior problem" as an administrative category serves as a basis for impugning their character and increasing control over them. This is a useful device in dealing even with lower-status youngsters, since it permits the school administration to fall back upon a "guidance" position[12] if it lets hostility get out of hand; a boy who has been pushed around by an angry teacher can, for example, be turned over to the guidance counselor as "disturbed" if he protests. But it is an essential weapon in containing the divergent behavior of upper-status youth. It is effective, because it cuts off his access to alternative upper-status norms, acceptable to the community at large, that he might otherwise use to defend his conduct or his privacy. A student who might be willing and able to take his chances and, if necessary, his punishment for a clear-cut breach of regulations, as a part of the process of growing up and defining his relationship to authority, may well be intimidated by the prospect of being treated and filed as a case study in "need to defy authority" or "compulsive drive toward pseudo-maturity." All this goes in the record; it just isn't worth it. The more "understanding" attitude of the con-

[11] *Ibid.*
[12] Cf. Aaron V. Cicourel and John I. Kitzuse, *The Educational Decision Makers* (Indianapolis: The Bobbs-Merrill Co., 1963).

temporary school expresses something very different from acceptance or tolerance, and may, indeed, express a greater hostility than the overt punitiveness of earlier times. Certainly, it gives greater scope for the expression of whatever hostility exists.

Even Sexton's book, which is concerned primarily with the bias of the schools against lower-income students, includes one rather dramatic bit of evidence of teachers' distaste for, and avoidance of, upper-status students. While physical facilities of high schools in Big City (Detroit) steadily improve as the average income of the families whose children attend them rises, and student dropout rates as steadily fall, the absentee rate of teachers, as estimated from the proportion of classroom time covered by emergency substitutes, is twice as high in the school attended by the wealthiest students as in those in the next lowest income category, though this index, too, falls steadily as income rises through the rest of the range. There seems to be a "tip point" at which increased student affluence ceases to make the school more desirable to teachers and instead makes it much less desirable. The percentage of total teaching time covered by substitute teachers in the high schools in each of Sexton's income categories, in relation to other variables she considers, is given in the following table:[13]

Income group	No. of high schools in category	Average age of buildings	Ave. no. of facilities substandard or lacking	Annual proportion of dropouts	Percentage of teaching time covered by substitutes
I. ($5,000—)	5	45.0	23	19.2%	7.4%
II. ($6,000—)	3	38.0	19	15.8%	2.6%
III. ($7,000—)	4	18.5	14	7.9%	2.2%
IV. ($8,000—)	4	24.5	17	7.2%	1.5%
V. ($9,000—)	1	10.0	11	3.6%	2.9%

[13] Adapted from Sexton, *op. cit.*, Chapter 4.

Since there is only one school in the open-ended ($9,000—) category, it is perfectly possible that its remarkable unattractiveness to teachers could be due to some entirely idiosyncratic factor. It *is* remarkably unattractive, however; the proportion of substitutes, instead of being lower than in the preceding category, virtually doubles and is higher than in any category except that having the lowest-income students. And from the dropout rate the school is clearly not comparably unattractive to its students. Professor Sexton comments merely:

> School 17 has an unexpectedly high percentage of ESRP's [emergency substitute teachers] as compared with other high income schools. Whether true or not, it is at least *claimed* [italics hers] by many teachers that students in school 17 are "hard to handle"; because of this the school may have trouble holding qualified teachers and may have to accept ESRP's instead.[14]

These indications of anti-aristocratic bias should be interpreted in the light of the manifest economic bias of special programs for "the gifted child." As Sexton justifiably stresses, programs for gifted children overwhelmingly serve youngsters from more affluent families; in Big City about ten times as high a proportion of children from families with incomes over $7,000 per year as from families below that figure were chosen; and above $7,000 the rate approximately doubles with each $1,000 increment.[15] Considering that selection is made on the basis of IQ scores, this is hardly surprising in itself. But if a higher IQ, whatever it may be, is both regarded as a gift and strongly associated with high status, how can the school be called anti-aristocratic when it provides lavishly for the gifted?

The problem lies in the precise nature of the gift. IQ tests

[14] *Ibid.*, p. 212.
[15] *Ibid.*, p. 60.

reward a cognitive style that is especially bourgeois. While they demand a verbal facility and a familiarity with abstract symbolism and with the goods, services, and proper social attitudes of the middle class that make it very difficult for lower-status children to give the right answer, they also penalize any youngster who approaches the test with the stance of the amateur, however gifted. Fanciful, original, or unduly perceptive answers are wrong, as are those that ignore or reject the commonplace assumptions of middle-class daily life. When the test includes items like "Policemen are usually . . ." it isn't only lower-status children who pick answers like "down on kids" in preference to "glad to help us when we need them." To get the right answer you have to be not only middle class, but square.

For ambitious American youth, test-taking is a very serious business. The youngster to whom the high-IQ style comes most easily is the junior organization man, the specialist in goal-directed behavior. Nobody has to lash him to the mast to keep him from wandering off course. Except during civil-defense drills, he does not listen to the sirens. *These* are the students most likely to be classified as "gifted" and assigned to gifted-student programs. It is true that their parents are likely to be fairly rich, and that they themselves are likely to become even richer. But anything less like an aristocrat would be hard to imagine.

The most systematic examination of the high-IQ style in contrast to what might equally well be—but in school is not —regarded as giftedness is to be found in Jacob W. Getzels and Phillip W. Jackson's research study *Creativity and Intelligence; Explorations with Gifted Students.*[16] This study, though it deals directly with the point under discussion, is based on a seriously limited sample. The study was

[16] New York: John Wiley & Sons, 1962.

not made in a public school, or even in a typical residential private secondary school, but in a university-affiliated laboratory high school. The mean IQ of their entire sample was 129, so that an average or even a low IQ in their sample would still have appeared at the "gifted" end of the public school spectrum. Nevertheless, the work is a quite unparalleled source of insight into the distinctive characteristics of the high-IQ intellectual operation and the view of the world and the school to which it is related.

From a sample of 449 students, Getzels and Jackson selected 28 who were in the top 20 percent in IQ, but not in creativity, to compare with 26 who were in the top 20 percent in creativity, but not in IQ. Creativity scores were computed from the students' performance on measures of "divergent thinking," as J. P. Guilford[17] defines this term, in contrast to the "convergent" thinking demanded by conventional IQ tests. In many ways the tasks required by the creativity test were the exact converse of those IQ tests usually call for. Thus, where IQ tests commonly require the student to *select* the correct meaning of each word in a long list containing both familiar and recondite words from five given alternatives, the Guilford procedure requires the student to write as *many* different meanings as he can think of for each word in a short list of very familiar words like "sack" and "bolt"; the smaller forms of hardware are perhaps peculiarly useful as source words for this task. Where IQ tests require subjects to solve mathematical problems of increasing complexity by selecting the right answers from among a number of possible answers, the Guilford procedure supplies the subject with a small number of highly

[17] J. P. Guilford *et al., A Factor-Analytic Study of Creative Thinking:* I, Hypothesis and Description of Tests (Los Angeles: University of Southern California Press, 1951).

complicated sets of data, and gives credit for the number of different problems that the student can identify as capable of solution with these data and no more—but does not require him to work out the solution. The Guilford procedure, then, is designed to identify individuals with exceptionally flexible and varied approaches to problems, who are not "stimulus-bound" and limited to conventional categories of thought, and who cannot merely tolerate but make use of ambiguity in solving them. People who score well on such tests do so by attacking new situations from various and often quite-unexpected angles, though they may also seem less systematic and thorough than their colleagues who use the convergent, high-IQ style. The speech or writing of the "divergent" thinker is not only more colorful but richer in all allusions and connotations, often derived from preconscious or unconscious sources; there is less constriction—and sometimes less precision and order.

The fact that the intellectual processes underlying "divergent" and "convergent" thinking are converse and complementary *does not mean* that the two skills are opposed, or that a person who is good at one is likely to be poor at the other. Getzels and Jackson simply set up artificially a procedure that selected adolescents with contrasting cognitive styles, much as a biologist studying human metabolism might canvass the population for a sample of short, fat people to contrast with a sample of tall, thin ones, even though tall people usually weigh more than short.

It follows also that the practice of admitting students to programs for the gifted on the basis of IQ score does not exclude the creative; in fact, it probably leads to the inclusion of a much higher proportion of youngsters capable of "divergent thought" than is present in the total school enrollment. What it does is establish the cognitive style of the high-IQ as a *precondition* for being considered gifted. Unless a student is a good "convergent" thinker he is not treated as gifted, whatever other endowments he may have.

Getzels and Jackson's findings discredit this precondition. Both their high-IQ low-creative and their high-creative low-IQ groups did equally well on standardized subject-matter achievement tests (not school grades) and better than the total sample of students from which they had been selected. The teachers, however, preferred the high-IQ students to both the high-creatives and the general run of students when asked whom they would prefer to have in class. An indication as to why is given by another of Getzels and Jackson's experimental procedures.

They asked their subjects to make up stories in response to a series of pictures that were shown them—a standard psychological procedure derived from the familiar Thematic Apperception Test, though using different pictures. One of these was perceived most often as a man in an airplane reclining seat returning from a business trip or conference. A high-IQ subject gave the following story:

> Mr. Smith is on his way home from a successful business trip. He is very happy and he is thinking about his wonderful family and how glad he will be to see them again. He can picture it, about an hour from now, his plane landing at the airport and Mrs. Smith and their three children all there welcoming him home.

A high-creative subject wrote this story:

> This man is flying back from Reno, where he has just won a divorce from his wife. He couldn't stand to live with her any more, he told the judge, because she wore so much cold cream on her face at night that her head would skid across the pillow and hit him in the head. He is now contemplating a new, skid-proof face cream.

To find how the students themselves perceive their position in life and their teachers' expectations of them, Getzels and Jackson devised an instrument they called the Outstanding Traits Test. This consists of thirteen thumbnail descriptions of such traits as social skill, goal-directedness, and good marks, identified by phrases like "Here is the student who is best at getting along with other people," "Here is the student who is best able to look at things in a new way and discover new things," "Here is the outstanding athlete in the school," and so forth. The students in the experiment were asked to rank these thirteen descriptions in three different ways: "as preferred for oneself," as "favored by teachers," and "believed predictive of adult success." There was *complete agreement* in the rankings assigned by high-IQ and high-creative students on how these traits contributed to adult success; on what teachers preferred, the agreement was virtually complete—the correlation was 0.98. But the correlation between the two groups' ratings of the traits as "preferred for oneself" was only 0.41. This can only be interpreted to mean that one or both of these groups believed that pleasing teachers and becoming successful was just not worth what it cost, even though they agreed completely as to what the cost would be.

Which group rejected the image of success that both shared? The components of correlation *within* each group on the three possible bases of sorting answer this question very clearly.

Components of Correlation	High-IQ Students	High-Creative Students
Personal traits believed "predictive of success" and "favored by teachers"	0.62	0.59
Personal traits believed "predictive of success" and "preferred for oneself"	0.81	0.10
Personal traits believed "favored by teachers" and "preferred for oneself"	0.67	—0.25

Though both groups agree about what pleases teachers, neither believes that this is very likely to bring success in later life—yet, they also agree about what will do that. From the two other standard tests of the intensity of the urge for successful achievement,[18] Getzels and Jackson infer that both groups want success equally strongly; I would infer, therefore, that the high-creatives just cannot bring themselves to be what they believe success requires, and are even more strongly repelled by what the teachers demand. The high-IQ students are willing to come to terms with the school in order to succeed; the high-creatives are not.

It should be recalled that these are students in a private school run by a distinguished university noted for its intellectual emphasis; their teachers, presumably, are willing and able to work with such students. In a public school sample, the high-creatives would presumably have felt far more alienated and disaffected; and Getzels and Jackson's findings would apply *a fortiori*. But the importance of their study depends less on its general applicability than on the precision with which it permits us to identify the factor that gets rich or poor, bright or dull students into trouble with school and society.

The best name for this factor is something like "inwardness," or "subjectivity"; the capacity to attend to and respond to one's inner life and feelings, to the uniquely personal in experience, to personal relationships. This is not "inner direction"—there need be nothing rigid or puritanical about it; the superego in such people may be so weak as to be virtually nonexistent, though it may likewise be strong and commanding. Nor does this "inwardness" necessarily make

---

[18] Using David McLelland's "need : achievement" and Fred L. Strodtbeck's "V-score," they found no significant difference between the two groups, or between either and the total sample of 449 students; the high-creatives were actually slightly higher for both measures.

people who have it more self-directive or truly autonomous; it may, by leading them to a more vivid understanding of their existential plight, flood them with such severe and chronic anxiety as to make them almost unable to cope. Such "subjective" people are often unusually self-centered and self-indulgent, whimsical and eccentric, disagreeable and demanding. Yet, in their own way, they are peculiarly trustworthy; they are present, they connect, and they treat other people as people, rather than as things, even when they treat them badly.

"Subjective" people have very little use for the school, and vice versa. Particularly in adolescence, they are trying to realize and clarify their identity; the school, acting as a mobility ladder, assumes instead the function of inducing them to change or alter it. They want to discover who they are; the school wants to help them "make something out of themselves." They want to know where they are; the school wants to help them get somewhere. They want to learn how to live with themselves; the school wants to teach them how to get along with others. They want to learn how to tell what is right for them; the school wants to teach them to give the responses that will earn them rewards in the classroom and in social situations.

No social or economic class has a monopoly on "inwardness," and none is composed primarily of "inward" people. Millions of poor adolescents still welcome the help of the school in moving ahead in the world; thousands of rich but socially insecure adolescents rely on it to confirm them for life in the stance and the skills of the Big Man on Campus and in Corporation. But among the poor and such of the rich as may be called aristocratic, "inwardness" is at least recognized and tolerated as the basis for a possible human life-style; both the rich and the poor can conceive of better ways to spend their lives than in self-improvement, if only because the rich already have much of what they need and the poor have comparatively little expectation of getting it. The rich and the poor often speak different dialects of the same language that is quite different from middle-class speech: more sensuous and direct, coarse rather than vulgar; rich in nouns and sometimes verbs but poor in adjectives and qualifiers; less passive and less conditional. Evasions are objectionable. The rich and the poor more easily accept the fact that strong feelings, tender or hostile, are likely to be expressed in direct physical action.

The rich and the poor, in short, can sometimes tolerate and even enjoy direct access to and expression of their feelings and senses in a way that the middle classes regard as disorderly. In school, as our subjects' reluctance to send Scott Cowen or Johnny Adams on "The King's Visit" illustrates, such expressions of subjective passion are taken as evidence of poor socialization or illness: as immaturity or, in the language of the counselor's specialty, as contributing to "underachievement" by frittering away time and energy that could be put to better, or at least more social, use.

This concern about "underachievement" has reached pretty high levels. Cicourel and Kitzuse[19] discuss in detail its use by high school counselors to monitor competent but undeserving blithe spirits out of line for strategic college admissions in a primarily upper-middle-class suburban high school. But even more significant is the comparison, by Charles McArthur,[20] of Harvard students who are graduates of high schools with others with similar measured IQ's who had graduated from private schools, especially the archetypi-

[19] Cicourel and Kitzuse, *op. cit.*, Chapter 4: "The Bureaucratization of the Counseling System."

[20] Charles McArthur, "Subculture and Personality During the College Years," *Journal of Educational Sociology*, February 1960, pp. 260–261.

cal New England schools that are usually referred to, collectively and derisively, in the literature of educational sociology as "St. Grottlesex" schools. McArthur notes that this difference in secondary-school background is associated with striking contrasts in almost any psychological data that can be gathered about the two groups of students. McArthur does not attribute these contrasts to the influence of the schools, but to differences between the total pattern of upper-status and middle-status life of which school attendance is a part. This point, I think, is very important; because spokesmen for private schools defending their enterprises before a primarily egalitarian public speak as if they would like to obliterate many of these differences as snobbish. The fact that they persist and can be strikingly observed by the technics of experimental psychology, which are not of a poetic subtlety, attests to their vitality. They are rooted in a life-style that transcends the willingness of St. Grottlesex to play down its own distinction.

McArthur himself interprets these findings as a credit to the public high school, and the "core American values" it represents, for laying more stress on effort and achievement. The private school boys, he finds, tend to be very serious "underachievers" when compared to high school boys of the same IQ, especially in science and the quantitative disciplines; St. Grottlesex holds its own or excels a bit in the humanities. But their cognitive styles are so different that it may be misleading, he notes, to speak of them as having the same IQ; St. Grottlesex boys and the kind of high school boys who made it into Harvard in the late 1950's think totally differently:

> We have some evidence that, with the same IQ being obtained by both men, the private school boy will have more intellectual range and power for his speed, while the

life of the possible. . . . The world of today, the "now" world, is a world of concretes, of boundaries, of limited possibilities among which one can roam. But the "if" world is—the world of what might happen, the world of the possible rather than the world of the probable, and that is seen quite differently. For in the world of the possible, one might get the lucky breaks, or settle down for the training which is necessary. But for almost all the boys, the important world is the "now" world; when they think of the "if" world, they are aware that it is not "now" and they have to live immediately in the "now" world.[22]

These observations apply as well to Getzels and Jackson's high-creatives. In contrast, the success-oriented high-IQ lives in a "now" world and a "when" world, and the connection between them is very clear to him indeed. When the claim of one must be pressed against that of the other, the "when" world always wins. The rich less often have to choose; the "now" world can be vividly accepted and acted upon without much fear of future risk. When they do get into trouble it is likely to be through a sensationalism that grossly underestimates even that small risk. They commit violent *actes gratuits* that particularly offend public morality because they are purposeless—at worst a Leopold-Loeb case; more commonly the peculiar delinquency of wealth: drunken, sporadic, sadistic. Much of this sort of thing was formerly institutionalized and contained, if not controlled, in the college fraternity subculture; but even fraternities are now defensive about their exclusiveness and former Dionysian character, and are seeking to create a more purposeful, industrious, and egalitarian public image. Their undoubted

---

[22] S. M. Miller and Ira E. Harrison, "Types of Dropouts: 'The Unemployables,' " presented at the Annual Meeting of the American Orthopsychiatric Association, Washington, D.C.: March 1963.

guilt in rejecting first-rate candidates on racial or religious grounds may now be leading them reactively to underestimate the influence, and the significance, of previous—and prospective—conditions of servitude.

Our ideological commitment to equality of opportunity implies to us that the school is obligated to devote itself to a continuous search on behalf of that equality, while defining opportunity in such a way as to place it beyond the reach of privilege. It prevents us from seriously considering that any individual or special group may make us richer simply by being what it is. Yet, adolescence is a stage of life in which every human being must come to terms with his own being, his own divergence, and the meaning of his relationship to other individuals. The meanest and most-cringing sycophant, the blandest and slyest bureaucrat, were closer to being human in adolescence than they were ever to become again. Self-definition is the prime developmental task of adolescence; indeed, it is the process of adolescence itself. The animus directed against the "inward" and the "subjective" is directed against such elements in all youth. But these are the elements that make adolescence possible, and that lead to *personal* growth and maturity, to acceptance of life as a unique and momentous sequence of actively monitored experiences, each contributing to the richness and relevance of the next.

As we grow older and see the ends of stories as well as their beginnings, we realize that to the people who take part in them it is almost of greater importance that they should be stories, that they should form a recognizable pattern, than that they should be happy or tragic. The men and women who are withered by their fates, who go down to death reluctantly but with no noticeable regrets for life, are not those who have lost their mates prematurely or by perfidy, or who have lost battles or fallen from early promise in circumstances of public shame, but those who have been jilted, or were the victims of impotent lovers, who have never been summoned to command or been given any opportunity for success or failure. Art is not a plaything but a necessity, and its essence, form, is not a decorative adjustment, but a cup into which life can be poured and lifted to the lips and be tasted. If one's own experience has no form, if the events do not come handily to mind and disclose their significance, we feel about ourselves as if we were reading a bad book.[23]

I have found the life of the high school to be, in this respect, very often like a bad book; sentimental, extrinsically motivated, emotionally and intellectually dishonest. The animus is directed against those of the young who are too fully alive, too completely realized, to fit among its characters. They are disparaged; by its disparagement the school wastes its opportunity to help youngsters create a style suited to their romantic age. The essential first step in encouraging growth in adolescents is surely to link their new sexual energy and their occasionally flamboyant quest for identity to the meaningful larger aspects of past and present culture, which is what taste means and disciplined self-expression requires. If the baroque manifestations of adolescence elicit instead an attitude of sulky oppression, as they do in Milgrim or Hartsburgh, the adolescent is thrown back upon resources he has not yet developed. The school then grudgingly supports the numerous more conformist and emotionally dependent youth within the youth

[23] Rebecca West, *Black Lamb and Grey Falcon* (New York: The Viking Press, 1940), p. 55.

culture itself against the occasional youth who retains his exuberance; using them to help isolate him and deny him the only valid source of status: recognition that his actions and his work express a personal view of reality, for which only he can be responsible. In his ensuing despair, the school helps him—helps him to become assimilated within the "teen-age culture." In a little while, it is as if he had never been.

awareness, precise self-expression, and personal commitment lead to success, greater power, or higher status in this country. Executives do not seek such schools for their children, and children who go to such a school—if they can find one—are not likely to become executives. The youngsters in Getzels and Jackson's high-creative sample who saw no significant correlation between the personality factors that lead to success and those they desired for themselves were probably quite right, and the opportunity to cultivate the traits they desired for themselves through disciplined instruction would not advance their careers.

Yet, it is elite education in the sense that its goals and its functions were formulated and accepted by social groups secure enough to be more concerned with their present life and its meaning than with their future chances. It is elite education in the sense that it is to such education that people turn when they finally feel themselves in the position to seek learning as an end in itself, rather than as an instrument to be used in performing a service or gaining an advantage. It is also elite education in the invidious sense that self-direction and inwardness in our society are likely to be extremely costly. One might say of autonomy and spontaneity in an open, mass society what Pierpont Morgan said of his yacht: if you have to ask what it costs, you cannot possibly afford it. The kinds of people who want help in penetrating more deeply into the meanings of their lives and communicating that meaning to others while receiving in their turn a comparable intimacy and confidence are less likely to be members of a recognized elite than socially marginal, and often economically so as well. Intellectuals, as Karl Mannheim long ago suggested, generally are; complicity inhibits insight. For just this reason, those youngsters now classed as gifted would probably reject the kind of education I am discussing; it would lie within their range of competence, but it would not take them where they wish to go.

This kind of education is merely what we have always called liberal, in the sense of education appropriate to free men. These are fewer than might have been expected in the Free World, and most of its education is not, and is not intended to be, liberal. I have avoided using the term "liberal education" because the very conditions that have led so many to rank freedom low among the possible benefits of education have also caused them to define liberal education as if it did indeed refer to a "decorative adjustment" rather than to "a cup into which life can be poured, and lifted to the lips, and be tasted," to return to Rebecca West's earlier-quoted comment on the necessity for art and form. This trivial conception of liberal education is also the source of the false notion that liberal education and vocational education are in conflict. Since what a man is in our society is so largely defined both by himself and by others in terms of what he does for a living, vocational education is in fact an indispensable part of liberal education—the part on which everything else rests; its hindquarter. Whether vocational education strengthens liberal education or cripples it depends on the spirit in which it is undertaken. If it includes a rigorous analysis of what the job for which the student is preparing means to its holder and to society, it is liberalizing; if it merely trains the student in the techniques he will be expected to know and indoctrinates him in the ideology that will make him acceptable to his colleagues, it is like much teacher education, slavish.

For most students, in any case, the issue may no longer arise, because most people must expect to earn their living in jobs that permit no personal style, require no skill, and are often not worth doing. There is no way education can make such work meaningful, though education can deal with it liberally by scrutinizing the economic arrangements, and their underlying social and moral assumptions, that condemn people to do it. One can, however, blame too much on automation and even on our profit economy, archaic as it is. Part of the problem, surely, lies in the passivity which schools encourage in their determination not to demand anything that would put the "culturally deprived" at a further disadvantage or require their teaching staffs to transcend their present cultural limitations. Much automation—especially of services, as distinct from production—is undertaken because the machines have become more trustworthy than the people available for the post, even though people, if they wish to, can perform the service more efficiently. There is cold comfort in vending machines, but they are less unpleasant than surly or incompetent waitresses. Machines are incapable of the highest craftsmanship, but they can be trusted more safely not to fall below their built-in minimum.

Liberal education, then, includes vocational education; it must, because it must take full account of any factor so central to the lives of its students. What it cannot do is serve students who are interested in the job purely for external reasons. Liberal education cannot assist in the conscious pursuit of happiness or social mobility, though it may —or may not—lead those who cherish it within reach of these. Any fundamental improvement in American education, therefore, depends on weakening the present total connection in the minds of both students and teachers between schooling and economic opportunity. This means, of course, a reversal in the historic role of education in this country and a replacement of its traditional social function by one which has never been taken seriously before. Such reversals do not occur easily, naturally, or suddenly on a wide scale; and it would be totally unrealistic to expect public education to transform itself or to attempt to transform it. One may even argue quite reasonably, as Ralph Turner has, that in *any* mass, open society, what people generally expect of their schools will be almost completely determined by what they think the schools can do to help them get ahead in the world.[1] But even if this is true, it merely raises the more fundamental question of just what education can be worth, and to whom, in a mass, open society. One of the most objectionable features of such a society is precisely that it does lead people to expect nothing of education—and, indeed, to accept nothing from it—except assistance in getting on.

Certainly, this is what we *do* demand of education, and nearly all that we demand of it. From small-scale research studies to the decisions of the Supreme Court against segregation, this becomes the fundamental issue by which education is judged. Nearly fifteen years ago Joseph Kahl, in a study gemlike in its size and precision, demonstrated this quite clearly in the course of a major investigation of processes of social mobility in a New England city. From the large sample included in the study, Kahl selected just twelve pairs of bright, academically successful boys for more intensive scrutiny. All these were from the "common-man" level of society; their fathers were semiskilled workers or held minor white-collar posts. All were in the upper 25 per-

[1] Ralph H. Turner, "Sponsored and Contest Mobility in the School System." *American Sociological Review*, December 1960. Turner convincingly argues that striking contrasts between the British and American patterns of education reflect not a *different* conception of the function of education, but different approaches that have evolved to perform the same function—recruiting lower-status pupils into middle class—in two quite different societies. As these differences diminish, the two educational systems become increasingly similar.

cent of their high school class, and could reasonably have counted on admission to college in the Boston area. But Kahl selected twelve who had definitely decided *not* to go to college, for comparison to twelve others who had definitely decided that they would go.

He found that the only factor that distinguished between the members of his two groups was their attitude toward social advancement. The boys who were headed for college were seeking a better job and a better position in life than their parents had; those who had decided not to continue on to college expected to find a place near their present social level. They were not altogether contented there; they expressed vague longings and occasional feelings of dissatisfaction with their lot as common men. But they had elected not to break out of the network of social and human relationships that had become familiar and enjoyable to them and face the hazards of a new way of life and the adaptations that this would have demanded.

Kahl also found that the role of the school in affecting their decision was secondary, though essential. It was the attitude of the boys' families that made the difference, though the school had been instrumental in bringing the superior potential of their son to the families' attention. In some cases Kahl reports that the brother of a boy in his sample who was going on to college had received no encouragement from the school, and hence none from his family, and was settling down to his accustomed life. "I suppose they figure," one of the boys remarked calmly, "if ya got it, ya got it; if ya haven't, ya haven't."

But to none of these able boys of "common-man" status had the school suggested that they might get anything out of education except greater social and economic opportunity. This was true *both* of those who had decided to continue and of those who had decided against it. "School and the possibility of college," Kahl reports, "were viewed by all the boys as steps to jobs. None was interested in learning for the subtle pleasures it can offer; none craved intellectual understanding for its own sake. . . . There were no cases in which the boy found in schoolwork sufficient intellectual satisfactions to supply its own motivation. And there were no cases where a sympathetic and understanding teacher had successfully stimulated a boy to high aspirations."[2]

In a study of "The Psychodynamics of Social Mobility in Adolescent Boys," published in 1958 by Elizabeth Douvan and Joseph Adelson,[3] there is further evidence that only the upwardly mobile boy is likely to find that school and society have anything much to offer him. I find this work particularly interesting because its authors write from a value-position expressly contradictory to mine, and are concerned with somewhat different issues. They note:

> . . . a general disposition to treat *upward* mobility in a vaguely invidious fashion. It would seem that, in this country, the Horatio Alger tradition and the "dream of success" motif have been pervasive and distasteful enough to have alienated, among others, a good many social scientists. The upwardly aspiring individual has apparently become associated with the pathetic seeker after success or with the ruthless tycoon. This image of success is, much of it, implicit—assumption and attitude, and not quite conviction— but it seems to have dominated the thinking of our intellectual community.

Except, I trust, for the imputation of vagueness, and the fact that I associate success in America with shiftiness more

[2] Joseph A. Kahl, "Educational and Occupational Aspirations of 'Common-Man' Boys." *Harvard Educational Review*, Summer 1953.

[3] *Journal of Abnormal and Social Psychology*, 56, 1958, pp. 31–44.

than with ruthlessness, this admonition applies quite justly to the present discussion. Douvan and Adelson interpret their findings as providing a rebuttal of this point of view, and—especially since they deal specifically with adolescents —their argument must be carefully considered. Douvan and Adelson interviewed a thousand high school boys fourteen to sixteen years old, asking them these two questions:

What kind of work would you like to do as an adult?
Are you pretty sure about this or do you think that you're just as likely to go into something else?

Other "open-ended questions and projective questions were used, and interviews lasted from one to three hours. . . . Each boy's aspiration was classed on the occupational scale and compared to his father's position to determine whether it was equivalent to, or higher or lower than, the father's job in the hierarchy of skills and status."

Since Douvan and Adelson quite correctly eliminated from their subsequent statistical analysis boys whose fathers held professional and managerial or unskilled jobs, on the grounds that these subjects, in the nature of the case, *could* show aspiration in only one direction and would therefore artificially distort the findings, they reduced their sample size to 518. Of these, 183 were the sons of white-collar workers, and 335 of "manual skilled" workers. This sample, then, is occupationally very similar to that from which Kahl's 24 boys were drawn. Douvan and Adelson classified 277, or over 53 percent of these boys, as aspiring to a higher-rated position than that of their father; 168, or just over 32 percent, as "stable" in their aspirations; and 73, or 14 percent, as wanting to do work that would class them as downward-mobile.

In nearly every respect the upward-mobile boys were

better adjusted and more effective members of their current
society than the downward-mobile:

> These boys seem humorless, gauche, disorganized—rela-
> tively so, at least. Perhaps the most telling and poignant
> datum which the study locates is their response to the
> possibility of personal change, their tendency to want to
> change intractable aspects of the self, and the degree of
> alienation revealed by their desire to modify major and
> fundamental personal qualities . . . the boy[s] give evidence
> of an ambivalent tie to the parents, a mixture of overt
> dependence and covert aggression.

The upward-aspiring boys, in contrast, showed greater self-
sufficiency; trust in, and tolerance of, their parents; participated in and enjoyed more activities; dated more; read more
and better materials; and showed, in general, what Douvan
and Adelson call a "higher energy level." It seems that the
potentially downward-mobile boys, though afraid to excel
or differ from their parents, also resent them and blame
them for contributing to their passivity and sense of failure.

All this is undoubtedly true. I have already cited evidence
that the mental health of low-status youngsters tends to be
much poorer than that of higher-status youngsters.[4] In view
of the findings of Richard Centers,[5] Kinsey in his familiar
studies of sexual behavior and attitudes, and others that
people assume the characteristics of the social class to which
they aspire rather than those of the class to which they
objectively belong, it is hardly astonishing that both the
low-aspiring and high-aspiring youngsters should already re-

[4] James V. Mitchell, Jr., "Identification of Items in the California Test
of Personality that Differentiate Between Subjects of High and Low
Socio-Economic Status at the Fifth and Seventh Grade Levels," *Journal
of Educational Research*, December 1957.
[5] *The Psychology of Social Classes* (Princeton: Princeton University
Press, 1949).

semble the people with whom they identify. On a common-sense basis, too, one would expect both groups of youngsters to be feeling the effects of their own self-fulfilling prophecy, in euphoria or in depression as the case may be. But I hardly see how these findings constitute a compelling argument that for a youngster to wish to advance in the world is in itself a fine thing—or even the normal thing, apart from the value the society places upon it. What is normal is to want what the prevailing values of the society establish as desirable, while it is invariably distressing and frightening to feel fundamentally at odds with the milieu in which one must live.

There is, in short, a circular ambiguity in Douvan and Adelson's findings that they do not resolve. Are their downward-aspiring boys downward-aspiring, as they conclude, because life and family background have made them sad sacks? Or are their despondency and *maladresse* attributable to their increasingly poignant awareness, as they grow older, that what they want they are unlikely to get without being severely punished for wanting it? Both, undoubtedly; but they would not be so certain of punishment or abandonment if their schools and their society were less completely preoccupied with self-advancement, and less completely disparaging of those who prefer security and stability.

Douvan and Adelson's findings, in fact, suggest that social stability does not occur as a *distinct* possibility to the adolescents in their sample. On nearly all their indices, the boys who aspire to jobs similar in status to those held by their fathers simply fall between the upward- and downward-aspiring youths; though one would expect the "stable-aspiring" boys to show a distinct pattern of their own if their aspirations represented a specific, positive attachment to a familiar style of life. The "downward-aspiring" young-

sters, after all, can hardly regard lower status and impover-
ishment as desirable in themselves, and one would expect
boys who saw such a future for themselves to have some
special difficulty. It is astonishing that the proportion who
did was as high as one-seventh, and almost a foregone conclusion that these would be anxious and troubled. The
"stable-aspiring" boys ought to have been different from
them in kind, rather than degree, if stability itself were what
appealed to them.[6]

Douvan and Adelson's data include two hints—and only
hints—that it may be. They cite no tests of statistical significance in comparing their "stable" group to either of the
others, so one cannot judge the probability that these differences may be due to chance. But out of nearly a hundred
comparisons made, only two show the "stable" group falling
well outside the range set by the "upward"- and "down-
ward"-aspiring youths. Fifty-nine percent of the "stable"
group said that they "particularly enjoyed" half or more
of the activities in which they participated, as compared
to 55 percent of the "upwards" and only 41 percent of the
"downwards." And 78 percent of the "stables" thought that
the most important reason for selecting a job was that it was
interesting, as compared to 70 percent of the "upwards"
and 58 percent of the "downwards." Both these suggest that
the "stables" find positive rewards in their lives that they
wish to retain.

But if they do, they are working against the purposes of
the school and the expectations of society. The primacy

[6] Kahl's sample, who appeared calmer and more rational in their choice
to retain their present status, *were* different, in that they were well-
enough adapted to the school they attended to have placed into its upper
quartile; an achievement which, one suspects, would have been beyond
the ability of many of the "stables" in Douvan and Adelson's academically unselected population.

in the public mind of the school's mobility function need not be inferred simply from the research reports of social scientists. It is explicit in the Supreme Court decision contravening school segregation, and this is a fact of the greatest importance in assessing the influence integration is likely to have on the social function of American education. Integration has become such a popular rallying point for liberal thought in this country, and the injustices against which it is directed are so serious and so manifest, that even scholarly discussion of it tends to resolve itself into slogans. But the form the struggle for school integration has assumed from the beginning, had it not been obscured by the urgency of the moral imperatives that surround it, would have revealed that its central issue was not racial, but a basic question about the priority to be assigned among the schools' social functions. It could not have been otherwise; for, if we have indeed abandoned the slander that Negroes are genetically inferior, then we must agree that the problems that arise in connection with integration originate entirely in the invidious social status which has been assigned to Negroes in this country.

Integration then simply brings forward—massively, and in politically explosive terms—our chronic conflict among the services different social classes demand of the public schools. The fact that the victims of discrimination are Negro, and have been victimized on racial grounds, makes their position morally unassailable; the extraordinary self-discipline and awareness of themselves as a separate social group which segregation has imposed upon them and the militance and capacity for direct aggression which they have been helped to retain by their exclusion from middle-class status make them politically irresistible. Their challenge is the first major moral demand to be made on our society during this century; and the example has provided a salutary contrast to the wheeling and dealing that constitutes our usual political style, though this refreshing innovation seems to be passing as the conflict moves into more advanced stages and integration leaders make use, in their turn, of more flexible and sophisticated political and public-relations techniques. But the conflict is nevertheless essentially a class conflict, and the issue on which it is drawn is that of equality of opportunity. Integration, then, raises acutely the question of the place of equality of opportunity in the hierarchy of values to which education can contribute. "Jobs and freedom; freedom and jobs!" the demonstrators led by CORE and SNCC chant; for most of the demands of the Negro movement are made in terms of freedom. Yet, "whoever demands of freedom more than freedom itself is born to be a slave," de Tocqueville observed, though it is perhaps too much to expect the validity of his point of view to be apparent to a people who have actually been subjected to that experience.

Whatever their historical source, the differences that distinguish white and Negro Americans today are largely social-class differences, which disappear when members of the same social class are compared. But most Negroes and whites are members of different social classes. Most Negroes have been retained by discrimination in lower-class positions; those who have escaped, up to now, have most often been individuals of extraordinary quality who skipped over the "common-man" level, proceeding rapidly to positions of distinction in the arts, in academic posts, and, more recently, in federal bureaucracies. Most whites, however, in our affluent society, have washed ashore at the "common-man" level without having to show much in the way of special characteristics; in Ortega's sense, quoted earlier, they are truly mass and resist nothing so strongly as being forced to define and affirm the purpose of their own existence.

This is a serious difference, with serious consequences, especially for education. Although the "common man," under our ideology, is expected to "better himself," this betterment does not obligate him to become more aware of himself and his own reality, or to take more responsibility for his own being. If he did so, he would cease to be "mass" and would jeopardize his role in a mass society; he would not "advance." The school, therefore, avoids challenging the values and assumptions underlying the "common-man" pattern, leaving its students to pick up the fashions of higher status as they need them, and to treat these as "decorative adjustments" to life at a higher level. For the present, while in school, the shabby-genteel life is exactly what the students are required to enjoy.

Integration is therefore likely to have a curious effect on the public school's already feeble power and irresolute will to help people understand the meaning of their lives and become more sensitive to the meaning of other people's lives. There may well be a net gain; there is certainly very little to lose.

Clearly "common-man" children — mostly white — and lower-class children—mostly Negro—cannot very well become more sensitive to the meaning of one another's lives or relate to one another if they never meet. Unfortunately, the best evidence we have on intergroup relations indicates strongly that contact between different groups results in increased understanding and acceptance between them only if they share a common culture to begin with. If the two groups contrast strongly in their styles of life the result is likely to be antagonism and increased stereotypy and misunderstanding: the middle-aged tourist returns to Gopher

Prairie from his first trip to Europe more than ever convinced that you can't drink the water and that only his continual vigilance kept thieves from stripping him of his luggage. This is especially true if the encounter is forced. World War II probably prolonged Midwestern Anglophobia by a decade. It not only confirmed the impression GI's had been gathering since childhood from the Chicago *Tribune*, it convinced them that, unlike most of what the *Tribune* complained of, the British actually existed. Nor did actual experience with the GI substantially reduce anti-American feeling among the British.

What usually happens, in fact, is that stereotypy is increased by selective observation and self-fulfilling prophecy, whether it be favorable or unfavorable. Groups of widely disparate status see in one another what they expect to see; they do not notice conflicting evidence. Whether lower-class Negro children will find the hostility of threatened and snobbish middle-class whites harder to bear than the solicitude of young liberals determined to help them solve their problems only Jules Feiffer, perhaps, knows. But neither group is likely to feel that members of the other see them as they see themselves.

Members of social groups that are uncomfortable with one another, as lower-class and middle-class people often are, work out technics of avoidance and rituals for keeping unavoidable encounters smooth and superficial; they do not become intimate. Traditional Japanese politeness, for example, is not a form of friendliness. It is a way of avoiding friction on an overcrowded island whose population has been made culturally very heterogeneous by rapid but uneven technological change. If the politeness holds, and there are no incidents, people may begin to step out of role and explore one another as individuals; but first, the cultural differences between them must be reduced below the shock level.

Our tendency to see in people what we expected to find and our devices for maintaining social distance from groups we fear have always limited the effectiveness of the public school in bringing children of different ethnic or class groups into real contact with one another, though this is one of the major claims made for comprehensive public education. Furthermore, the school does this less and less effectively as it becomes more and more heterogeneous and egalitarian.

The high school today is a far less exclusive place than it was when most of us were in it. The present furor over school dropouts is not a result of any increase in the proportion of youngsters who do not finish school, but the fact that there is no place for the dropout to go in our economy. Among American adults, age is quite consistently *negatively* related to the level of schooling completed; the older an American is, the more likely he is to have dropped out of school early. But those who remained were more likely to have found the school clublike and personal: to feel that they knew, understood, and liked or disliked their classmates and could trust one another.

As the school has become more heterogeneous, it has also become more liberal ideologically. Not only are the people in it more likely to be strangers, they are more likely to be cultural relativists and to feel that they have no right to uphold their own values and folkways, even though they do not really accept any other. The nineteenth-century middle-class English tourist who enjoyed Paris partly because it was full of interesting foreigners too ill informed to know that what they called *un cheval* was, in fact, a horse has vanished, to be replaced by grantholders so eagerly homeless in their transit that they can no longer distinguish bread from pain.

Under these circumstances students of contrasting social status, as in Milgrim, respond to one another with distant, generalized, potentially hostile uneasiness. The middle-class youngsters have far too little confidence in themselves to respect the lower-status youngsters in their human wholeness, with good qualities and bad. They vaguely dismiss them as a threat—"the hoody element"—and wish they were not there. They do not profit from the lower-status kids' more confident sexuality and concrete practicality, or learn from them when direct, violent action is more appropriate and legitimate than filing a petition. Nor do they get on good enough terms with the lower-status youngsters to be able to tell them, when the occasion warrants, to scrub up and calm down. The lower-status youngsters reject out of hand the social skills that the middle-class kids possess, and the comparative ease with which they handle symbols and get places on time—their genuine and useful administrative sense—and likewise never get close enough to shake or coax the middle-class kids out of their cool noncommittal stance for the sake of the greater warmth they might share.

But not only do the youngsters usually refuse to make real personal contact across class lines, the superficially pleasant but essentially noncommittal ways they evolve for dealing with each other without getting involved also inhibit them from making intense commitments or deep friendships with others of their own background. Some schools actively discourage cliques based on "mere friendship"; public schools commonly require that any official school organization be open to any student in good standing. Cliques continue to dominate the informal social structure of the school,[7] and school administrations, for practical political reasons, may be reluctant to intervene in the affairs of those composed chiefly of higher-status youngsters. But the youngsters nevertheless know that their relationships are disapproved as undemocratic and become guilty and defiant about their own exclusiveness; the members lose, or never develop, confidence in their right to choose their own friends, and their clique then becomes a more exclusively political instrument than it otherwise would have been. Fraternities are outlawed, or choose to operate informally without school recognition rather than surrender their right to choose their members, or they turn themselves into the equivalent of service clubs and send their pledges out on dreary missions of impersonal philanthropy instead of risking the intimacy of hazing them. The school encourages extensive social contact, but discourages intensive relations between small numbers of self-selected individuals.

Undoubtedly, this is an effective way of making the young ready for easy social and geographical mobility. But it makes the high school as impersonal as a waiting room. It combines the costly, well-appointed discomfort of the airport terminal with the atmosphere of a bus station. Waiting rooms are neither really middle class nor really lower class, nor are they compromises between the two. Their style is residual; everything that would be meaningful to either class is removed, along with anything that might make people too comfortable and get them to thinking they owned the place.

---

[7] James S. Coleman, *The Adolescent Society* (New York: The Free Press of Glencoe, 1961), especially Chapter VII, "Structures of Association and Their Relations to the Value-Systems."

Personal relationships do not flourish in this climate. Even friends and lovers become rigid and self-conscious in their anxiety to be on their way.

The crucial lack of our society is not opportunity but intimacy. There is nothing it needs less, at the present time, than another wave of status-striving and a further alteration of its social institutions—especially the schools—to accommodate it. Already, we have become a people at once casual and sly; searchers for angles who discard one another like old Kleenex after use. We must take time to settle down and learn to use our affluence and our leisure to redefine ourselves and reform our institutions—and, to some extent, the other way round.

In short, one of our most urgent needs is for more gentlemen. The term is no longer taken seriously; the species is on the verge of extinction. Our grubby, puritan prejudice against the whole idea of a gentleman and our extravagant willingness to excuse defects of craftsmanship in self-made men have blinded us to the fact that gentlemen were not parasites; they had a social function as defenders and exemplars of liberty, properly called civil. These were the people who really did have middle-class values in the sense of keeping their word, doing their job as they understood it, and having too much confidence in their present position in life to wish to evacuate it in quest of a better one.

Integration ought to open up to our society a whole new source of gentlemen. If few Negroes in our society have been permitted to become gentlemen, a very large proportion of such few gentlemen as survive are Negroes. Indeed, one hardly ever encounters examples of aristocratic bearing among any other contemporary Americans. Who have there been besides Dr. King, the murdered Medgar Evers, and a small band of less familiar patriots? Is there a living white man who shows any of the qualities of John Adams or Thomas Jefferson? Conservative, today, means someone like Barry Goldwater.

Negroes have so much more often developed and retained an aristocratic personal style and sense of responsibility, I believe, primarily because they have been excluded from the pettier temptations of the opportunity structure; it hasn't been worth their while to sell out; and by the time they reach maturity they can no longer be offered what they know they are worth. Yet there have been enough exceptions in public life to suggest that, granted equally degrading conditions, Negroes are no better than whites. It is just those conditions that a pattern of integration which emphasizes the use of the public schools as a means of making up for lost economic opportunity is most certain to reinforce.

The more hysterical segregationists sound as if they expected integration to result in violent assaults on public decency, making the schoolroom what the New York subway has already become. The very contrary is the case; integration, if undertaken with enough vigor and determination to seem real, will eliminate Negro violence and misbehavior in schools, though it may arouse a few last-ditch outbursts from disaffected whites. What disturbs me is quite a different probability.

The indoctrination of Negroes with the values already dominant in the school, and accommodating them in the lower reaches of the status structure, may well inundate us further with yet another wave of presumptuous, conscientious minor functionaries who will be the more oppressive for having been worse insulted. I neither fear nor expect to meet Negro hoodlums. But I do not relish encountering a newly recruited army of internal-revenue agents, assistant principals and assistant district attorneys, librarians, social workers, and teachers, thirsting for compensation, advancement, and respectability. This might be just; but it would certainly be extremely unpleasant. Former prisoners make bad jailers, though they sometimes make good judges.

Most Negro leaders would doubtless be proud to relinquish their moral advantage for the sake of more widespread opportunity and greater social equity; and this is understandable. But there may be a real conflict of interest here between what the Negro leadership wants and what the nation needs from it. From being a burden on the conscience of America, the Negro leadership has gone on to become, as well, the conscience itself. We have seen people sustaining beatings, imprisonment, and murder—and also fighting back—because they knew their dignity required it. One would hope that this spectacle has reminded the spectators—which is all most of us have been—of what dignity is, though there isn't much evidence, in the form of a changed spirit in our daily life, that it has. What is certain is that this has been an exotic spectacle, quite unlike anything to be seen, so far, in suburbia. When it ends, as such conflicts must in our society, in committee, there is a real sense of loss; the subsequent claims of progress, though valid, sound hollow and sickly.

Is this, then, to be yet another struggle over access to suburbia? Do the chants of "Freedom! Freedom!" refer to freedom to live in little boxes and go to summer camp and then to the university? It is presumptuous for a member of a social group that can take these things for granted to question their value to people who have been denied them; and I do not mean to suggest that it would be possible—much less desirable—to transform the Negro from the role of untouchable to that of a priestly caste, thus preserving segregation on an honorific rather than a pejorative basis.

But this is undoubtedly our society's last chance to transfuse into itself a stream of people whose moral vision has been—relatively, at least—preserved and sharpened by exclusion from opportunities for self-betrayal as well as self-advancement. The Negro is the only American whose loyalty to his country has not made him an accomplice in a succession of dubious enterprises from Cuba to Southeast Asia. If the vision of the Negro leadership is sometimes distorted by hatred, it is seldom blurred by guilt and the need to rationalize past policy.

Integration, by devices like "in-busing" and reverse quotas, is designed to assimilate the Negro into mass culture: to make him, indeed, a part of "all that which sets no value on itself—good or ill—based on specific grounds, but which feels itself 'just like everybody' and nevertheless is not concerned about it." This, if effective, will squander the last aristocratic element that might have countervailed, however feebly, against the severe and debilitating demosis that now cripples our culture. Abraham Lincoln's familiar observation that God must have loved the common people best because he made so many of them seems less self-evident than it must have when he made it. The demographic changes wrought by the passage of a century are enough to suggest that Mr. Lincoln's comment may have encouraged God to excessive zeal. It is difficult to accept mass society as evidence of Divine Love.

The schools, in any case, have a more specific social function than to assist and offer Him guidance in His mission. That function is the respectful and affectionate nurture of the young, and the cultivation in them of a disciplined and informed mind and heart. Schools are not primarily instruments for the redress of social and economic grievances, or escalators on which the victims of injustice and discrimination may be brought to parity, much as these are needed. Yet—though I do not want to overstate the case—it is precisely among the presently "underprivileged" and "culturally deprived," Negro and white, that I would expect to find most of those who would be benefited by a more aristocratic education. The converse of this statement is not true; most of the "culturally deprived" would probably find aristocratically run schools very little, if any, more congenial than they do the present ones, though the things that "bugged" them would be quite different. But a very large proportion of those students now in public school who would find a more aristocratically-run school better suited to their needs might, I believe, be drawn from among the most disadvantaged.

A bright slum child, whatever his race, is likely to fare much better at Hotchkiss or Choate[8] than in a school like Milgrim, provided he has the money to maintain himself while he is there and the technical skills and study habits to do what the curriculum requires. The first can be provided and the second can be developed more easily in a protected atmosphere. The characteristics that threaten high school teachers and expose the lower-status child to the rejection or derision of his classmates are more likely to arouse inter-

[8] This certainly depends, however, on the assumption—which may well be false—that Hotchkiss and Choate accept their own functional aristocracy. I have not derived any observations comparing the social climates of private and public secondary schools from my own research, because two private schools, neither of them very typical, would be an absurd sample from which to generalize. We did try to extend the study to several of the St. Grottlesex schools, but they refused us politely, I suspect both because they dislike having brain watchers intrude on their students and because they are snobbish about education professors. There is, after all, something to be said for both points of view. The private schools that we did include, however, seemed to be bending over backward to be more democratic than the public schools—though the *students* in the private boarding school were more frequently concerned with their own distinction, fought bitterly with the administration, and fantasied that they would have more freedom in public school.

est and win him distinction in an upper-status environment, where social attitudes are generally more liberal and lower-class competition is on the whole too remote to be felt as a threatening encroachment. The teachers, like the students, are less frequently themselves fugitives from the working class, and less likely to use their energy and instructional time imposing "common-man" patterns of language and behavior on "culturally deprived" students for their own good. The adjustment from lower-status to upper-status standards is in many ways far less severe than from either status to the standards of the "common man"; there are tremendous differences in usage but the basic style is much the same: more subjective, forceful, and warlike; less bureaucratic and inclined to qualify; more concerned with the present and less with the future. Whether these are qualities or defects is a matter of individual judgment and depends on the context in which they are displayed and the total state of society. The traits and behavior that are stigmatized as delinquent in street gangs bent on organizing conflict become qualities of aggressive leadership when displayed in the corporate board room, where the steady decline in *machismo* seems to be going too far.

The slum, then, is a most promising source to canvass for youngsters who have already begun to develop the foundations of an aristocratic bent. There are serious difficulties, to be sure, in trying to develop that bent even in good schools. I am not referring here to technical problems like "poor study habits," or those like "low level of motivation," that are used to explain "underachievement" in "culturally deprived" children as if they were innate to the children themselves rather than aspects of their relationship to the school they are obliged to attend. I mean more stubborn aspects of the culture itself. The better private schools now deprecate their aristocratic function and undermine it in efforts to be more equal than anybody—not merely in their admissions policies, which is a good thing as far as it goes, but in maintaining an atmosphere of austerity and a dedication to what the late J. P. Marquand, with tongue in cheek, called "The Social Future of the Harvard Man in the Free World of Tomorrow." The primarily upper-middle and upper-status suburban public high schools, like Cicourel and Kitzuse's Lakeshore, have responded to parents' anxieties about getting their sons and daughters into college by becoming citadels of bureaucratic manipulation. There are no schools in this country that proudly maintain an aristocratic ambiance. "American schools," Martin Mayer justly observes in *The Schools*:

> are always going to promote middle-class values because the national community they serve is overwhelmingly middle-class in orientation and even in "self-image." It is more than a little unrealistic to expect teachers who are fighting hard for recognition as "professionals" to cultivate in their classroom the values of an unprofessional subgroup in the community.[9]

This is as true of aristocratic as of lower-status values; and indeed, there is something inherently adaptive and ambitious about institutionalized formal education as such. Even the vaunted British public schools, though popularly accepted as a symbol of upper-class education, came into power not to serve the aristocracy but to train the expanding middle class to fill the posts of the civil and military services required to man an expanding empire. As Matthew Arnold sadly observed,[10] aristocracies have no interest and develop

[9] New York: Harper & Row, 1961, p. 117.
[10] In *Culture and Anarchy* (1869). Quoted in *Passages from the Prose Writings of Matthew Arnold*, William E. Buckler, ed. (New York: New York University Press, 1963), p. 86.

little skill in handling general ideas—in this, too, they resemble lower-status groups more than they do the middle classes. But the British model did undertake to imbue these middle-class aspirants with a sense of style and personal integrity on an aristocratic model.

A further difficulty—this time an ideological one—results from the fact that only a small proportion of "culturally deprived" American youth could soon be placed in the kinds of schools that might best nurture their latent aristocratic potential. There are few such schools, and it takes time to develop them. It takes a reasonable degree of initial self-confidence to profit from them; they can easily and swiftly train up the illiterate but not those who feel themselves already defeated. Such schools can manage very nicely with children who have been brought up—or not brought up—to swear and fight; but not those who have learned to cringe and slink. No school could continue to benefit "culturally deprived" children if it accepted so many as utterly to alter its own character. Any attempt to locate among slum children those with greatest unimpaired aristocratic potential and groom them would constitute in itself a form of inequality of educational opportunity. Though in the nature of the case such a canvass would tend, as far as it went, slightly to offset the effects of earlier deprivation, it would, in principle, bestow an educational privilege, albeit among members of a social group that had thus far been stringently denied it.

So be it. I am not seeking to eliminate privilege, but to create it and distribute it more intelligently—not necessarily more equitably—than the exigencies of race and economic opportunity have done. I am not trying to be fair, or to identify and reward the most deserving, but to find educational means for sponsoring and nurturing more trustworthy and humane people than those among whom our lives now seem destined to be spent, and spent utterly. There are no serious technical difficulties in locating the slum adolescents to be singled out to receive this special favor, should they wish to undertake the difficult and protracted task of accepting it. The techniques used by Getzels and Jackson to identify the creative can easily be modified to select adolescents whose heads, though bloody, are unbowed. Indeed, they can usually be identified by a cursory examination of school records. They are not, of course, the youngsters whom the school favors or who have good records—those are the gifted. Neither are they the most consistent troublemakers, who are likely to suffer so severely from a compulsive need to behave defiantly, and from severely eroded self-esteem, as to be even more rigidly conformist than the gifted, and even less promising. But the records also show which students have a sprinkling of good grades despite a low citizenship rating, which youngsters have been disciplined for offenses that require superior imagination and executive ability to conceive and perpetrate, which have in their folders, among a preponderance of adverse clinical and academic judgments, occasional enthusiastic reports from teachers who themselves failed to get tenure. These are the ones to look for.

But once identified, these youngsters could not, I believe, be nurtured within the limitations of the public school system in its present form, for reasons I have already discussed. If education is not to go on making adolescents "mass" more and more thoroughly and destructively, the young and the schools must be given a wider range of alternatives with respect to one another. The young must not be compelled to submit to year after year of education that denatures them. The schools must not be compelled to accommodate the hordes of youngsters unqualified by earlier experience to participate in its specialized educational functions, and to permit them to disrupt those functions for which they are unqualified and in which they see no value. The young must not be worn into submission, during their most vulnerable and crucial years of growth, to the ignoble view of life that dominates the schools. They must not be constrained to relinquish the precise and significant image of themselves that can only be developed when personal experience is privately explored under conditions of trust and intimacy.

Basically, then, I disapprove of compulsory school attendance in itself. I see no valid moral reasons to single out the young for this special legal encumberance. The economic reasons are compelling enough; but they are likewise contemptible. A people have no right to cling to economic arrangements that can be made halfway workable only by imposing an infantile and unproductive status on adolescents and indoctrinating them with a need for trashy goods and shallow, meretricious relationships that they know to be degrading. There are social reasons, too; the family has lost many of its functions through adaptation to social change and now has no more place for its young than any other social institution has and no real basis for dealing with them. If the children were not in school, many parents would go mad; and the schools, for all their defects, are more orderly and safer places, with a little more care and better food, than many homes.

Nevertheless, I find it odd that children should be confined because adults are incompetent to design, or too grossly impaired emotionally to accept and operate, a society that works. It is, I would very strongly stress, the *compulsory* feature alone that I object to. Public education, in the sense of a system of publicly supported schools open without charge to any student who wishes to attend them, is not a debatable issue. I should like to see the schools supported more lavishly so that they might function as an amenity as well as a social obligation; and to hire what we used to call a better class of people to operate them.

I do not believe that a school should be required to admit students who are not, in the professional judgment of its staff, qualified for the kind of work it offers; and I do believe that the state has an obligation to provide a substantial service to all its youth, even the least qualified. There does come a point at which one either ceases to call the institution that provides the service a school or admits that the word has no meaning except that of a place specially intended for young people. Be that as it may, it should be there and it should be free. This implies, then, a decided preference for a diversity of schools, each serving a specialized, rather than a mass, clientele. The students of each school and their associates would approximate, I hope, what Ortega called a "specialized minority" and C. Wright Mills "a public" when he spoke of a functioning democratic society as composed of a "community of publics."[11] Among them, the schools would try to meet the widest possible variety of social demands, including the demands of the gifted and ambitious for assistance in getting ahead.

But I do not believe that any student should be compelled to attend any particular school. Should the young be compelled to go to any school at all? I should prefer that they be left free; that youth be provided with a wealth of diverse opportunities for employment and self-employment, with school attendance prominent among them and left to work out their own arrangements to meet their own needs with

[11] *The Power Elite* (New York: Oxford University Press, 1956), pp. 302–304.

the assurance of a reasonable level of state support—both financial and in the form of services of trained personnel available to give *solicited* advice. In short, I would rather treat youth as farmers are treated. Farmers are provided with a wealth of technical services of high quality that they are free to ignore, and subsidized against the economic catastrophe that would otherwise result from their ignoring it. They are encouraged to believe that their way of life is in itself a moral resource of value to the nation, and protected from the worst consequences of their own smugness or selfishness, as well as against disasters of nature. The result is an embarrassing abundance of good food, and somewhat more stable agricultural communities than our rate of technical development and demographic change would lead one to expect. If this coddling tends to sap the self-reliance of farmers, or subvert their devotion to the philosophy of free enterprise and the open, competitive market, no responsible statesman from the Farm Belt has ever said so.

But farmers, unlike youth, vote, and are concentrated in certain states and congressional districts from which it is easier for them to make their needs known; and they enjoy, on the whole, a far more favorably disposed press—Billy Sol Estes is the only person I can recall who ever became famous as an agricultural delinquent, though there must be others. So it would be unrealistic to expect youth to be treated as well or trusted as far. It would also be risky. Few members of contemporary society, whatever their age, know how to organize their leisure to serve their own ends; and, indeed, it is almost impossible to do it, especially if you have too little money or equipment. Society depends on the school, as it later depends on the job—or the sometimes-marginal farm—to give individuals a sense that there is some place they ought to be and something they are supposed to be doing. The very futility of much school experience is profoundly effective in preparing youth to avoid excessive expectations of the work-opportunities that will be available to them in adulthood. No state is going to risk leaving its youth at loose ends. They will certainly continue to be compelled to attend school.

What one should look to, then, is an improvement of their range of choice, so that no student could be compelled to accept the kind of treatment that some students receive at Milgrim. The most obvious way of going about this would be along lines similar to those of the late President Kennedy's Medicare bill or the old, familiar GI bill for veterans' education. Neither of these set up additional publicly operated facilities. Both simply provide public support that individuals could draw on to widen their selection among public or private facilities. Both also set up minimum standards which any facility had to meet in order to be qualified to receive such support. Among these, at the present time, it is clearly essential that there be included a provision that no school could qualify that discriminated against applicants on racial grounds; and de facto segregation should be accepted as presumptive evidence of such discrimination, on the complaint of any clearly qualified applicant who had been rejected or subjected to administrative delay.

In our society, a particular problem arises with reference to church-supported schools. These are certainly not generally superior to the pubic schools by quantitative criteria or perhaps by any other. Class sizes tend to be larger, and the teachers even more poorly prepared. Minimum standards for these and other relevant criteria would have to be set by church schools or any other that wished to accept students whose fees were to be paid from public funds. But if they did qualify, I would most certainly include them. They need not be superior. In our uniformity, we so desperately need alternative life-styles and ethical models that are related to a particular community and to the experience of life within it, rather than more recipes for tearing away from one's roots and learning to function smoothly among successively more affluent groups of strangers. To seek one's education within institutions sponsored and controlled by the church in which one has been reared is often unwise: parochialism is properly so-called. But at the present, parochialism seems to me far less of a threat to either the individual or society than rootlessness. Church schools which, by their very nature, combat this may well contribute more to the moral stability of society than they do to their own constituency; and they ought certainly to be eligible for public support.

But neither church schools nor the St. Grottlesex schools are adapted to the needs of the mass of youngsters now deemed "culturally deprived"; and they cannot be so adapted without destroying their own character and essential social function. A new range of publicly supported institutions of an entirely different character is needed. For one thing, the academic difficulties of poor adolescents are seldom academic in origin, and they cannot be attacked by academic means. The first need of poor youth is to live better. It is rather stupid to discuss the educational problems of youngsters who live in wretched homes with bad and irregular nutrition, no privacy and no place to study, in contact only with adults who are too exhausted and disturbed by the difficulties of their own lives and in homes that are often not so much broken as never intact in the first place, in terms of teaching techniques, programmed instruction, and changes in the course of study. Slum children need the *alternative* of attending a residential institution, though they certainly should not be compelled to leave their home to attend one if they prefer to remain in a regular, day public school. And this institution should be quite different from a St. Grottlesex school in attitudes and physical arrangements. Such children are likely to come from a home in which the mother has been obliged to fill her own function and that of the father, and provide what stability and sustenance she could. In such homes deprivation is a matter of stark necessity, but it is not held to be good for character. Generally speaking, slum children may be assumed to have received already whatever virtues austerity might confer. Any residential institution designed with their needs in mind ought to be prodigal with food, care, and facilities. In its smoking room, there should be installed the largest and most brilliant color TV that money can buy. Its rules should be concrete, and as few as is consistent with the maintenance of order; there should be none whose purpose is primarily that of indoctrinating them with the behavioral code of the middle classes, or of insuring good public relations. These youngsters, in short, should be treated in a way that means respect to them, and for the deprived this must include a large measure of material and sensual indulgence. They would have to be given allowances of pocket money. A Spartan life is a luxury that only the rich can afford; it costs the poor too much in self-esteem.

There is certainly no economic difficulty in providing such facilities; they are just the support our economy needs, both in themselves and in view of the lavish tastes they would engender. They would still be cheaper than missile bases, though for political reasons it might be necessary to disguise them as such and restrict access to them to authorized personnel. Certainly, they would arouse too much resentment and anxiety to permit them to be locally supported or controlled. Conditions that would be regarded as intolerable violations of local autonomy and folkways if locally sponsored are, however, much more readily accepted if they are imposed by a central authority and locally perceived as a form of economic subsidy.[12] The crucial factor here appears to be structural; the dynamics øf consent must be set up so as not to require local political leadership to violate established local prejudice, while permitting it to claim credit for inducing the central authority to establish and maintain costly facilities where they will benefit the community. In a mass society, freedom consists very largely in managing to avoid having to ask the consent of authorities who may be afraid to accept the responsibility of giving it. In this respect the large bureaucracies of the executive branch are highly effective instruments of policy. They are big enough to maintain officials specially trained to deal with Congress and complicated enough to shield their working personnel from having to deal with anyone else.

I would favor, then, the formation of a Federal Educational Authority to control and operate such boarding schools as an open, public facility. There is, in fact, pending legislation to assume a comparable responsibility; but

[12] Arthur J. Vidich and Joseph Bensman, in *Small Town in Mass Society* (Princeton: Princeton University Press, 1958), present a superb and brilliant case study of the social and political dynamics by which small communities rationalize their dependence on state and national political and economic forces, preserving an illusion of grass-roots autonomy while nevertheless bringing their policies into line with the requirements of state-aid formulae in crop control, road construction, education, and virtually any other applicable area. Even the most segregationist areas of the South, similarly, have usually avoided trying to impose their folkways not only on federal military installations—which may be thought of as foreign bodies—but even on such facilities as those of the Veterans' Administration, which serve a primarily local clientele.

the facilities under consideration are objectionable. They are paramilitary, modeled on the Civilian Conservation Corps of the great depression of the thirties; it is even proposed that they be located on disused portions of existing military bases. They are invidiously designed; these camps are intended to toughen up school dropouts, keep them off the streets, discipline their delinquent tendencies out of them, and turn them into God-fearing citizens. All of us, I would agree, have ample reason to fear God and not least in our capacity as citizens. But I am not convinced that a scheme for remanding the children of the poor to military camps will please Him. In any case, it does not please me; and though it might be made to please the youngsters it would also perfect them as a threat to civil liberty; they could too easily be trained to serve willingly as a kind of storm trooper. I am aware that it is easier for the government to provide extravagantly for disagreeable and destructive purposes than to provide amenities, especially for those elements of the population other people enjoy feeling superior to. But if such camps are financially possible, so are my schools.

I envisage, then, three kinds of public support for education. (1) The existing, locally supported public school system, altered insofar as it would no longer be the only place in which compulsory schooling could be acquired without charge, and would be deprived of state subsidy calculated on the basis of average daily attendance to the extent that students decided to withdraw from it; (2) direct payment of fees to private schools, secular or church-supported, that met established standards and were designated as recipients by students who chose to attend them and were qualified for admission; and (3) totally federally supported boarding schools—which might, like private boarding schools, also accept day students—open to any student, and designed to be very comfortable and attractive, though unfashionable. I would expect the public school to serve—as it now does most effectively—ambitious, conventional youth who accept with equanimity the commonplace folkways of their community. This would include gifted and talented youth who found it comfortable to express their talents in conventional ways. I would expect the private schools to serve their present clientele, greatly enhanced and complemented by the presence of students too energetic, creative, and original to flourish in the public school and too poor or "disadvantaged" to attend these schools without subsidy. The new boarding school I would expect to attract initially poor youngsters who needed the physical and emotional support it provided and the special instructional techniques and patience it could afford them. As they grew accustomed to it and to the use of its unfamiliar space and tranquillity, I would also expect their academic achievement to rise, and initial distinctions in curriculum between it and the public school to diminish. It seems to me likely—though I do not particularly care about it—that a larger proportion of these students would discover in their senior year that they had the SCAT scores required by the best colleges if they chose to continue than would have been the case had they continued in the public school. Public schools tend to underestimate the potential of lower-status youngsters, and steer them out of college preparatory courses or honors tracks.[13]

But the public school, itself, would, I think, rapidly change and improve. These proposals, if carried out, would be (in the language of pedagogy) a real challenge to it and

[13] Cf. Aaron V. Cicourel and John I. Kitzuse, *The Educational Decision Makers* (Indianapolis: The Bobbs-Merrill Co., 1963), for a detailed discussion of this process.

might lead its staff and administration (in the language of Dr. Johnson) to concentrate their minds wonderfully. They would relieve it of the burden of those students whom it finds, and who find it, least congenial. And they would force the public school to regard the student as a client with alternatives, rather than as a conscript. The individual adolescent himself would become one of the political factors the administration would have to consider. He would no longer be, as he is now, the easiest victim to sacrifice in any conflict of interest.

The school, however, like any other organization, is limited by what it has to work with. Here, I think simple, substantial alteration in the process of recruitment and conditions of employment would be particularly helpful. When this issue is discussed, as it frequently has been by Conant, Koerner, and others, it is usually in terms of certification requirements, which are certainly relevant. But they do not get to the heart of the problem. By altering certification requirements it is possible to withhold certification from candidates who are not qualified, but it is not possible to produce candidates whose qualifications are what one would desire. The wrong kinds of people now seek to become teachers for the wrong reasons. They are, to be sure, exactly the right people to perform the traditional function of the high school. But I am suggesting that this function alter.

I would suggest, then, that the teaching cadre be both upgraded and reduced. It is here, I believe, that programmed instruction has a real role to play, and it is here that the conformity of the high school plays into the hands of the proponents of programmed instruction. The opponents of teaching machines quite properly maintain that only a teacher can stimulate original discussion, contribute to its richness and subtlety, take account of the individualized responses of students and guide them to a perception of truth and meaning that is unique for them. But conversely, only a teacher who does at least some of these things much of the time is a better teacher than a machine can be. The machines themselves are getting better, too; while they do not respond to human emotion or subtle variation, they are no longer limited to rote response, either. They don't have heart, but they do have complex capacities to take account of feedback.

There is very little that a good high school ought to do that can be done as well by programmed instruction. But programmed instruction can do a great deal of what the school actually does, as well as or better than the teachers now do it. A careful analysis of the actual processes of instruction would, I suggest, permit the school to be staffed by far fewer people providing students with more, sensitive, highly skilled service. Suppose that the home-room teacher, instead of serving as a kind of room clerk and door check, were given the responsibility of a senior tutor and required to have the academic and personal qualification necessary to permit him to guide, say, sixty students in independent study. In any given year he would be the central figure in the students' academic life; he would help them plan their work, assess their progress, and know and be known by them; he would have no other duties. Assuming that he taught for a five-period day, he would then be meeting with these students in seminar groups of twelve. For much of the rest of their time, they would work either with programmed instruction or in the library, under the general supervision of a specialist in the area of instruction that concerned them during this period, who would be available for consultation; but this specialist would be responsible for providing this limited service to a much larger number of students than he would teach in an ordinary class by discussion—not a larger *group* of students because, except in home-room tutorial and a small number of specialized, advanced classes, they would not meet as a group.

I do not put this forth as a plan or model—it is much too casual for that, and I am not concerned here with high school administration as such—but simply as an example of the kind of approach that might permit the high school to operate with a smaller number of more highly skilled individuals while still providing the individual student with a personal focus and link to the school. It would also be essential to quit using teachers in menial roles—hall and cafeteria duty, for example—and to provide them with office space suited for consultation with students, and secretarial help. I suspect that these police and stenographic functions have been included in the teachers' role less because it is cheap—even under present conditions—than to make a status point and keep the teacher from forgetting himself and getting as hard to handle as a college professor. I suggest, however, that the school would be better run if the teachers had at least the dignity and competence of university professors, had more status, and were fewer.

This means an enormous decrease in the utility of the teaching profession as a vehicle for the gentle ascent of common men, or as an anteroom in which poor but respectable girls can occupy themselves while awaiting the possibility of marriage; what has been essentially a lower-middle-class vocational preserve would become more nearly an upper-middle-class profession. This is exactly the consequence I would seek.

It is particularly important that pretentious but vulgar-minded lower-middle-class staff be excluded from the public boarding schools I have proposed. Their effect there would be sheer murder. The consequences of putting lower-status youngsters in the custody of respectable lower-middle-class people in a boarding school have been amply demonstrated by the experience of Indian children in schools—also run by a central federal authority—of the Bureau of Indian Affairs. Here the teachers insist enthusiastically that the children have no culture at all: no music, no language—they can't even speak English; no ethical code—they *help* each other on tests!; and no experience of life—they have never seen an escalator or a supermarket! For the Oglala Sioux themselves, and their way of life, most of the teachers express contempt and fear; and they avoid any contact with the Indian community outside of school as the teachers quoted in Becker's study of Chicago would have avoided the slum from which their charges came.[14]

At the cost of whatever damage to the mobility ladder, this sort of thing must be stopped. It will tend to stop if teaching can be made a higher-status occupation; but it

[14] Murray L. Wax, Rosalie H. Wax, and Robert Dumont, Jr., with the assistance of Roselyn HolyRock and Gerald OneFeather, *Formal Education in an American Indian Community*, SSSP Monograph published as a Supplement to *Social Problems*, Spring 1964, Chapter V: "Schools, Ideologies and Teachers" and Chapter VI: "Within These Schools" are especially relevant.

The authors, in their one-page Preface, "A Guide to the Reader," state explicitly:

> The reader who is familiar with the problems of schools in urban slum communities will be struck, as we were, by the marked parallels between these educational institutions and those of Pine Ridge. In both, scholastic achievement is low and dropout is high, the major loyalties of the children are to their peers, and the children are confronted by teachers who usually see them as the inadequately prepared, uncultured offspring of an alien and ignorant folk. In view of this marked similarity, we hope that our analysis will contribute to an understanding not merely of Indian schools but also of the many urban schools which serve as the reformative, custodial, and constabulary arm of one element of society directed against another.

cannot be unless the schools can be run with fewer though costlier personnel. Here, as critics like James Koerner have long maintained, difficulties do indeed arise with reference to the teacher-education programs of schools and colleges and the way in which these programs have been institution-alized. Much of this complaint has been directed at the sheer mass of the "professional" requirement—that is, the number of education courses, which are held to take up so much of the student's time as to deprive him of the oppor-tunity to become academically qualified. This is hardly true of students preparing to teach in high school, who must usually fulfill the same subject-matter requirements in order to graduate as any other major in his field of specialization. But the problem goes deeper than any conflict over the allotment of the student's time.

Koerner identifies it correctly in stating:

> It is an indecorous thing to say, and obviously offensive to most educationists, but it is the truth and it should be said: the inferior intellectual quality of the Education faculty is *the* fundamental limitation of the field, and will remain so, in my judgment, for some time to come. . . . One's principal impression of educationists . . . is that of a sincere, humanitarian, well-intentioned, hard-working, poorly informed, badly educated, and ineffectual group of men and women.[15]

As a holder of a Ph.D. in Education, who taught for more than a decade in one of the largest departments of education in any college anywhere, I come within the scope of his condemnation. But despite my respect for many colleagues, whom any reasonable person would likewise esteem as the intellectual and scholarly peers of the members

[15] James D. Koerner, *The Miseducation of American Teachers* (Bos-ton: Houghton Mifflin Co., 1963), p. 37.

of any academic discipline, I must endorse not only the accuracy of his judgment but its relevance. An intellectually honest educationist learns to respond to criticism of the general level of scholarly activity in his field as the British respond to criticism of their climate by foreigners. One dismisses it with a kind of pride that no foreigner, outraged though he might be by it, could possibly imagine how bad it really is; and one laughs, politely, but hollowly.

It could scarcely be otherwise. Since Americans insist on thinking of the high school as both comprehensive and college-preparatory, they must be allowed to think of teachers as college-educated—"normal school" graduates could not prepare students for college. And since an educational enterprise that tries to be simultaneously comprehensive and college-preparatory must be both huge and enormous—if not downright egregious—and must run to common-man standards, the colleges must, in effect, run an intellectual economy-class service to meet the needs and suit the style of teacher-candidates. It isn't that these are necessarily less able, although by ordinary standards (such as norms on standard intelligence and achievement tests) they do tend to be less able than liberal arts or science and engineering students in the same institution. But their ideology and mental texture are different and less distinguished, and the education curriculum has evolved to match their experience and peculiar intellectual style. It is frequently hortatory and pontifical rather than analytical; pompous and philanthropic but basically contemptuous of intellectual distinction and insensitive to its demands. The intellectual atmosphere of ed courses is, in fact, much the same as that of the high school itself. Critics who charge that it repels able students who might otherwise become teachers—and who would, to be sure, be pretty unhappy in the average high school if they did—are, I think, right. Occasionally, a gifted—or creative—English major responds to our offering in the words of e.e. cummings' Olaf; and we can only wish ourselves braver and blonder.

When our critics go on, however, to maintain that we educationists are the *cause* of the public schools' intellectual vulgarity they are being, I believe, far too simple. This thing, as the saying goes, is bigger than any of us. The quality of teacher-preparation might indeed be improved if we made ourselves—or were made—scarce; as we would be if the teaching profession were upgraded. No responsible adult should hesitate to commit suicide in a good cause. But neither should he assume himself to be, or permit his adversaries to convince him that he is, a First Cause or the center of the universe.

The replacement of the professional curriculum of education with courses in the liberal arts or social sciences and with more intensive training in the teacher's prospective special field might well do more good than harm; though it would certainly do some harm. The very prevalence and ubiquity of public education suggests that there is at least a worth-while administrative advantage to be gained from designing special courses in the social and psychological issues that arise in connection with that peculiar institution. It is perfectly true that the sociological and psychological principles that affect the school are the same as those that affect the operation of every institution, and that these might very well be taught in departments of psychology or sociology. But the school is the institution in which teachers must apply them and understand their functioning; and there are enough teachers to justify a special vehicle for their conveyance. The question is not so much whether such courses are useful to teachers as whether educationists can teach them without making them intellectually shoddy ideological instruments and whether prospective teachers could pass them if they did. There is even less debate over the desirability of special methods courses. Clearly, there is a special body of vocational skills that teachers need in order to carry on their work—particularly in schools for "culturally deprived" clientele—that they are not going to pick up serendipitously as part of their academic training. A teacher in a primarily middle-class school may depend on her pupils' "learning skills" and their sophistication in handling themselves in a school situation; but in other schools, teachers need what they learn in "methods courses" even to keep the classroom situation going. This isn't "content"; it is group-dynamics or penology, and I do not mean to defend it in principle. But if public education is essential, this is essential to it.

But even if a liberal education of high academic quality were all that is needed to teach school, and certification requirements were amended or abolished to permit the schools to hire any academically competent college graduate as a teacher, the present cadre of applicants would not get much better academically. Their reasons for seeking a liberal education are not congruent with the education itself. Granted that a second-generation American from Park Slope or Cobble Hill who wanted to teach English would have more chance to learn her field if she could read Henry James instead of taking ed courses, it is hard to imagine what she and Mr. James will make of each other on first acquaintance so late in life. It isn't enough to give prospective teachers more chance to read in college. It is rather more important to attract into teaching people who read before they came to college because they had learned from their parents or their friends that this would give them pleasure. Our present teacher-candidates do not as a rule have such parents or friends. They have peers.

This is not a situation that seems to be on the verge of imminent change. For the difficulties of improving the public schools, and their attendant teacher-training curriculum, illustrate precisely, though in microcosm, the basic difficulties that always impede any attempt to initiate social change —on behalf of adolescents or anybody else. The undertaking is always essentially a bootstrap operation. Proposals to alter the way a society works are, perhaps, essentially unrealistic. Societies do not develop their defects by making wrong choices that they were free to avoid. They become what they are through very stubborn processes of organic growth. Though they constantly alter, the process of alteration follows, for better or for worse, the pattern already inherent in the tensions that exist among their components.

Human potentialities, so poignant and literally crucial in adolescence, really are trapped and vitiated in a mass society. But American society, just because it is so very mass, is attached to mass institutions like a factory to its parking lot, or a church to its graveyard. Ortega's definition fits it, but not with the finality of the Law of Conservation of Mass. American society, it sometimes seems, is composed of elements that can neither be created nor destroyed.

The Law of Conservation of Mass has, to be sure, been superseded by other, more modern and comprehensive physical principles. But these, in the context, are less suggestive, and perhaps do not embrace our society. The least probable fate one can imagine for the American mass is that it might be converted to energy, or light.

APPENDIX

TEST I — THE CLARKE-BARTO INCIDENT

Suppose that your school is strict in enforcing the rule against students smoking in washrooms. The following incident takes place:

Mr. Arthur Clarke, a social-studies teacher at your school, is taking his mid-morning coffee break. On entering a men's washroom he discovers Johnny Barto, a junior, and a somewhat notorious character around the school, smoking. Mr. Clarke knows that Johnny should be in class this hour and furthermore, that he is a troublemaker, is having difficulty with his courses, is on probation, and that he is old enough to quit school. While Mr. Clarke and Johnny are approximately the same size, Johnny is not very strong. His whole attitude, though, is one of arrogance, as if to say, "Show me, buddy."

* * *

Turn to the cards you have been given for Test #1. On these cards you will find stated nine (9) possible actions which Mr. Clarke might have carried out on discovering Johnny. While it is also true that he might have undertaken to perform a combination of these, or might also have done something entirely different, disregard this. *For the moment*, think only in terms of each of these as separate and alternative actions. You will have sufficient opportunity, after completing the test, to discuss the adequacy of these separate actions. Please read *all the cards* through thoughtfully. Then, having read them through:

1. Select the *three* cards which, you feel, represent the *best* actions that could have been taken under the circumstances at that time.

2. From these three, select the *one* which, you feel, would be *best* of all.

3. Returning to the cards remaining, select the *three* cards which, you feel, represent the *worst* actions that could have been taken under the circumstances at that time.

4. From these three, select the *one* action which, you feel, would be *worst* of all.

You should now have the cards for Test #I arranged symmetrically in piles of 1, 2, 3, 2, 1, along an axis indicating the significance you would attach to them. Now, turn to the test entitled, "The LeMoyen Basketball Team," Test #II, and complete it.

[Cards for Test I]

1. Mr. Clarke orders Johnny to put the cigarette out and return to class. Johnny responds by taking a swing at Clarke. Clarke, angry himself now, knocks Johnny down. Afterward, he helps Johnny to his feet, apologizes for his anger, but warns Johnny he will report him if he catches him smoking illegally again.

2. To teach Johnny a lesson Mr. Clarke strikes him several times. This he does coolly and with emotional restraint. After finishing, he gives Johnny a lecture, telling him what happens to young men like him when they don't mend their ways.

3. Mr. Clarke orders Johnny to report to his (Clarke's) classroom the next period. At that time, Clarke describes the incident to the class, and then orders Johnny to apologize to the students for having brought the good name of the school into disrepute. After the apology, Mr. Clarke asks the class members to suggest appropriate punishment for Johnny. This is all presented as a kind of object lesson in social studies.

4. Mr. Clarke takes Johnny to the principal's office and turns him over to the person on duty there for punishment. He also requests of the office that it notify him as to the nature and severity of the punishment to be administered to Johnny.

5. Mr. Clarke reports Johnny to the Student Court at their meeting that evening. At the time he calls on the officers of the Court to remember their responsibility for the maintenance of order in the school, warns them not to be swayed by sentiment, and then requests that suitable punishment be administered.

6. Mr. Clarke calls Johnny's parents, describes the incident to them, informs them of the seriousness of the offense, and suggests that they take appropriate measures to get Johnny in line. He also warns them that if they do not succeed, it will reflect against Johnny.

7. Mr. Clarke has Johnny report for after-school detention, at which time he (Clarke) has Johnny write the following statement on the blackboard 500 times: "I, Johnny Barto, am sorry and will never smoke in school again."

8. At the faculty meeting that afternoon, Mr. Clarke discusses the "Johnny Barto problem" with the school psychologist, and the school psychologist agrees to set up a counseling program designed to get at Johnny's "anti-social" behavior and straighten him out. The psychologist then calls Johnny in for counseling.

9. Mr. Clarke acts as if he hadn't noticed Johnny and leaves the washroom as soon as possible.

TEST II—THE LeMOYEN BASKETBALL TEAM

At LeMoyen High School, about a fifth of the students are Negro; the rest include young people of Irish, Italian, and Eastern European descent—the latter chiefly of the Jewish faith—as well as some students from families that migrated from Northern Europe several generations back and think of themselves as just Americans. Because of the way the neighborhood served by LeMoyen High School has developed, the Negro students come from homes in which the father, on the average, earns more money and has had more years of education than the fathers of the average white students at LeMoyen, who are mostly from working-class families.

For the past two years, LeMoyen has had the best basket-ball team anywhere around and has won the regional championship. The seventeen-man squad has ten Negroes on it and five boys from Irish families. Three of the four regular starters on the highly successful team are Negro players, while the fourth is a white student named Johnny Adams. The coach, Mr. Regan, who also teaches shop, passes the fifth starting position around among the Irish lads on his bench. There has never been a Jewish boy on the basketball team at LeMoyen. Mr. Regan says the Jewish boys are "fine students, but too short to make good ball players."

This year, there transferred into LeMoyen, as a junior, a boy from an Irish background whose father was recently sent to the community as director of plant operations from the oil refinery that is by far the biggest industry in town. The only LeMoyen student this boy, Kevin McGuire, knew before he came to town was Grant Eubanks, the captain of the basketball team and the son of a Negro physician who is the chief heart specialist at the local Veterans' Hospital. The two met at a camp in France where students from other countries go to spend the summer and work with French people and get to know them. McGuire, who as a sophomore was already a basketball star at his old high school, was drawn to Eubanks by the game; during the summer, they taught about 50 kids of various nationalities, who had never seen a game, to play fairly good basketball. Eubanks has told Mr. Regan that the six-foot-five McGuire is without a doubt the best basketball player ever to come anywhere near LeMoyen, and that they must get him on the team. At this moment, McGuire is driving over to the gym to try out for the team, and Mr. Regan is trying to decide what to do next.

*   *   *

Turn to the cards you have been given for Test #II. On these cards you will find nine (9) comments concerning Mr. Regan's problem about Kevin McGuire. *For the moment*, think of each of these comments as being separate and distinct from the others. Again, do not concern yourself about comments you might think of that are not covered by these nine, for you will have ample opportunity to discuss your own ideas about the situation after you have completed the test. Please read *all the cards* through thoughtfully. Then, having read them through:

1. Select the *three* cards which, you feel, represent the *best* comments on the situation described.
2. From these three, select the *one* comment which, you feel, would be *best* of all.
3. Returning to the cards remaining, select the *three* cards

which, you feel, represent the *worst* comments on the situation described.

4. From these three, select the *one* comment which, you feel, is the *worst* of all.

You should now have the cards for Test #II arranged symmetrically in piles of 1, 2, 3, 2, 1 along an axis indicating the significance you would attach to them. Now, report your results on the two tests, I and II, to the person administering the test.

[*Cards for Test II*]

1. The only important thing for Mr. Regan to consider is whether McGuire is as good a player as Eubanks thinks he is. This is what should determine whether a boy gets on the team; the rest of the story is irrelevant.

2. If he doesn't want things to get out of hand, Mr. Regan had better take a good, hard look now at what basketball is being used for at LeMoyen. The business of a high school basketball coach isn't to win games but to give every boy his fair chance to participate, even if he isn't such an expert.

3. If Mr. Regan is the kind of coach who puts competence above race or religion, he and the LeMoyen team will surely welcome young McGuire with unmixed delight.

4. There doesn't seem to be too much of a moral issue here, but, politically, Mr. Regan is certainly on the spot.

5. Mr. Regan might find it very helpful if it were pointed out to him that letting young McGuire join the team would not really be in the best interests of either the boy or the school. Having the richest boy in school as a star athlete as well would be very likely to lead the basketball team to think of itself as a group of privileged characters which, under the particular circumstances described, would be most unfortunate.

6. Mr. Regan is being offered another top-flight player who comes sponsored by his captain and has the same national background as the boys on the team who haven't been doing so well. McGuire sounds like just what he needs.

7. A basketball team is an official school organization, and official school organizations should be representative. It is the responsibility of the principal and the board to see to it that the basketball coach—no matter who he is—runs the team for the benefit of the whole school and not as his private club.

8. It is too risky to take McGuire on the team, especially if he is as good as Eubanks says he is. Coming from a rich home, and as Eubanks' friend, it would be the last straw for the poor Irish boys. You can't really expect them to take a thing like that. A team may like to have stars, but it needs its back bench, too.

9. This story shows how two boys who share the same skill and enthusiasm in sports and general social background can accept each other as individuals, without getting involved in an irrelevant racial issue. Their problem now is just to finish what they have started; Mr. Regan will be risking upsetting his team by letting McGuire on it; but if he is really a good teacher and a good man he must do it.

TEST III — THE LeMOYEN DANCE

The Student Council at LeMoyen High School is planning the annual Spring Dance. This event is held in the high school auditorium, and about one fourth of the cost of it is covered by a subsidy from the school. The rest of the money must be raised by selling "bids" (or admission tickets) and refreshments. The dance has been held every year for the past six years and has become more and more popular each year. It is open to any LeMoyen student. Bids are generally $1.50 per couple, or $1 stag. Refreshments have consisted of hot dogs, hamburgers, and pizza slices at 35¢ each, and soft drinks at a quarter. The music for the dance is recorded. Last year, a large proportion of the junior and senior classes attended the dance—over three hundred couples and about seventy-five stags. Except for an occasional girl dated by an older boy, freshmen and sophomores rarely attend.

However, last year's dance was marred by the obstreperous behavior of several stags who appeared to have drunk their fill, and whom the teachers designated to act as chaperons were unable to keep at bay. Afterward, a rumor went around the school that these boys had been "troublemakers" from the school's vocational track, though vocational students have generally supported the Spring Dance enthusiastically. "They get *so* much out of it," Miss Leigh, the speech and drama teacher who has served as chaperon since the first dance was held, had earlier observed, "It's the one big event of the year for them." And, in fact, the only students who were actually identified as contributing to the disorder that broke out on the floor were seniors, now in college, who, the dean of boys reported sadly to Miss Leigh

afterward, "come from some of the finest homes in the city—
I never thought I would have to call them into the office."
"I'm sorry, sir," one of these boys told the dean; "we didn't
particularly want to spoil anybody's good time, but the
whole thing was so jammed you couldn't move, and it has
gotten so *corny* it didn't even seem real. I mean, like we go
to dances all the time, and, *you* know."

Though the dean accepted this explanation and let the
boys off with a reprimand, pointing out to them that their
conduct had shown them to be deficient in just the qualities
of leadership he had counted on them to have, the Student
Council is anxious to avoid any repetition of the disaster this
year. Accordingly, one faction of the students on the Council has proposed a radical revision of the plans. These suggest
that the price of the bids be raised to $7.50, a couple or
stag, and that the cost of the refreshments be included. For
this money, they calculated that they could provide a tempting cold buffet, or *smörgåsbord*, and that they could also
hire a small orchestra that the school jazz club has said is
the coolest in town. Although the Student Council has final
responsibility for planning the dance, it has held a survey
of school opinion to guide it in reaching a decision. The
survey indicates:

1. A majority of the entire student body oppose the new,
   more expensive plan.
2. A small majority of the students who attended last year's
   dance, however, favor the new plan.
3. Enough students indicated that they would still attend
   if the price of bids was raised to $7.50, with supper
   included, to give a predicted attendance of about a
   hundred couples. This is enough, by a wide margin, to
   pay for the dance.

*   *   *

Turn to the cards you have been given for Test #III. On these cards, you will find nine (9) comments concerning the proposal before the Student Council for the Spring Dance. As before, you will have ample opportunity, after completing the test, to discuss these comments in detail. Please read *all the cards* through thoughtfully. Then, having read them through:

1. Select the *three* cards which, you feel, represent the *best* comments on the proposal for the Spring Dance.
2. From these three, select the *one* comment which, you feel, would be *best* of all.
3. Returning to the cards remaining, select the *three* cards which, you feel, represent the *worst* comments on the proposal for the Spring Dance.
4. From these three, select the *one* comment which, you feel, is the *worst* of all.

You should now have the cards for Test #III arranged symmetrically in piles of 1, 2, 3, 2, 1 along an axis indicating the significance you would attach to them. Now, turn to the test entitled, "The King's Visit," Test #IV, and complete it.

[*Cards for Test III*]

1. It is hard to see how the Student Council can persist with such an undemocratic plan, when their own study shows that a majority of the student body oppose it. It is their duty as elected representatives to find another, more acceptable selection.
2. It is unfortunate that the Student Council should be obliged to consider making the Spring Dance a more exclusive affair, but they may have to do it. Evidently, as the dance has gotten more and more popular, it has attracted the

kind of "teen-ager" who does not know how to act at a dance. The somewhat greater formality and higher cost of attending the dance under the new proposal should limit its appeal to the kind of student who belongs there.

3. A serious disadvantage of the new plan is that some youngsters would be excluded from the Spring Dance who would enjoy it, simply because they couldn't afford it anymore. But this may be outweighed by the fact that it would be a much better dance, even if you had to save up or go without something else. If the dance is allowed to turn into a brawl or a rat-race, it isn't worth holding.

4. There is nothing undemocratic about the Student Council's new plan. A majority of the students who are qualified to pass judgment, and who have shown their interest by supporting the dance last year, approve the new plan. And it would still be open to any student who wanted to spend the money.

5. The Student Council has been left holding the bag for the Dean of Boys' reluctance to treat kids from influential families like everybody else. If he had cracked down on these boys after last year's dance, there wouldn't be any problem.

6. Everything the school sponsors is a part of its educational program, and should be open to all. It is good for the Student Council to have the experience of running the dance, as this helps them to learn to be responsible. But they must not be permitted to turn public education into an exclusive social affair.

7. Maybe the dance is pretty corny and crowded. But it wouldn't be fair to turn it into a college-type affair that most of the students would not feel at home at, especially those who have not had the advantages of the youngsters from better homes. Chaperon the dance a little more closely, if necessary, but keep it down to earth and unpretentious, the way it is now.

8. Unfortunately, the Student Council is not the proper body

to get to the root of a problem like this. Youngsters have to learn—sometimes the hard way—to bear the responsibility for their own misconduct. The school authorities should suspend the dance for a year, to teach the students that the privilege of holding it depends on their power to discipline their own conduct. This is a far more important question than what kind of dance they have.

9. If you are planning a dance, the first consideration is to make it a good one. Dances don't break up into brawls unless the kids are pretty bored with them. The new plan would make this a really enjoyable occasion, and might especially benefit the less privileged kids, who can get awfully tired, too, of cheap, commonplace institutionalized entertainment.

TEST IV — THE KING'S VISIT

Several weeks ago, the Governor wrote to the principal of LeMoyen High School to tell him about the impending visit to Capital City of the King of a country not unlike Denmark and of the King's notable interest in spirited young people. He also informed the principal of the King's expressed desire to meet with some interesting and representative high school students during his visit. The Governor then went on to say that he had selected LeMoyen as one of the ten high schools chosen from throughout the state which were to pick several students to meet with the King when he visits the Governor at the Executive Mansion. The Governor added that the King speaks English fluently, and then concluded with the suggestion that such young people as were to be chosen should be persons to whom the school could point with pride as expressing what was finest and best about their school.

At LeMoyen, where such things are always done as democratically as possible, the students were to have a voice in the choice. First, nine individuals and groups were nominated by a committee composed jointly of faculty members and students with the Dean of Men, Mr. Blakely, serving as Chairman. These nine were to stand for election as candidates for the post of school representative (or representatives). The student body was to choose from this list of nine the person or persons they thought would best represent them at the meeting with the King. This vote was not conclusive, however, but was primarily advisory, for the principal reserved the right to make the final nomination for the

school, guiding himself in his choice by the committee rec-
ommendations and the student vote.

*   *   *

The committee has just acted and the nine candidates have
been chosen. Each of the nine cards you have been given for
Test #IV describes one of the nine candidates or groups of
candidates selected. Please read the descriptions on *all the
cards* through thoughtfully. Then, having read them through:

1. Select the *three* cards which, you feel, describe the
   persons who would best represent the school at the
   meeting with the King.
2. From these three, select the *one* person or group who
   you feel would be best of all in this role.
3. Returning to the cards remaining, select the *three* cards
   which, you feel, describe the persons *least suited* to
   represent the school at the meeting with the King.
4. From these three, select the *one* person or group who,
   you feel, would be *worst* of all in this role.

You should now have the cards for Test #IV arranged symmetrically in piles of 1, 2, 3, 2, 1 along an axis indicating the
significance you attach to them. Now, report your results
on the two tests, III and IV, to the person administering the
test.

[Cards for Test IV]

1. Nancy Harris

Nancy Harris is a violinist. This year she has been accorded
the signal honor of being first violinist and concert master of
the all-state orchestra. She has also performed as soloist for
several of the local symphony orchestras. Nancy is gifted with
artistic sensibility and quickness in all things. She is a very

good student, and still manages to keep her course work up while practicing three or four hours a day. Unfortunately, her schedule does not allow her much opportunity for social activity, which is too bad because she is really an attractive young lady who, with a little effort, could easily be very popular. But her enthusiasms are more for things than for people and she prefers artistic creation to success with her fellow students.

2. *Eric Pratt*

Everybody at LeMoyen loves Eric Pratt. He's cool. He has a great line and really knows how to make the girls happy. He's always lots of fun, anywhere, anytime. He's up on the latest record, in with the newest fad, and on to the easiest way to do the hard things. Eric's sharp, he sure is, you should see the way he dresses. Man, you should see. If you had money like Eric has you could pay for the clothes, but I'll bet you couldn't get it right, most likely you wouldn't. It's something you've got to know how to do, and Eric does. He's got style in everything he does. Don't get the idea that this kid's just popular with the gang, though. He's more than that. The teachers think he's great, too, especially the women teachers. He knows how to talk to them, and make them love him, and make them do anything he wants them to do.

3. *Elfrieda Eubanks*

Elfrieda Eubanks is so sweet you couldn't help liking her, and everybody at LeMoyen does. She's president of the Girls' Athletic Association and a sure thing for the Chamber of Commerce's best All-Around Girl award this spring. Elfrieda is tall, slender, and very graceful. She has a beautiful voice and sings regularly at several local churches. A better-than-average student, she's also a volunteer nurse's aide at the hospital, chairman of the school hostess club, and LeMoyen's number one cheerleader. She dances beautifully, too. One thing you can say about Elfrieda, she's always smiling, always a good guy, no matter what. That's what makes her so popular. Even her twin brother,

Grant, who was the best basketball player LeMoyen had until Kevin McGuire came along, isn't as popular as Elfrieda, and that's saying something.

4. *Johnny Adams*

Johnny Adams is something of an enigma. It isn't easy to figure out how he managed to make the basketball team. He's not big and he's not fast. It's not clear why he wanted to, either. He doesn't hang around with the fellows on the team. The kids he runs around with are what are called beatniks at LeMoyen, the kind, you know, who usually don't care about things like sports and dances. But when Johnny decided he wanted to make the team, he did. He has drive, and he's smart, too. If he wanted to, he's one fellow who could give Karen Clarke or Scott Cowen a real run for it academically. But most of the time he doesn't feel like it. When he does, though, watch out. It was a big surprise, last year, when he won the veterans' club oratorical contest. He did it against odds, too. No one would ever call him good-looking, he has a sort of squeaky voice, and most of the time he could use a haircut and shave. He's not always an easy guy to be with, either. Still, he took on the best the county had to offer and showed them all how to do it.

5. *Ronnie, Big Joe and Pink*

Ronnie, Big Joe and Pink have just cut their second platter. Known as the Combo, they play and sing with a fast, easy beat that's sometimes subtle and sometimes frantic. It's easy to like, too. The Combo is so good, actually, that it was featured on a coast-to-coast TV network last month. About the members of the Combo, well, they're not just ordinary: Big Joe, Joe White, that is, is the first Negro ever to be elected president of the school honor society. Pincus Peabody is going to a music school in New York on a scholarship next year. He's quite a composer and works up the arrangements for the Combo. He can write in the classical mood also, and is the composer of the violin sonatina Nancy Harris in planning to play at graduation. One can't say too much for Ronnie, though, except that he organized the Combo and writes the lyrics. And really, the lyrics are great; they have a twist to them that gives them class, something like the Kingston Trio, and still it's different.

6. *Karen Clarke*

Karen Clarke will be giving the valedictory at graduation for this year's class. As she should. Always well groomed and polite, she is completely in command of herself in any situation. She is the perfect model of what a high school student ought to be. Her work is neat, correct, and unlike that of so many other students, in on time. It really has to be, because her dad, Mr. Clarke, teaches here and he makes sure Karen doesn't get any special favors. He makes certain that she stands up for herself and does her work. In student activities she is Treasurer of the Senior Class. She is also a teacher's aide for Mr. Pottitone's chemistry laboratory and a member of the Ethics Committee of the Student Government. Where others are concerned, Karen always tries to be helpful. She wants to go to a good college like Vassar or Smith, and plans everything she does carefully, with this in mind. At LeMoyen everybody feels that she has a real chance to get into the kind of a college she would like to go to.

7. *Mill and Jill Bernstein*

Mill and Jill Bernstein are two of the craziest kids you can imagine, crazy in a great way, that is. While they aren't really twins they look so much alike that they might as well be. It really gets you, you never know which one you're talking to, and they are always pulling gags on people that way. They've got so much talent they can do anything, and almost do. They both play instruments in the band, they have their own vocal duet, and they are really wonderful with their mimicry. They are a must at any party because they usually make it go. At LeMoyen, they're for the school all the way, the real boosters.

They're the in-everything girls, cheerleading, the school paper, debating, the works. They also run everything; they should, too, because they get things done. Right now Mill is organizing the Senior Class trip, and Jill is chairing the Junior Clambake Committee. LeMoyen has a lot to thank Mill and Jill for, and it's going to remember them for a long time.

8. *Nicky Galetti*

For the past three years the right side of the line of the LeMoyen football team has been practically impregnable. The reason is right tackle, Nicky Galetti, two hundred and twenty pounds of solid bone and muscle. Nicky is a great team man, hard-working and loyal, and never an angry word. This year Nicky played every minute of every game, except for the last two in the game with City High. It was really Nicky's game, and against LeMoyen's traditional foes, too. Nicky led the offense, and on defense, he was, as usual, the key man. Unfortunately, LeMoyen's backfield was weak this year, and the game was scoreless until the last few minutes, when Nicky blocked a City punt. Joe White recovered it for a touchdown. Everybody felt that it was too bad that it wasn't Nicky, just so he could have scored at least once. When the coach took him out a few minutes later, the stands went mad cheering for him—a great team man if there ever was one.

9. *Scott Cowen*

Scott Cowen is supposed to be a genius. When he was twelve years old his parents arranged for him to take a special course in mathematics at the university nearby and he did very well, indeed. Although all the other students in the course were either specially selected senior high school students or college freshmen, Scott came out first in the class. According to the instructor's report, "Mr. Cowen is potentially a mathematician of the first order and with proper training should be able in the future to do work of great significance." At LeMoyen, Scott has continued to do well. His entries in the Senior High

School Division Science Fair won first prize both last year and this. He is a brilliant chess player and managed a draw with the state champion. And he is editor of the LeMoyen *Xantippe*, the school literary magazine. Scott's work at LeMoyen is always original and always competent, although it does tend to be sloppy. He's sloppy, also, in the way he dresses, and he does manage to argue with some of the teachers. If it weren't for this he would probably be valedictorian of his class. He has the ability to be.

TEST V — MISS POST'S ENGLISH ASSIGNMENT

Miss Elsie Post is, by consensus, the finest teacher Le-Moyen has and probably ever has had. Her subject is English, and her skill lies in drawing the best out of even the most reluctant student. Under her guidance young people develop a real respect for literature, no matter what their background, and for many of them her class is the first time in their lives in which they have attempted seriously to express their thoughts with style and distinction. Miss Post is often gay and sometimes even frivolous while teaching, but underneath there is a resolute spirit. She is stern and surprisingly demanding in her assignments. "You know, she expects the impossible," is an often-heard student comment the first day of class. Yet, when the year is over, many own up that she'd gotten that impossible. "It makes you feel proud to do well for Miss Post," is the way Ronnie Jackson said it to Scott Cowen one day, while they were working at putting *Xantippe* together for publication. "Yeah," answered Scott. "I never thought I'd go for poetry and all that stuff, but after you've heard about it from her, and then read some of it, well, it's great, it's something she does that makes it real."

Miss Post is just as demanding of herself as she is of her students. She spends hours each day correcting class themes and homework assignments. And she has a reputation for uncovering each and every error the thoughtless, ignorant, or deceitful student has let slip into his work, this despite her advanced age and notably weak eyesight. Her comments on the papers are in themselves something of a form of art, always precise and to the point, and yet affectionate, amusing, interesting, and, where necessary, devastating. As the students at LeMoyen soon discover, Miss Post is not an easy person to fool.

Miss Post has taught at LeMoyen for many, many years. A number of the parents of the present student body had her as a teacher when they attended LeMoyen, and they always seem to remember her much as she is today. However, Eric Pratt, exercising a scientific bent he generally kept well under wraps, found her picture in the 1934 annual, and announced—much to his surprise he claimed—that she had once been a most attractive young lady. After Eric's discovery had gained currency throughout the school, rumors of a tragic love were rife around LeMoyen, but nothing was ever proven. Whatever her private life though, Miss Post must always have been a very good teacher. For, only last summer while attending a summer basketball clinic at a famous Eastern university, Mr. Regan met an eminent scientist who, on hearing of LeMoyen, asked about Miss Elsie Post, his once-upon-a-time teacher. The scientist then went on to say that she was the finest teacher he had ever had, bar none, and this despite his many years of education in college and graduate school.

*   *   *

Assume that you are a student in Miss Post's class. Today she told her class that each member was to bring to class tomorrow several lines of poetry which he felt best expressed what *love* means to him. She indicated that the students would be expected to read and discuss their selections in class the next day. Assume further that it is evening, and you have come up with nine possible selections. The nine

cards you have been given for Test V are the nine selections
we will assume you have found. As usual, you will have
ample opportunity to discuss these selections later. Please
read *all of these cards* through thoughtfully. Then, having
read them through:

1. Select the *three* cards which, you feel, have poems
   which *best* express what love means to you.
2. From these three, select the *one* poem which, you feel,
   would be *best* of all.
3. Returning to the cards remaining, select the *three* cards
   which, you feel, have poems which express *least* or
   possibly even the opposite of what love means to you.
4. From these three, select the *one* poem which, you feel,
   is *worst* of all.

You should now have the cards for Test #V arranged
symmetrically in piles of 1, 2, 3, 2, 1 along an axis indicating
the significance you would attach to them. Now, turn to
the test entitled, "Alan Slade and His Friends," Test #VI,
and complete it.

[Cards for Test V]

1. Yet in herself she dwelleth not,
    Although no home were half so fair;
    No simplest duty is forgot,
    Life hath no dim and lowly spot
    That doth not in her sunshine share.

    She doeth little kindnesses,
    Which most leave undone, or despise;
    For naught that sets one heart at ease,
    And giveth happiness or peace,
    Is low-esteemed in her eyes.

　　　She hath no scorn of common things,
　　　And, though she seems of other birth,
　　　Round us her heart intwines and clings,
　　　And patiently she folds her wings
　　　To tread the humble path of earth.

2.　　True love's the gift which God has given
　　　To man alone beneath the heaven;
　　　It is not fantasy's hot fire,
　　　Whose wishes, soon as granted, fly;
　　　It liveth not in fierce desire,
　　　With dead desire it doth not die;
　　　It is the secret sympathy,
　　　The silver link, the silken tie,
　　　Which heart to heart and mind to mind
　　　In body and in soul can bind.

3.　　No man is an island,
　　　No man stands alone,
　　　Each man's joy is joy to me,
　　　Each man's joy is his own.
　　　We need one another
　　　So I will defend
　　　Each man as my brother,
　　　Each man as my friend.

4.　　No thorns go as deep as a rose's,
　　　And love is more cruel than lust.
　　　Time turns the old days to derision,
　　　Our loves into corpses or wives;
　　　And marriage and death and division
　　　Make barren our lives.

5.　　When our two souls stand up erect and strong
　　　Face to face, silent, drawing nigh and nigher.

6. He prayeth best, who loveth best
    All things both great and small;
    For the dear God who loveth us,
    He made and loveth all.

7. Breathes there the man, with soul so dead,
    Who never to himself hath said,
        This is my own, my native land!
    Whose heart hath ne'er within him burn'd
    As home his footsteps he hath turned,
        From wanderings on a foreign strand?

8. There is a pleasure in the pathless woods,
    There is a rapture on the lonely shore,
    There is a society, where none intrudes,
    By the deep sea and music in its roar;
    I love not man the less, but Nature more.

9. Ah, love, let us be true
    To one another! for the world, which seems
    To lie before us like a land of dreams,
    So various, so beautiful, so new,
    Hath really neither joy, nor love, nor light,
    Nor certitude, nor peace, nor help for pain;
    And we are here as on a darkling plain
    Swept with confused alarms of struggle and flight,
    Where ignorant armies clash by night.

TEST VI — ALAN SLADE AND HIS FRIENDS

Early in his senior year, Alan Slade, a short, well-proportioned boy who is captain of the tennis team at LeMoyen High School, and has been an honor student through his whole high school career, began to run into trouble. His grades have fallen off sharply, though they are leveling off at a point well above passing. He has been seen around town in one or two taverns that have records of violating the law against selling liquor to minors, and which the principal of the school has been trying unsuccessfully to have permanently closed. He was picked up a few weeks ago for drunken driving, but the lab test showed an alcohol content just below that necessary to establish intoxication. His father, a lawyer with a reputation for sharp legal technique, was quick to point this out and prevented the boy from being formally charged. But he also forbade him the use of either of the Slade cars for an indefinite period, until "he got himself straightened out." Not being able to drive now, Alan seems to spend most of his time hanging around the house or a candy store near the school that few students patronize, not doing much of anything. His tennis game is shot, and so are LeMoyen's chances for the year.

Nobody seems to know just how Alan's trouble started, though Monica St. Loup, another senior who is a cheerleader and president of the girls' Pan-Hellenic council, has hinted to several of her intimate friends that she does know, although she would rather not talk about it. She did, however, overcome her aversion to doing so long enough to go to Mr. Blakely, the dean of boys, and plead for help for Alan before anyone else had even noticed that there was anything wrong with him. Despite his encouragements—"The kids all know my door is always open," Mr. Blakely has often said—not many LeMoyen students feel free to go to the dean unless sent for. But the dean of boys is also, *ex officio*, in charge of student activities at LeMoyen. Mr. Blakely's admiration for Monica St. Loup is well known in the school. "Monica is about as close to an All-American girl as you can get," Mr. Blakely once observed. "Pretty as a picture; smart, too; any group she's in seems always to have a lot of fun. But her mother doesn't have to worry about her a bit; Monica can be trusted. She knows just how far she can go and not lose her self-respect. If this school had more like her, my job would be easy."

It was to Mr. Blakely, then, that Monica turned, not on her own behalf, but on that of Alan Slade. The discussion was, of course, confidential, but immediately afterward Mr. Blakely sent, separately, for Johnny Barto, a junior with a bad reputation in school as a troublemaker, and for Alan. Mr. Blakely took no formal action; but when Johnny left school that day, he never came back. Some of the kids say he has left town; he has certainly not been seen around school. To Alan, Mr. Blakely spoke gently but firmly, if somewhat ambiguously. "I'm here to help you, son," he said. "I think you know that. This kind of situation isn't a disciplinary matter; intelligent people don't think of it that way any more, really. But you do need professional help. During the year, you'll be applying for college; then there's the army to think of; these people count on us to be honest with them about the emotional adjustment of our students.

You have such a good record here, Alan, and I'm going to see to it that you don't spoil it. I don't even want you to worry about it, son; normal growth is our business."

Mr. Blakely's tone became less warm, however, when Alan insisted, and continued to insist more and more anxiously, that he did not understand what Mr. Blakely was talking about. "It would be better, son," said Mr. Blakely, "if you could trust me. It would be better if you could trust *yourself*; the only way out is to face up to this like the man we hope you will become. The first step is to be absolutely honest; and that is what you'll have to do. I'll tell you what we'll do, I'm going to set up an appointment for you with Dr. Bruch [the visiting school psychiatrist for the LeMoyen district] when he comes next month. I'm not a psychiatrist, and I don't pretend to be. But I am Dean of Boys, here; and I am responsible for your well-being and for that of the other boys you are in contact with here. Until we get this report—and I'm afraid Dr. Bruch is a pretty busy man—I'll do what I can for you. Meanwhile, don't worry."

This was three months ago. Whether or not Alan took Mr. Blakely's advice not to worry, he is, as has been stated, in trouble now. Dr. Bruch's report, when received, recommended regular psychotherapy; but the school has no program for providing this. Mr. and Mrs. Slade, when Mr. Blakely told them of Dr. Bruch's recommendation, were unco-operative and ungrateful. "I'm afraid you interpret your responsibility and your mandate both too broadly and too loosely," Mr. Slade replied. "I'm not certain that I know what you are talking about any better than Alan does, but if I do I can well understand your vagueness, since you are quite right in supposing that a more forthright statement would be libelous." "If we *should* think—as we do not—that our son needed psychiatric help," Mrs. Slade added, "we would send him to our own analyst. Dr. Liebig has kept our marriage going for twenty years, which is a tribute to his competence if not to his judgment. We know that Alan has been miserable at school this year and we have been worried sick about him, but we didn't know what was wrong and he doesn't seem to be able to tell us. Now that you've told us what you've put him through, we can begin to understand it. All we ask of you is that you attend to his education, which seemed to be going pretty well, by your own account, until you brought all this up."

Here, however, Mr. Blakely was adamant. His responsibility, he said, extended to all aspects of the welfare of LeMoyen boys while they were in school. Mr. and Mrs. Slade could ignore Dr. Bruch's recommendation if they chose, but if they did he would insist that Alan report to him for a weekly conference, at which "I will try to help him as much as he will let me." Otherwise, he would be forced to recommend to the principal that young Slade be suspended from school, "without prejudice, for reasons of health." So far, there have been six of these conferences. During them, after polite greetings, Alan sits silently, while Mr. Blakely waits patiently "for you to get tired, Alan, of your resistance."

No one at LeMoyen supposes that Monica St. Loup asked Mr. Blakely to help Johnny Barto also. Nor did she. Monica's usually inexhaustible good will never extended to young Barto, except for a brief period early last year when Monica did try to take an interest in him. "He could amount to something, you know," she said to one of her sorority sisters who had warned her against getting "mixed up" with Johnny. "He's bright, even if he is a couple of years older than the other boys in his class. That's just his background. And he's attractive, in a kind of feline way, like a tiger. He could learn, if he had somebody to take him in hand. Don't worry about me. It's Alan you ought to be worrying about. He's such a sweet boy, and so shy; I really wish I knew how to help him. I've tried, but I can't seem to reach him, somehow. I'm sure he hasn't any idea what he's getting into."

But Monica had no more success with Johnny than with Alan. The two boys were discussing her, rather casually, late one night during a camping trip, which they often took together. "You watch out for her, Shrimpboat," Johnny told Alan. "She isn't what she thinks she is. Oh, she's all for good, clean fun, and no passes accepted. But just fail to make them when she expects them, and see what happens. I know."

Monica was not the only person who disapproved of the friendship between the two boys. Mrs. Slade had also complained about it to her husband, but he had disagreed with her. "I can't go along with that, dear," he said. "If you'll remember, Johnny's grandfather just about got my career started for me; though if Johnny knows it he never said anything to Alan. There was always a streak of the gentleman in those Bartos. Oh, they have no talent for legitimacy, and the whole line has just gone to hell since repeal; it was probably a blessing the old man got bumped off when he did. There was nothing any lawyer could have done for Johnny's father, and I'm glad he didn't come to me. But there's plenty of people jumped all over the boy since he's been down, and you know, I don't think we'd like to join them. Alan can take care of himself as well as I could at his age, and he'll have to, won't he, against people more dangerous than Johnny Barto?"

*   *   *

Turn to the cards you have been given for Test #VI. On these cards you will find nine comments concerning Alan Slade's situation. As before, you will have ample opportunity after completing the test to discuss these comments in detail. Please read *all the cards* through thoughtfully. Then, having read them through:

1. Select the *three* cards which, you feel, represent the best comments on the incident.
2. From these three, select the *one* comment which, you feel, would be *best* of all.
3. Returning to the cards remaining, select the *three* cards which, you feel, represent the *worst* comments on the incident.
4. From these three, select the *one* comment which, you feel, is the worst of all.

You should now have the cards for Test #VI arranged symmetrically in piles of 1, 2, 3, 2, 1 along an axis indicating the significance you would attach to them. Now, report the results on the two tests, V and VI, to the person administering the test.

[Cards for Test VI]

1. Bad off as he seems to be, the root of Alan's trouble is probably basically self-pity. Certainly, he is lucky at least to have both a friend and a counselor so devoted to helping him. If he won't let them, he can't expect things to get much better.

2. The attitude of Alan's parents illustrates how necessary it is that parents co-operate with the school, if as much as possible is to be done for students when they need help. In a world as interdependent as ours, the individual must co-operate with the legitimate institutions of society if progress is to be made.

3. Neurotic parents rear neurotic children, this is the iron law of psychoanalysis. The older Slades' hostility to getting any psychiatric help for their son is but an extension of their guilt for the entire situation.

4. At the heart of Mr. Blakely's attitude is essentially middle-class prejudice. If Johnny Barto were Alan's social equal, their friendship would appear perfectly natural to him.

5. The worst thing that can be said about Mr. Blakely's policy in this case is that it is too soft and compromising. Knowing what he evidently does—or he wouldn't have dared to go this far—he ought to have kicked both these young punks out of town, rather than just one. Of course, under the circumstances, he has to watch his step legally.

6. Mr. Blakely seems to be on the right track, but the school's resources do not extend far enough to back him up. When the school psychiatrist recommends that a student be given psychiatric help, the school should require that he accept it and, if necessary, provide the funds for facilities to make it possible.

7. Mr. Blakely's action is both unprofessional and a gross invasion of privacy. He is allowing himself to be influenced by one student against another, has used his office to break up a private friendship between two students, and has done grave injury to both. To call this "helping" is either hypocrisy or lunacy.

8. The most remarkable factor in the situation is the Slades' wonderfully democratic and tolerant attitude. Despite their apparent wealth and success, they recognize that a boy with Johnny's background should be encouraged to make some-

thing of himself, and, despite their misgivings, permit their son to befriend him closely. This is the kind of thing that America means.

9. The most hopeful factor in the situation, so far as Alan is concerned, is that his parents basically respect and care for him so much, and can still say no when they have to, both to him and to the school authorities. Nobody is proof against fools, busybodies, or a woman scorned; but with this kind of home life to draw on, Alan will probably come through, scars and all.

EDGAR Z. FRIEDENBERG was born in 1921, and grew up in Shreveport, Louisiana. He received both his B.S. (Centenary College, 1938) and M.S. (Stanford University, 1939) in chemistry. Of his further education, Mr. Friedenberg writes: "I switched to the School of Education at Stanford, which, in the social climate of the late thirties seemed a reasonable thing to do, particularly to a person who had never attended public school and had no way of knowing that he was thereby entering complicity with that peculiar institution. I was drafted into the Navy in 1944—too late to improve Japanese chances significantly—and entered the University of Chicago on my release, receiving a Ph.D. there in 1946."

Mr. Friedenberg has taught at the University of Chicago and Brooklyn College, and is now Professor of Sociology at the University of California at Davis.

VINTAGE HISTORY—AMERICAN

VINTAGE POLITICAL SCIENCE
AND SOCIAL CRITICISM